PRAISE FOR
DAUNTED NO MORE

Daunted No More had me at the opening paragraph. I had to read it in a single sitting. The beautifully-structured format lends itself to a several-session read... if you think you can do that. The story's flow is seamless; the rhythm, engaging; and—beware—the pacing will alter your heartbeat. The author artfully weaves the culmination of a family's multi-generation tale into a riveting journey through the reader's emotional spectrum. You will fear, love, hate, fret, hope, and cheer... and then some. I loved this book... and hate that it needed to be written.

— Mark Bracich, Screenwriter, Actor,
Filmmaker, and Retired USAF Colonel

Daunted No More takes readers on an emotional journey through the mind games, manipulation, and self-doubt of unhealthy relationships into a place of bravery, courage, and discovering self-love. This thought-provoking story has the power to inspire deep conversations in groups, clubs, and classrooms. It's a must-read novel demonstrating the importance of devoted support and unconditional love from friends and family.

—A. Van Donk, 911 Dispatcher

This tale brings home a message in a viscerally relatable fashion. A difficult subject addressed with the finesse of an expert storyteller, *Daunted No More* proves to be a thought-provoking, yet highly entertaining read.

> — Michelle Murray, COO at KMP Entertainment, Screenwriter, Novelist, Veteran's Advocate

Daunted No More is a captivating, fast-moving story with truths sprinkled in that are profound and can be applied to our lives in positive ways. Great reading for high school students as well as adults. It's an important message immersed in rich authenticity and a page-turning plot. Riveting!

> —Marlys Johnson, Author, Highschool Teacher, and Former Family Life Weekend to Remember Director

A page-turner I could not put down, *Daunted No More* is for every survivor currently walking the path looking for a new road, and, more importantly, for every woman who has said, "That will never happen to me!" In an emotionally raw way, S.R. Luviek has intricately woven three unique perspectives around one sadly taboo topic. The nuances, the lies, the empty promises, and delusions are all addressed in a vulnerable way that begs for light to be shed where darkness and secrecy have usually prevailed.

> —Kristy Bingham, English Language Arts Teacher

A moving story that hooks you from the beginning, *Daunted No More* is engaging and well written. It paints a sobering picture that is too often ignored, brushed-aside, or explained away. May it stir up grace and action in the hearts of its readers.

> —Kirby Alfaro, Pastor

Daunted No More is a gripping story depicting the generational impact of choices on those who follow.

—Kristi Byrd, School Counselor

Daunted No More exposes terrors that tragically affect millions of people from every demographic. This captivating, moving, and relevant novel sheds light on the inner thoughts and emotions of both the trapped and the survivors, yet also offers truth and hope that can help sufferers escape. Adults of every age should take time to read, ponder, and digest this story so we can better recognize the signs and help end the vicious cycle.

—Jennifer Walling, School Principal

DAUNTED NO MORE

S.R. LUVIEK

AUTHOR ACADEMY elite

Printed in the United States of America

Published by Author Academy Elite
PO Box 43, Powell, OH 43065
www.AuthorAcademyElite.com

Identifiers:
LCCN: 2020914517
ISBN: 978-1-64746-418-9 (paperback)
ISBN: 978-1-64746-419-6 (hardback)
ISBN: 978-1-64746-420-2 (ebook)

Available in paperback, hardback, e-book, and audiobook

Scripture taken from the New King James Version®. Copyright © 1982 by Thomas Nelson. Used by permission. All rights reserved.

Any Internet addresses (websites, blogs, etc.) and telephone numbers printed in this book are offered as a resource. They are not intended in any way to be or imply an endorsement by Author Academy Elite, nor does Author Academy Elite vouch for the content of these sites and numbers for the life of this book.

Dedicated to the survivors.
Never doubt that you are noticed,
loved, valuable, and wanted.
You matter.

And to those who didn't make it.
You are not forgotten.

It's time to break the cycle.

CHAPTER ONE

The bedroom door slammed upstairs. Bethany Garcia tried to disguise the way her body twitched by scooting back on the couch and pulling her five-year-old daughter against her chest. As she rested her lips on top of Gloria's thick, dark hair, she drew in a slow, lavender-filled breath. Everything faded except the heavy footsteps retreating to the far end of the house until she could no longer hear them.

Gloria's sigh brought Bethany back into the family room. Bethany's heart gradually stopped slamming against her ribcage. Everything would be fine. Bethany pecked Gloria's temple with a loud kiss. "You smell just like your shampoo. Yummy."

Gloria picked at her mom's sleeve. "Don't Daddy work today?"

Bethany wished for the same thing as she wiped a tear from her little girl's cheek and shook her head. "Not today. It's Saturday."

"*Can* he?"

Bethany chuckled and squeezed her daughter. *If only it were that easy.* "No." *Time to cheer these girls up.* "Now, let's see if your sister will join us." Strawberry blonde waves cascaded over the arm of the couch as Bethany leaned over and looked for her hiding three-year-old.

Maria held chubby legs in a tight ball and pressed her back into the corner between the couch and the wall. Bethany smiled. "It's okay, Maria. Daddy's upstairs now. Wanna snuggle with me and your sister? There's room on my lap for you."

Maria scooted forward and peeked around the front of the couch but darted back to her corner with a thud. Gloria leaned into Bethany and whispered, "Mommy."

Carlos stood just inside the room. The thick fingers of one hand clutched the case of his new, long barrel revolver while a small box of bullets rested in the curled fingers of his other hand. His eyebrows shot up, along with his chin, as if beckoning her.

Bethany held Gloria tight, wary eyes searching Carlos' face.

He nodded toward the door. "Let's go."

"Go where?" Her eyes darted to the gun case as heat swirled up from her belly. She shook her head. "No. I can't."

Carlos tucked the case under his arm and closed the distance between them. He jerked Bethany off the couch by one arm, dumping Gloria to the side. Gloria scrambled to the other end of the couch without taking her wide eyes from her parents.

Color crept up his face as he growled into Bethany's ear. "Why don't you ever listen?" He gave her a little shake and let go as he tipped his head back and yelled at the ceiling. "Kenny! Come watch your sisters." Storming to the front door, he opened it and looked at her with impatient eyes. "Let's go."

She dropped a kiss on top of Gloria's head. Better to get him away from the kids until his mood improved. Relief washed over her when she saw Kenny Evans, a sixteen-year-old boy version of herself, dressed in his typical knee-length beach shorts and plain tee-shirt. He rushed down the stairs and scooped Gloria up.

If only Carlos weren't bringing the revolver. A knot grew in her belly. Where were they going? At least the girls would be okay. She couldn't let worry find a crack in her armor.

Her best defense was a level head and a casual attitude. She took one last look at her beautiful children. Kenny's face was creased with concern as he watched her shut the door.

• • •

Twenty minutes later, their four-door truck lurched from smooth pavement to dirt road. Bethany opened her hands and wiped the palms on the front of her jeans. Carlos had been strangely silent since they'd left. He drove with one hand draped over the top of the steering wheel, smoking, and periodically looking at himself in the rearview mirror. Years ago, she'd found his infatuation with himself amusing. The amusement had long faded, and now she was repulsed by it. Mirrors. Sometimes he'd raise his eyebrows, frown, or pretend to laugh.

He took one last drag off his cigarette before flicking the butt out the window. The truck hit a long washboard causing the gun case and box of bullets to rattle on the center counsel and nearly push Carlos' army cap over the edge. He snatched the cap, flung it into the back seat, popped open the gun case, and stroked the barrel. The corner of his mouth twitched when he caught her watching him. She forced a smile, but when he winked at her, the back of her neck tingled and goosebumps popped up on her arms.

Dry grass and weeds seemed to choke out the road as they drove. She cleared her throat and faked cheerfulness. "How much farther?"

"Far enough that no one hears."

She coughed. He shot her a curious look. "So much dust."

He pulled off the trail and drove into the dusty weeds and turned off the engine. "This will work." Grabbing the case and little box, he hopped out.

It was stupid to come out here with Carlos while he was still angry. But what else could she have done? She didn't know how to refuse his demands when he was upset. Sooner or later, he always got what he wanted. Sooner seemed to be less painful for everyone. She shook her head to quiet her conflicting thoughts. She jumped out. Her shoes created a little puff of dust that grew and followed her when she hurried to check the truck bed. Nothing but a little dirt and a bendy straw. "Where's the target?"

"Thought I had one." Carlos lowered the tailgate. "See anything we can use?"

Bethany searched the cab. Whew. An empty soda can was stuck under the backseat. "Found something!" Her nervous giggle annoyed her.

He loaded the bullets into the chamber and glanced around. "Great." She watched him from the back door until he gestured with the revolver. "Put it on that log over there."

Uh-huh. Nice. She forced herself to jog the short distance and dropped to her knees. She'd be filthy, but her legs were getting wobblier with each bullet Carlos loaded into the chamber. The can shook in her hand. Dumb can didn't want to stand up on the pitiful little log. When she finally got it to stay, Bethany took a deep breath and blew it all the way out. She popped up and jogged toward Carlos.

He lifted the gun and pointed it in her direction. What happened to all the gun rules he'd taught her?

She pushed out a fake laugh. "Hey, baby, don't aim that thing at me!" The cheerfulness in her voice sounded so exaggerated when it reached her ears that she wasn't sure Carlos would buy it.

But he laughed with her as he lowered the gun. "Then get your sweet bottom back over here and shoot this thing."

Just like that. Back on his good side. *Now, let's keep it that way.* When she reached him, she took the gun and kissed him in one fluid movement. It had been a few years since they'd went shooting together. They didn't own guns in those days. But they'd enjoyed shooting whenever they went on military leave. Carlos' parents had a piece of property in Arizona.

She'd fired her first shotgun to the sound of Carlos' cheers and encouragement. His dad, Antonio, was always there, and they usually had Kenny with them. It had been fun. Back then. "It's got a strong kick. Get a good grip with both hands. Don't drop my new toy in the dirt."

"I haven't forgotten how to shoot, honey."

"Sí, but this kicks harder than Papá's guns."

Bethany nodded and aimed. She squeezed off a deafening shot as her arms pulled back and her ears rang. *Wow.* "We should have brought earplugs." She clutched the revolver, terrified she'd drop it and set Carlos off again. How had she ever enjoyed this? Trembling, she shot a glance at him. His eyes twinkled, and most of his perfect teeth showed behind a boyish grin. He didn't look dangerous. He loved her. It was all over his face.

Carlos pointed at the can and laughed as he pulled her close. "I thought you didn't forget how to shoot." He smacked her butt and nudged her. "Try again."

Bethany went along with his contagious enthusiasm. Was she losing her mind? Moments like this made her wonder why she was scared of him. She missed again and laughed. "Guess you better show me how it's done."

Carlos smiled and took the revolver. "This would be more fun with a moving target." He missed his first shot, but the can flipped off the log on his second. He jumped with a fist pump. "Whooo! Still got it." Turning, he shoved the revolver into Bethany's hands and rushed out to set the can up. When he jogged back, his face was glowing. "Try again?"

Bethany shook her head. "Too loud. I'll watch." He looked so happy. If only she could keep him that way. She must be the worst wife ever. How did other women do it? She'd read about being a good wife, but everything she tried only seemed to make things worse. Why didn't any of it work for her? What was she doing wrong?

Carlos lined up his next shot. "Wonder if I'll get to shoot anyone on this deployment."

She hopped onto the tailgate, drawing her knees to her chest, and covered her ears. Another loud shot and the can sailed. She wanted to get home to the kids. Hug them. Make sure they were okay. She wanted to let Kenny know how much she appreciated him. Her thoughts drifted to the upcoming deployment as she chewed one side of her bottom lip. She could hardly wait to have Carlos out of the house for a whole year.

He was new to the unit, and, as usual, everyone seemed to think he was an amazing guy. He was unbelievably charming and helpful. Saying all the right things. It was always like that. But gradually, he would lose all but one or two friends. She'd already seen it happen at their last two duty stations.

Carlos grabbed her ankles and slid her toward the edge of the tailgate. Stepping close, he pulled her legs around him and wrapped her in his arms as he set the revolver on the truck bed behind her. He gave her a long, wet kiss. "Let's go to that new Italian place for dinner."

"What about the kids?"

"They'll be fine."

Bethany groaned inwardly. She was glad Kenny was there to pick up the slack, but she hated ditching them. The cold revolver sat behind her, the sun was sinking, and she was eager to get back to town. *Just give him what he wants.* "Let's go eat. I'll call Kenny and let him know."

He reached under her and lifted her with her legs still wrapped around him. "But what if I'm not done with you yet?" His eyes scanned the emptiness around them while he licked his lips.

If only the thrill of being desired wasn't tainted by fear.

CHAPTER TWO

BETHANY   **Monday, May 23**

The next afternoon, Bethany smiled as she watched Gloria and Maria sit on stools at the large kitchen island and clumsily ice fresh cookies. The warmth and smell of baking cookies were two of Bethany's favorite things. It brought back fond memories of the times she'd watched her mom bake.

She glanced at her phone on the counter, where Stacie smiled through the screen. Clearly, her mom loved video chatting with her granddaughters from her home in Cedar Park, Texas. "You'll have to take pictures and have Mommy send them to me."

Maria nodded. Gloria showed off her latest cookie covered in purple icing. Maria tipped the bowls of icing, looking in each one. "Where purple?"

Gloria grinned. "I made it. Watch!" She stuck her first finger in the blue icing. "Make one finger blue." She scooped a glob of red icing up with the fingers next to her blue one, being careful not to get too much blue mixed in with the red. "Get some red." With a big smile, she grabbed a bare cookie and wiped the red on top of it. As she stirred it with her blue finger, she laughed. "See! I make purple!"

Maria was mesmerized until Gloria sucked the purple off her fingers. "Mm. My turn."

Stacie's laughter floated from the phone's speaker. "Such big girls!" Bethany's mom had the best laugh. Deep and full. It had a way of filling up any lonely spaces in Bethany's heart.

Bethany handed Gloria a disinfectant wipe before she could pick up her next cookie. Gloria nodded at the phone. "We're growing, Grandma. Wanna come see how big we are?"

"I sure *do*."

Bethany squinted and pulled her lips to one side. "Yeah, if only it were closer."

There was a pause before Stacie responded. "It's just a flight, sweetie."

"I know. We've been so busy with Carlos' training for deployment. End of the school year ..." Bethany's voice trailed off. She was rescued when the front door closed and Kenny's voice reached them just before he came into view.

"Something smells good!" He only had eyes for cookies when he stepped into the kitchen.

Gloria and Maria were always happy to see their half-brother come home and made enough noise to let him know it. "Kenny's home!"

"We're making cookies!"

Stacie greeted him from the phone. "Hi, Kenny."

The first cookie was in his mouth before he said another word. "Mmmm." He closed his eyes and chewed.

Gloria gasped. "Mommy, Kenny ate one!"

Bethany struggled to suppress the smile that refused to hide. There wasn't much Kenny could do that bothered her, and he probably knew it. She shook her head anyway, more for the sake of Gloria and Maria, and tried to use a firm voice. "No more cookies till after dinner."

Kenny gasped and clutched his chest as he stumbled behind his sisters. His hand jumped through the space between them, and his fingers wiggled over the cookies. They both squealed and grabbed his arm. "No, Kenny!"

"That's it. You're gonna get it." He tickled their sides until he had to block them from falling off their stools as they flung around laughing. Bethany giggled and glanced at her phone screen to see her mom doing the same.

No one heard the front door, but Carlos' angry voice cut through the laughter. "Honey!"

A hush fell on them as the children looked at Bethany's face. She leaned over the phone. "I gotta go, Mom. Love you." She hung up before Stacie could respond. Kenny ducked out one side of the kitchen as Carlos entered from the other.

STACIE

Stacie Newfield lowered the phone to her lap with a creased forehead. Her stomach knotted as she mentally replayed the last ten seconds of the call with her daughter and grandkids. The kids were so cute, and she loved hearing them laugh together. She wished there had been more laughter when her kids were still home. They were all grown now.

Bethany was the oldest, thirty-five, and on her second marriage. The first husband was a doozy. Stacie thought Carlos was an upgrade. He was an Army guy, and they were stationed at Fort Bragg, North Carolina. The twinges of concern she'd had over the years were easy enough to explain away.

Holly was her thirty-two-year-old middle child. She only lived about twenty minutes away, in the little town of Liberty Hill. She'd never been married but was rarely single for long. Stacie never knew when the next call would come in that Holly and her twelve-year-old daughter, Felicia, needed a safe place to spend the night.

She'd lost track of how many times she'd taken Holly to the courthouse to file protective orders. Every time, she hoped Holly would pick herself up and focus on Felicia and work. Every time, Holly would either drop the protective order or get picked up by a new loser. There were countless options fishing the local clubs and bars she was drawn to on lonely nights.

Nate was Stacie's baby. He was a single military man, thirty years old, stationed at Fort Hood with a modest house in Copperas Cove. Close enough to home to see him often. He lived for God, country, and family. She was proud of him.

Stacie hadn't set a good example for her children. She wanted to deny knowing what her husband had been doing. Admitting she knew made her hate herself. Sure, she didn't understand just how far it had gone back then. But she had known enough that she now felt guilty for keeping him around for so long. Oh, how she wished she could go back and let them see her take action. Instead, she'd shown them how to put up with mistreatment continuously. How to hide it and how to protect the abuser.

People say it's best for children if their parents stay married. But Stacie had learned the hard way. There was something far worse for kids than divorce.

And now, the hardest person to forgive was herself.

She stared at the contact info on the screen of her phone. The picture of Bethany's smiling face didn't warm her this time. She was sure she'd heard Carlos' voice just before the laughter died. Bethany had said she had to go and hung up before Stacie could respond. Stacie had heard that same tone from Holly many times over the years. But why would Bethany be afraid of Carlos?

Stacie hadn't gotten a chance to get to know Carlos much herself. She hadn't known Bethany was in a serious relationship until she was suddenly married. No one had even been invited to a wedding. That was seven years ago. They'd never been back to Texas since. Bethany said it was too hard. Too many bad memories. Stacie had flown over to help out after Gloria and Maria were each born. But every other time she wanted to visit, Bethany gave her dates when Carlos would be training away from home.

He was a little loud and opinionated for Stacie's taste, but Bethany seemed to know how to deal with it. She brought his mood up with a simple touch that visibly relaxed him or a light joke to get him laughing. It had been obvious to Stacie that Carlos relied heavily on Bethany for his happiness.

Carlos loved Bethany. She was in good hands. But now... Stacie shook her head. Couldn't be. But then again... Bethany only called and took calls when Carlos wasn't there. Why? Stacie was missing something. She'd heard it in Bethany's voice right before she'd hung up.

Stacie never wanted anyone to feel the way she'd felt when her late husband had finally been arrested. She'd quickly become the topic of gossip. She'd been embarrassed and ashamed. The things he'd put her kids through were worse than anything she could have imagined. How blind she'd been. How selfish. Wrapped in a blanket of insecurities, it had been too hard to see past his lies and accusations. She knew now that she'd *wanted* to believe him.

Afterward, she'd wondered why so many people told her they'd suspected all along. If they'd suspected, why hadn't anyone said anything to *her*? Why hadn't anyone helped? If someone had confronted her, she would have questioned his deception.

But would she have? She wanted to think so.

Now, she shook her head. She hoped she was wrong, but if there was even a chance this sinking feeling had merit, she refused to become one of those people to sit by and wait for something to happen. Maybe Holly or Nate knew more.

Stacie wandered into the kitchen to make tea as she listened to her phone ring Nate's line. Just when she thought she'd have to leave a message, he picked up.

"Hey there, handsome. Got a question for ya. What do you think of Carlos?"

"Bethany's Carlos? Hardly know him. According to Bethany, he's Prince Charming in the flesh. Why?"

Stacie examined the various boxes of flavored tea without seeing them. "Was on the phone with her. He came home and she suddenly had to go. Something in her voice."

"Seriously, Mom?"

"I know. Silly, right?" She shook her head and grabbed the spiced chai.

"About to leave. Got anything good goin' for dinner?"

Stacie chuckled. "I'll put something on."

They hung up, and Stacie pulled two chicken breasts from the freezer. Her phone rang. Felicia's cute face lit the screen. "What's up, pretty lady?"

"Grammy, can I spend the night? Mom said she needs time alone with Danny. He's upset again and Mom's been cryin' all day. I don't wanna be here anyway."

"Need a ride?"

"Yeah. Can ya come right now?"

Stacie pulled another chicken breast from the freezer. "Yup. On my way, Princess."

FELICIA

Felicia tossed her phone on the edge of the bed and grabbed a backpack. Thank goodness for Grammy. After she dumped her binder and loose papers in the middle of the bed, she stuffed a pair of jeans in the bottom. She knew she had about a half-hour before her grandma pulled in, but she was eager to get out of the house.

Danny was such a jerk, especially when he was drinking. She couldn't stand the yelling and she didn't want to be around if Danny started breaking things again. Her hand froze with a pair of socks over the bag.

Maybe she should call Grammy back and cancel.

Danny and her mom had been seeing each other just over a year, and they'd all moved in together nine months ago. It only took about a week for Felicia to see that Danny wasn't any better than the other guys they'd lived with. The main difference was that Danny was *almost* okay when he was sober. Too bad that wasn't very often. Especially lately.

But about two months ago, there was this night when she'd been scarfing down her second corndog while sitting on the kitchen counter. Her mom had raced in with Danny yelling right behind her. There was no sneaking out unseen. Awkward.

Mom had turned on Danny and screamed back in his face. Danny had smacked her in the mouth. Next thing Felicia knew, the last half of her corndog launched out of her hand and bounced off Danny's face. Felicia had frozen while Danny covered his eye with both hands and roared. Time seemed to slow down. Felicia couldn't take her eyes off Danny. She was hot and trapped, and when Danny screamed the f-word and a string of names Felicia wasn't allowed to repeat, she was sure she was about to die.

Mom suddenly grabbed Felicia's wrist and yanked her off the counter. There was something wrong with Felicia's legs. Like she was trying to run through mud. Her mom kept pushing her from behind as they rushed to the front door. "Go."

As soon as their bare feet hit the rough wood of the front porch, Mom snagged Felicia's elbow and pulled. "Come on."

They'd barely made it to the sidewalk when Danny burst out the front door. "I'll get you, ya little—"

"Don't stop." Mom yanked Felicia's arm.

The neighbor had opened his door. "What's going on?" That's all it had taken to get Danny to shrink back inside and shut the door. *Coward.*

Her mom hadn't wanted her to tell Grammy what had happened. The only way Felicia agreed to keep quiet was if they moved out. That's when Mom had called Uncle Nate and asked if they could stay with him for a while. Even then, Felicia doubted Nate knew any details. For some stupid reason, her mom didn't want anyone to know just how horrible her jerks were.

As far as Felicia knew, that was the only time he'd ever done anything like that. Mom would be fine tonight. They were trying to make up now. Danny would be nice.

Grammy had come to Felicia's rescue all her life. Every time she didn't want to stay around the arguing. Different jerks. Same issues. Thank goodness for Grammy.

Felicia finished packing. Throwing her backpack over her shoulder, she went to wait on the couch. She could see the driveway from the window. Danny and her mom were in their bedroom. Felicia could still hear them every once in a while. She opened the music app on her phone and stuck her neon green earbuds in to block out the noise while waiting.

BETHANY

Bethany glanced at Kenny's back as he hurried out and then forced a smile for Gloria and Maria. She was relieved Kenny was safely in another room. "Look, Daddy's home!" She kept her smile in place for Carlos. "How was work?"

"I'm going out tonight." Carlos shoved a cookie in his mouth and talked around it. "One of my soldiers is in the hospital."

"What happened?"

"He was jumped last night and almost killed."

"That's terrible! Yes. Go visit him."

Maria fidgeted on her stool. Carlos shook his head while Gloria watched another cookie disappear into his mouth. His voice grew angry and loud. "Oh, I'm going to visit *someone* tonight—someone that will pay for this.

Maria bounced on her stool, making little noises with each bounce. Bethany helped her down. Gloria watched her sister run from the room and then licked her lips. "Cookie?"

Bethany shook her head and lifted Gloria off the stool with a peck on the forehead. "After dinner, sweet pea. Go play with Maria now."

Bethany's eyebrows drew together as she tried to understand. She smoothed her expression and busied herself placing cookies in a jar while her insides twisted. "Then, who will you visit?" She glanced at him.

"I know which gang did this. I'm going to kill at least one of them tonight."

Her wide gaze crashed into his piercing one as her throat tightened. *No!* The corner of his lips twitched. She'd given him a reaction but she couldn't help it. Murder was not a path she wanted her husband to take. He was scary enough as it was. There was a pinprick of concern for the intended victim, but she was far more worried about how murder might change Carlos. Guilt washed through her at her selfishness. She was a terrible person.

Cold, steady eyes examined her face. "It'll be easy." He shrugged one shoulder.

"You could get caught."

"I know how to kill people and get away with it. It's not that hard."

Her voice came out low and raspy. "Please, don't do this."

"Leaving after dinner." Carlos popped a cookie in his mouth and walked out, chuckling.

STACIE

Stacie grabbed her purse and keys from the little table by the front door and slid into flip-flops. She rushed to the blue Corolla parked in the garage and set off for the cute two-bedroom mobile home Holly shared with Danny.

She needed a distraction. She pressed a button in her car. "Call Rich."

A slightly robotic but confident voice replied through her car speakers, "Calling Rich."

Two rings and then, "Stacie! A pleasant surprise." She heard the smile in his deep voice and enjoyed the automatic upward pull of her lips in response. They'd attended the same church at least a decade. Their friendship had blossomed over the past three years. It started with the day they were put in charge of organizing the games at a big, singles-over-fifty event their church had hosted.

"I'm on my way to Holly's to pick up Felicia for the night."

"Oh? Fun plans?"

Stacie sighed. She'd long since confided her concerns about Holly's love life.

He seemed to understand. "I see. No plans yet, but you'll make it fun anyway."

She rolled her eyes with a smile, realizing why she'd called him. He had a way of turning her attention where she wanted it. Somehow, he brought out the best in her. "I suppose I'll have to." She sighed. "I don't know what I'm about to walk into."

"Just remember, you don't have to go in there alone. If it's not safe, call the police. I don't want anything happening to you. Any of you."

Stacie nodded. "Yeah. Thank you."

"If you need me, just call. I could come out there, but I don't have a badge, and I don't want to make things worse."

Ten minutes later, she turned onto Holly's street. Stacie longed to swoop her daughter far away from Danny and lock her in a tower somewhere. Keep her from finding another low-life.

As Stacie pulled into the driveway, Felicia's face disappeared from the front window. She jogged to the car three seconds later with a backpack over her shoulder. Stacie stood from the car and looked past Felicia. "Where's your momma?"

"Bedroom with Danny." Felicia hopped into the passenger seat and shut the door.

Stacie hesitated. She couldn't leave without making sure Holly was okay. She stuffed her phone in her back pocket as she strode to the door.

Inside, she strained to quickly adjust her eyes to the dim light before heading to the master bedroom and tapping on the door.

Danny hollered, "Felicia! Done told you already. Leave us be!"

Holly's broken voice didn't give Stacie a chance to respond. "Don't talk to her like—"

"—Knock it off!" Something banged on the other side of the door.

Blood rushed to Stacie's face. One hand-cranked the doorknob while the other slammed into the door, causing it to fly open and bounce off the doorstop. Danny spun toward her with his ugly mouth hanging open. He wasn't bad looking, but Stacie couldn't stand the sight of him.

She yanked her phone out of her pocket and held it up. "Got the police already dialed. Give me a reason to tap my screen." She hovered a finger over the black screen.

Holly wiped mascara-stained tears from her face and slid off the bed. "Whatcha doing, Mom? Danny just wanted some time alone with me."

"He hit you?"

Holly shook her head. "The dresser."

Danny threw his hands up. "I wouldn't hurt her. She drives me crazy, but I still love her."

"Done it before." Stacie glared at him.

Danny rolled his eyes and dismissed her with one hand and shot Holly a look.

Holly walked to Stacie and put a hand on Stacie's arm, steering her out of the bedroom. "Felicia going home with you?"

Stacie knew that forced tone in Holly's voice and nodded while her heart broke at the way Holly protected Danny. He didn't deserve it. She searched Holly's face, hoping for a sign that she wanted help. Even the slightest hint and Stacie wouldn't leave without her.

"Thanks for taking her. Can you get her to school in the morning? We'll be up too late for her to come home tonight."

Stacie covered the hand Holly had put on her arm with her other hand and allowed herself to be led toward the front door. She dropped her voice. "You okay?"

"Yeah. Danny needs me tonight. Some reason, he thinks I been flirting with one of my customers. Just gotta remind him that he's my one-and-only." Fake smile.

Stacie felt hot all over and nodded. "If you're sure."

Danny startled her when he poked his face between theirs. "Said she was."

It was all Stacie could do not to punch him in the nose. How much longer before Holly was finally done with this clown? She glared at Danny. "This is my daughter. Be good to her."

"Always am." He mocked a vampire bite to Holly's neck and laughed.

Holly giggled and pushed him away. She hugged Stacie while speaking into her ear. "It's okay, Momma. He loves me."

Stacie didn't want to hate anyone, but Danny made it hard not to. With a fire in her chest, she headed to the car.

Felicia cleared her throat as they pulled onto the street. "Can we get Chinese for dinner?"

Stacie glanced at her granddaughter's beautiful face and forced herself to shift from concern about Holly to quality time with Felicia. "I set chicken out, but ..."

Felicia smiled and leaned her head against Stacie's arm. "But Chinese sounds better, huh?" *Irresistible.*

Stacie laughed. "Let me call Uncle Nate."

"Uncle Nate's coming?" Joy filled Felicia's voice. She leaned back with a wide smile.

BETHANY

Carlos appeared to be in a good mood during dinner and even cleared his own dishes afterward. Bethany started to wonder if he'd changed his mind until he kissed her on his way out of the kitchen. "Time to get ready." His smile and wink turned her dinner to lead in her stomach.

A tornado of terror and hope churned her insides. The hope made her feel like a rotten person so she let her mind play over the root of her terror instead. Killing someone would change him. He'd be more dangerous with her and the kids. She was especially worried about Kenny.

But she wasn't convinced he could get away with it. And that led to hope. If he actually did it, he might get caught, and her prayers for change would finally be answered.

While she didn't want anyone to *die*, she couldn't help the joy at the thought of being free from Carlos' temper, control, threats, and criticism. But could she stand by and *let* someone be murdered for a *chance* at freedom? Had she become that selfish?

She worked to keep the rush of competing emotions from pushing out rational thought. What if he didn't get caught? If he got away with murder—She had to talk him out of it.

Bethany opened the door to the master suite with her heart pounding in her ears. The room was huge. Their bedroom furniture didn't quite fill the side left of the doorway. Against the wall, across from the bedroom door, was a small desk and office chair. The doorway to the bathroom and walk-in closet was to the right.

Carlos came out of the bathroom. He scooped up a rucksack as he walked toward her and slung it over his broad shoulder. Bethany cleared her throat and closed their bedroom door.

"Time to go." He stepped close but she remained between him and the door.

She bit her lip and wrung her hands. Now was the time to let him see how worried she was. He didn't need to know why.

He cupped her chin. "I have to do something. This kid is in the hospital."

The emotional tug-of-war was too much. Tears sprung to Bethany's eyes. "It's illegal. It's not your fight, Carlos. It's murder." She struggled with whether or not to voice her real fear. Finally, she whispered, "It could change you."

Carlos shook his head and wrapped his free arm around her shoulders. As he pulled her close, he whispered in her ear, "Baby girl, I'll be okay."

Her arms went around his waist. She clung to him as if her grip could somehow stop him from going. "Please don't."

"How will I live with myself if I do nothing?"

"How will you live with yourself if you get caught?" She tipped her head back, looked in his eyes, and then kissed him. "Just come to bed, honey. It's late." She buried her face in his chest. "Stay with me." She felt him relax in her arms. Her kisses became more demanding. He seemed to melt into them with a sigh.

Bethany pulled the rucksack off his shoulder. His arms reached for her as he watched her set it down. "How do you do this?"

She took his hand and led him toward the bed. He sighed. "You are the only one in the world I listen to. The *only* one that changes my mind."

"I love you, Carlos."

"Oh, I know you do. But I love you more."

CHAPTER THREE

BETHANY   **Tuesday, May 24**

The next afternoon, Bethany pulled warm clothes from the dryer and folded them on a long counter. Doing laundry relaxed her. The washer and dryer's rhythmic sound brought back the sense of security she'd always felt at her grandparent's house. She couldn't think of a single time her dad was anything but appropriately loving whenever they'd visited her mom's parents. They'd always been safe at Grandma's.

As she folded a tiny pair of pink jeans, a loud and long burp came from downstairs. Kenny's surprised voice held a hint of pride as he called out, "Wow, Mom! You hear that?"

Bethany shook her head with a smile. She opened her mouth to respond, but before any sound came out, Carlos' heavy footsteps charged from their bedroom and stormed downstairs.

"You think that's funny, Kenny? It was rude and disgusting!"

She crept to the landing above the stairs and held her breath. Something smashed into a wall. She ran downstairs on the balls of her feet. As her foot hit the last step, she forced herself to slow down and look as unruffled as possible. She wouldn't be able to calm Carlos down if he saw how frantic she was.

But what Bethany saw made her want to jump on him. He held Kenny against the wall with his meaty hand on Kenny's chest, fingers pressed near the base of Kenny's throat.

Kenny had recently grown slightly taller than Carlos but was still nowhere near his mass. Bethany shook. "Don't—" Her throat closed. She put a hand on Carlos' arm.

He let go of Kenny and flung his arms back. One side of his lip curled as he watched Kenny adjust his shirt. Carlos pushed his face close to Kenny's and jabbed a fat finger against his chest. "This is my house! You will respect my house."

Kenny side-stepped and dropped his head. Bethany wanted to reach out and touch him, let him know he wasn't alone, but couldn't risk making things worse.

Carlos glared. "You're disgusting."

Bethany moved to Kenny's side. "It was only a burp."

"It was rude!"

Kenny shuffled his feet. "No one was downstairs. Didn't know it'd be so loud."

"I don't care!"

Bethany sighed and looked beyond Kenny. *Oh no. Not again.* There was a large, shallow imprint in the wall where Kenny's shoulders and upper back had been. A heaviness settled in her chest. "Go upstairs, Kenny." He shot her a look of gratitude with pink, watery eyes.

Carlos' loud voice took on a mocking tone. "Aw, you need your mommy to come to your rescue again?"

Kenny's eyes flashed. He stood up straight, making their height difference more obvious, and took half a step toward Carlos with clenched fists.

Bethany immediately stepped between them, giving Kenny a tiny shake of her head. She jerked her chin toward the doorway and mouthed, "Go."

Kenny turned and hurried from the room with fists pressed against his sides.

Carlos taunted his departing back. "I see you running, Mommy's boy." When Bethany turned, Carlos was already glaring at her. "I can't believe you're not angry with him!"

"He's sixteen. He's going to burp."

His face darkened. "Not in my house. Why do you defend him?"

She traced the edge of the dent with her finger and sighed. She longed for peace and felt discouraged at her inability to maintain it. She couldn't stop Kenny from annoying Carlos, and she couldn't stop Carlos from overreacting. All she could do was jump between them and then try to smooth things over with each of them later. It was exhausting.

Carlos' face was rich with color. "I want to see *you* get angry with him." Heat crept up her neck. He pointed at the dent. "You think I *want* that?" His voice grew louder. "I buy you this big house. I give you all this stuff." He looked at the ceiling and screamed, "And I get no respect!"

He did spend a lot of money on them. Shame weighed heavily on her shoulders. "I'm sorry."

"What happens when I'm deployed? Kenny will run wild without me here."

A bump in the doorway drew her attention in time to glimpse Gloria's head dart out of sight. Feeling sick, Bethany tuned Carlos out to listen to Gloria's little footsteps race up the stairs. It didn't matter what he said. She'd heard it all before. Bethany caught another sound and held her breath. If only Carlos would shut up. Her head tipped sideways as if bringing one ear up would make it easier to hear. No doubt. The familiar sound, dull and steady, replaced every other emotion with sheer panic.

Thump. Thump. Thump. "Gotta check on the girls." She raced to the stairs.

Thump. Thump. She took the stairs two at a time. *Thump.* She ran softly down the hall— *Thump*—and around a corner. *Thump.* There were two bedroom doors down this hall. *Thump.* Bethany stopped at the first one. *Thump.* She relaxed her face as she opened the door.

The pink room held two twin beds, one on either side, with dolls and stuffed animals scattered on the floor. *Thump.* Gloria sat on a bed, holding a stuffed puppy in one hand and a faded baby blanket in the other. When Bethany stepped inside and shut the door, Gloria's eyes swung to the white closet door. *Thump.*

Bethany slid the door open. *Thump.* Maria, legs drawn to her chest, steadily bumped the back of her head against the wall. *Thump.* Bethany's stomach clenched. Was Maria giving herself brain damage? This closet-head-thumping had started a couple of months before.

Bethany hurried to put her hand between Maria's head and the wall, pulling Maria onto her lap with her other hand. "No, no, no, Princess." Bethany wrapped her arms around her youngest daughter and sat in the corner of the closet. Maria curled up in Bethany's lap. Her body gradually relaxed as Bethany stroked her soft hair.

A few minutes later, heavy footsteps passed in the hall. "Kenny. I need to talk to you."

Maria swung her face into Bethany's chest. "It's okay." Bethany whispered with her lips against the top of Maria's head, "Daddy just wants to talk with your brother." Maybe Carlos had cooled down, and Kenny would let him vent.

She let herself relax and leaned her head against the wall as silent tears flowed from her closed eyes. Once again, she looked forward to his upcoming deployment. Things would be so much sweeter during a nice long break from Carlos.

• • •

After crawling into bed that night, Bethany turned off the lamp and waited.

Carlos let out a big sigh. "Kenny said he thought about calling 911 today. You believe the nerve of that kid?"

He did? *And* he actually told Carlos? Wow. But then again, anything could come out of a talk with Carlos.

Disagreements could last hours and only ended when Carlos was convinced the other person knew he was right. He often bragged that he was always right and others would eventually realize it, even if it took a while. He seemed oblivious to the other alternative. Others just got sick of the conversation and wanted to end it at any cost.

Carlos turned to his side and propped his head up with his hand. "Told him he better not *ever* pull a stunt like that."

"You were hard on him."

"Bull crap. If he can't take that, he will never make it out there. I just toughen him up."

Bethany sighed. Another excuse for his cruel behavior. But the idea of Kenny calling 911 made Bethany's heart race. If only …

Carlos flopped his head on the pillow. "If he doesn't like the way things are around here, he can move out." He wrapped an arm around her waist and yanked her against him. "You'll never leave me, though." He chuckled. "You even *think* of leaving; I'll take our girls." His kisses were wet. He whispered with his lips still against hers. "You'd never see them again."

Bethany's face flushed and tears leaked from the corners of her eyes. She couldn't bear the thought of life without her kids.

Carlos rubbed his cheek against the side of her face. When he felt the tears wet against her temple, he moaned deep in his throat. "I love you so much." He groped her body and pressed himself against her. Why did her pain excite him? "You will never leave."

She cringed, but he was right. She couldn't. He would take her girls, and they needed her.

CHAPTER FOUR

Bethany woke up just before the scream of terror ripped from her throat. She controlled a couple of deep breaths to bring her heart rate back to a reasonable pace. *Just a nightmare.* She heard Carlos getting ready for work through the open bathroom door. She had to tell him about the dream. Hear his reassurance that it was totally unrealistic. He'd tell her that something like that could never actually *happen*.

She rubbed the sleep from her eyes as she walked to the bathroom. Carlos squeezed toothpaste onto his toothbrush. "I had a terrible dream last night."

He glanced at her in the mirror and put the toothbrush in his mouth.

"You grabbed your gun and were heading down the hall to kill Kenny."

He lifted one eyebrow and nodded. He brushed his teeth with one hand and flexed his other arm. Not the reaction she'd hoped for, but maybe he was trying to be funny.

"Then I was trying to find the phone to call the police—"

Carlos jerked the toothbrush out of his mouth and almost choked. "You called the police?" He spit in the sink. "Wow, first Kenny, and now you."

Bethany frowned as she remembered what Carlos had said the night before.

"You wouldn't really do that …?" His voice trailing off like bait. The reflection of his eyes focused on hers.

"If you were going after one of the kids to *kill* them, I would. You had a gun." Was he actually upset?

He studied his reflection as if considering his next words. His eyes snapped back to hers in the mirror. "Know what would happen if you did that?"

Her heart pounded the way it had in her dream. She shook her head, unable to break eye contact with his reflection.

"I'd shoot you." One firm nod. "Then, I'd shoot all the kids. When the police came, I'd start shooting them too." His cold eyes held her gaze.

The shaking started in her core and flowed to her arms, legs, and jaw. He meant it. Everything in his face, tone, and words all revealed how much he actually meant it. She had never been more terrified in her life. No matter how much he scared her, she could never call for help or he'd kill them all. For the first time, she wondered if counseling would be enough. How much worse would he be after another deployment? Bethany had to get out of the bathroom before her trembling legs failed her. She clenched shaking hands together in front of her, hesitating with one last hope that he would smile and tell her he was joking.

Carlos raked her trembling body with his eyes and grunted with a half-smile. He turned back to his reflection and continued brushing his teeth. The temperature must have dropped because Bethany was freezing. Her jaw was so tight it hurt. She caught her reflection in the mirror as she hugged herself. The terror in her eyes shocked her. So that's what Carlos saw. That's what he enjoyed. She turned and drifted from the bathroom. The police could never help her.

She wrapped a thick bathrobe around her body. She didn't want to die, and she couldn't lose any of her children to his selfish rages. She would keep him happy these last two weeks before he deployed. Then, she'd have a whole year to come up with a plan.

Stacie

Stacie grilled the chicken she'd pulled from the freezer two days before. After a Chinese dinner with Nate and Felicia, she'd tossed it in the fridge for later. As she lathered barbeque sauce on the chicken, she thought about her day. Her florist shop had been quiet, and none of her flower arrangements seemed quite right. How could flowers actually look depressed? Maybe it was her mood. She'd finally given up trying to be productive and closed shop early. She'd asked Nate to come over for dinner. Quality time with her son was just what she needed.

As he scraped the last bite of food onto his fork, he smiled at her. "Was really good, Ma. Thanks for dinner."

She loved feeding this man. She'd never cooked for a more appreciative person. Chewing, he moved the empty plate aside and reached across the table with his hand open. She grabbed it. Warmth spread through her chest. She didn't deserve a son like him.

"Okay, Mom. You ready to tell me what's up?"

She snickered. "What makes you think something's up?"

He squeezed her hand and raised one eyebrow. "How long I known ya?"

Stacy rolled her eyes.

Nate leaned back and put both hands behind his head, elbows out. "Holly or Bethy?"

A laugh burst from Stacie at his cocky, know-it-all attitude. She tossed her paper napkin in his direction. It only made it halfway across the table.

He smiled. "Couldn't really talk with Felicia around the other night. Was Danny there when you picked her up?"

Stacie nodded and told him about the incident. As she talked, Nate leaned forward and rested his elbows on the table. A crease grew between his eyebrows. When she finished, he growled and shook his head. "Momma. I don't wantcha going over there when Danny's home. Don't trust him."

"If Holly or Felicia need me, I will."

"No. If they be needing somethin', ya call me. I'll go."

"What if you're working?"

"Don't matter. I *do not* want you there without me." He leaned back and shrugged one shoulder. "Family emergency. I'll be there."

Stacie studied his expression. But what if he wasn't fast enough?

"I don't wanna go to jail, but if he ever did something to hurt you … Well, I suppose God could use me in jail too."

"You better not go to jail." She sighed and rolled her eyes. "I'll stay away when Danny's home. Unless I *have* to be there."

"Can't have no one hurtin' you." He rubbed his eyes and leaned back. "Don't want no one hurting *Holly* either, but I'm still workin' out how to keep *her* safe. Can't believe she went back after I had her all set her up at my place. This shoulda been over already."

"I know. First-time leaving doesn't usually take. She'll get sick of it and leave for good one of these days. Wish Felicia could move in with me until she does."

Nate nodded. "Can ya please do something for me?"

Stacie lifted her eyebrows and tipped her head.

"Next time yer around Danny." He dipped his chin and looked up at Stacie with a small shake of his head. "Don't challenge him."

"You think I *challenged* him?" Stacie's face flushed. Her eyes flashed.

"I think *he* saw it that way. Don't give him a reason to hurt you."

"A *reason*? That man doesn't *need* a reason, and there is *no* excuse for hurting people." She slammed her palm on the table. "Don't you go making excuses for men like that."

She stood and snatched their plates off the table. "Don't you do it, Nate. No excuses!"

He followed her to the kitchen with his hands lifted in surrender. "Didn't come out right. *Course,* there's no excuse. Just looking at it from *his* perspective is all."

Her eyes shot to his face. "But I don't *want* you to share *his* perspective. It's not right." She set the plates in the sink with a clatter.

"True." Nate put his hands on her shoulders and dropped his voice. "Just wanna make sure yer never his target."

Stacie nodded and hugged him. She understood. But if Holly or Felicia needed help faster than Nate could get there, she'd still go. She'd do anything to keep them safe even if Danny didn't like it.

Nate's arms felt good. How'd her son grow up so fast? After a quiet moment, he chuckled. She pulled back with a question in her eyes.

"Aren't ya glad we don't have to worry about Bethany like this?"

Uncertainty stirred in Stacie's heart. She smiled. "Yeah."

"She got her bad apple out of the way. Sheesh. I sure am ready for Holly to do the same. Maybe then I could actually consider finding me a good woman."

Stacie backed up, shocked. "*That* why you haven't found someone? Cuz of your sisters?"

"Partly." His eyes dropped. He traced a line on the tile with his toe. "Sometimes, I worry." He shrugged. "Might turn out like Dad."

She gasped. "Oh, Nate. You're *nothing* like him."

BETHANY

Bethany was making soup and rolls for dinner. The rolls had already filled the kitchen with a mouth-watering aroma that made it hard for Bethany to resist. At the stove, she popped a bean in her mouth to see if it was soft enough to add the other ingredients. She jumped when Carlos wrapped his arms around her from behind. "You're home early."

His breath tickled her ear. "Wanted to surprise you." Warm hands on her waist turned her around. His smiling face brought tingles to her belly that she hadn't felt in a while. "Brought you something." He side-stepped to reveal a massive bouquet of spring flowers on the island counter.

She gasped and covered her mouth with one hand. "Oh!" Burying her nose in the flowers, she sucked in the tangy scent.

Carlos pulled her close. "Couldn't find any as pretty as you." His kisses were tender and loving. No trace of the man she was scared of this morning. Maybe she'd misunderstood him. Bethany wanted to stop time. She sighed and leaned into his kiss.

Kenny strolled in, coughed, and opened the fridge. The moment dissolved but left a lingering warmth inside of Bethany. Carlos dropped his arms and leaned against the counter, watching Kenny rummage through the fridge. Bethany placed a tomato on the cutting board and went to work dicing it while shooting glances at Carlos.

Kenny pulled out an apple and took a big bite. He shut the door with his foot as he turned and walked to the kitchen window. Carlos crossed his arms and straightened, eyes following Kenny. What was wrong? Bethany silently pleaded with Carlos. *Please, just go upstairs.* Kenny took another bite and chewed while gazing out the window.

Carlos squinted. "What are you doing?" Kenny continued eating and didn't seem to realize Carlos was talking to him. Carlos raised his voice. "Hey!"

Kenny turned. Carlos repeated his question. Kenny tipped his head sideways. "Eating."

"Why not sit at the table?"

Kenny shrugged.

Carlos waved an arm at Kenny. "It's bad manners to eat standing up."

"But I like it."

Carlos moved closer to Kenny and put his hands on his hips. "As long as you live in *my* house, you will eat sitting. Now, sit down!" He pointed to a chair.

Kenny sat but only took one small bite before he popped up, tossed the majority of his apple in the trash, and strolled out.

Carlos swung around and looked at Bethany with a vein bulging on his forehead. "He has no manners." Carlos stormed out of the kitchen. Heavy footsteps indicated he was headed to their bedroom.

As Bethany added chopped veggies to the pot, Kenny strolled in from the other side with a smile. "Smells good. I'm starved."

Bethany nodded, wondering if he'd intentionally provoked Carlos. "Be ready soon." She tossed the last handful of veggies in.

Kenny took the spoon and stirred. "I'm thinking of moving in with a friend."

"What? No." She shook her head and grabbed his shoulder.

"I can't do this anymore. We all dread him coming home. Every. Single. Day."

"I know, but just wait a little longer. He needs help. He's trying, but he needs counseling or—" She shrugged. "Something."

"I don't know if I can."

Panic rose in Bethany's chest. "Two more weeks. Just wait till he deploys. While he's gone, I'll convince him to start counseling. He'll be better."

Kenny's face blurred on the other side of Bethany's tear-filled eyes. He sighed and wrapped his arms around her, resting his chin on top of her head. "Okay, Mom. I'll wait."

She wasn't sure how much longer she could juggle it. But she figured she could hold everything together for two weeks. Maybe. It was so close now. What could happen?

CHAPTER FIVE

FELICIA   **Thursday, May 26**

The next afternoon, Felicia was ticked as she sat on the kitchen counter and watched her mom's fingertip trace the wood grain on their kitchen table. Danny had pealed out of their driveway, making it safe to come out of her room and raid the fridge. But one look at her mom, wearing another fake smile, and Felicia was ready to spit fire. She was sick of this version of her mom. She missed her mom's laugh. Her *real* smiles. Real conversations. This sucked. "How much longer are you gonna put up with that loser?"

Mom's mouth dropped open. "Don't call him that."

Felicia groaned with an eye roll. "How long, Mom? Can we be done with this one yet?"

Tears filled her mom's eyes. *Oh please, for real?* Felicia leaned to one side and twisted to open the cupboard behind her. There was a box of cheesy crackers just waiting to be devoured. She popped three into her mouth and savored the burst of imitation cheese. *Yummy.*

"He's not gonna change, Mom. Let's just leave. Uncle Nate would probably let us stay with him again. Grammy would let us stay there. But her house is really small. I vote Uncle Nate's." Her mom watched her munch crackers, but Felicia couldn't tell what she was thinking. Wouldn't it be so cool if they *planned* to leave instead of always waiting until something happened?

Mom shook her head. "Can't ask Uncle Nate. And Grammy doesn't need to worry about us. Maybe it would be better to have a fresh start somewhere else."

Wait. What? Was Mom actually considering it? Felicia jumped off the counter and slid into a chair. Leaning over the table, she locked eyes with her mom. "Where? I'm ready. Can we go before Danny gets home from work?"

A spark lit her mom's eyes and ignited a thrill of excitement in Felicia's belly. This would be fun. Just the two of them again on an adventure. No jerks. "Can we go to Hawaii?"

Mom chuckled. Felicia's heart soared at the genuine sound of joy. She bounced in her chair like a child unable to contain her delight.

Her mom laughed and shook her head. "That would be fun, wouldn't it?"

Felicia's head bobbed. "Or Florida."

"Nothing so glamorous. Sorry." Mom's smile kept her words from disappointing Felicia.

"Then, *where?*"

"What about North Carolina?"

Felicia pulled back against her chair and drew her eyebrows together. Who ever heard of running away to North Carolina? She'd never heard anything cool about North Carolina. Both of Felicia's suggestions had been *south*. South equals warm and tropical, right? This was so far north they had to include it in the name of the state. She may as well have said, Alaska. Felicia failed to keep the whine out of her voice. "I want to go somewhere *warm*."

"North Carolina *is* warm. Your aunt Bethy's there. I hear they have a nice big house. You could hang out with Kenny again."

That actually didn't sound so bad. Kenny was cool. They'd spent a lot of time together before Aunt Bethy had moved when Felicia was little. Might be fun. But Aunt Bethy was married. Felicia didn't know Uncle Carlos. Was he a typical jerk? Or nice, like Uncle Nate? She tipped her head to one side as she thought about it. "Might be cool." She nodded and allowed a slow smile to grow.

"Okay, then. I'll call my sister and see what she says." Her mom looked happy and her voice changed when she said the word "sister." She made it sound like having a sister was something special.

North Carolina. What would it be like? She skipped to the freezer. While she waited for her Pizza Pocket to cook, she pulled her phone out to look up the weather in North Carolina. Not bad. She could hardly wait to go. Except, she'd miss Jasmine, the only friend that actually got her. Well, they'd always have the internet. They could still text and call each other. Even from the other side of the world. It would be worth it. *Goodbye, Danny.*

Bethany

Gloria and Maria were cute when they played in the bath together. They seemed to enjoy their ponies most. The bathing part finished, Bethany appreciated a few relaxing minutes before she'd have to pull them out against their will.

Her cell phone vibrated on the counter. Holly. Her sister didn't call unless something was wrong. But since she was rarely single, and tended to choose unstable men, Bethany heard from her regularly. "Hey, sis!"

"Hi. Um. How ya doing?" *Uh oh.* Holly wanted something. Bethany never liked this game. *Just get to the point.*

"Good. Getting ready to take the girls out of the tub. What's up?"

Holly jumped in but talked so fast it was hard to understand. Bethany let her ramble and tried to put the words and phrases together as she watched her girls make their ponies jump from the edge of the tub into the water with a splash.

Bethany shifted to a sympathetic voice and walked around the corner. "Danny being a jerk again?"

"Can I come stay with you for a few days?" Bethany's mind raced to Carlos. No way she wanted Holly to see him like this. Holly cleared her throat. "I would've asked Nate, but he wasn't happy when I moved back in with Danny. He'll just lecture me. Know what it's like to be lectured by your *younger* brother?"

"Holly—"

"*Please,* Bethy."

"I *want* to say yes, but Carlos is getting ready to deploy, and it's been crazy." She poked her head into the doorway long enough to make sure both girls' heads were above water.

Holly sniffed. "But I already told Felicia. She's so excited."

Bethany sighed. She couldn't even let her sister come because of *him*. As soon as Carlos was gone, Holly and Felicia could stay the whole year if they wanted. "I can't say yes until Carlos deploys. Two weeks from today." She tried to make it sound good. "You can come then."

Holly sighed. "One day, I'll get a great guy like Carlos. You're so lucky, sis." Her words were shovelfuls of sand, tossed into Bethany's belly.

Bethany was a fraud and a liar. "Great guys are hard to find." At least *that* was the truth. Bethany grabbed towels for her girls. How much longer could she put on this masquerade? The growing chaos under her roof had become difficult to wade through. Her love life was more messed up than Holly's. At least Holly was honest about it.

STACIE

Stacie was exhausted by the time she watched her last customer walk out the shop door. Time to lock up and flip the sign. Holly had been on her mind off and on all day. She'd planned to call and check on her during lunch. But a regular client was getting married, so instead, she'd spent hours looking through books and talking about colors and arrangements between her other customers. Now, Stacie had a headache, and her hunger pains had turned into cramps. The candied almonds in the glovebox would have to hold her over.

On her way to the car, she dialed Holly's number. Voicemail. Stacie pulled out of the little parking lot, discouraged. A hot cup of tea and the sofa called her name, but she wouldn't be able to relax until she checked on Holly.

Twenty minutes later, Danny's truck was the only vehicle in the driveway. Stacie had no desire to talk with him. Still … She was all the way out here. Danny opened the door. "Whatcha want?"

The stench of beer and body odor made Stacie cringe. "Looking for Holly and Felicia. Know when they'll be back?"

"Better not be coming back," Danny slurred. "Told Holly if she left this time, wasn't taking her back." A sneer lifted half of Danny's mouth as if he were proud of himself.

Good. Holly had finally left him. "Where'd she go?"

"Like I care."

She wanted to ask what time they left but remembered Nate's request and turned to leave.

"Tell your daughter she better come home tonight, or I'm gonna burn all her stuff."

Stacie stopped and turned. "Thought you weren't taking her back."

"What can I say? I love to hate her." Danny snorted and laughed, smacking his thigh.

Heat burst inside Stacie's chest. She closed the small gap between them and slapped his cheek so hard that she felt the vibration all the way up her arm. Her palm stung and throbbed. His eyes bulged. She couldn't believe what she'd just done. Instinct drove her legs toward her car faster than she'd moved in years. Her heart pounded so loud that she barely heard her tires screech as she sped away.

Oh, Lord, please forgive my lack of self-control. She had to find Holly and Felicia. She pressed the button on her iPhone and told Siri, "Call Nate."

Siri's soothing voice responded. "Calling Nate."

He picked up right away. "Hey."

"Is Holly with you?"

"Noooo."

"I just slapped Danny."

Silent pause as if he expected her to say more. Finally, "Like, a real slap?"

"Yeah. I was so mad. Now my hand hurts."

"Mom! You were supposed to stay away from him. You okay?"

"Where would Holly go?"

"I'll call Felicia." Stacie swung by a couple of hangouts she remembered Holly mentioning but didn't see her car. Nate called back to say he couldn't get either Holly or Felicia to pick up but left them both a message. He asked her to go home, but she wanted to check a couple more places first. After driving around another hour, she felt queasy and dizzy. She finally admitted it was time to head home when Rich called. She answered and filled him in.

He was quiet. Stacie wondered what he was thinking. "Stacie, I'm not sure what to say. I'm worried about you. Why are you trying to do all this by yourself? We could have covered more ground if you'd reached out to me or any of our other friends."

"I know, but this is sensitive. Private. It's my daughter."

"Please forgive me if I'm out of line for saying this but, isn't that way of thinking part of what kept you and your kids in a dangerous place before? I mean, I thought you'd realized we need the support of other healthy people in our lives."

"I called Nate ..." Her voice trailed off in shame as she realized Rich was right. Why hadn't she thought to ask for help?

From the end of the street, Stacie saw a car in her driveway. She squinted. It looked like Holly's car. "Holly's here!"

A rich aroma greeted her when she opened the door. Holly and Felicia were in the kitchen. She rushed to them with outstretched arms and squeezed them, one in each arm.

When she let go, Holly loaded a plate. "We were worried about you. Aren't you usually home by now?"

"You didn't answer your phone so I went to your place."

"Danny took my phone."

Felicia plopped down at the table with a huff. "Mine too."

Well, that explained a lot. Holly placed steaming plates on the little kitchen table. "You see Danny?"

Stacie shoved a bite of potato in her mouth and closed her eyes. Ah, food. "Yeah. I slapped his face. Hard." She cut a piece of chicken and savored the burst of flavor as Holly and Felicia stared at her. "Then, I left. Quick." She snickered.

"I would have loved to see that!" Holly burst out laughing. "I'm glad you're okay."

"What would he have done?"

Holly shrugged as her eyes teared. "Can we stay here a few days?"

"Don't want you going back to Danny." Stacie told Holly what he'd said about burning her stuff. "Don't go there without a cop."

Holly's hand went to her forehead. "He's so mean!" She smacked the table. "Wish he'd just stop drinking. Not so bad when he's sober."

Felicia rolled her eyes. "He's never nice." She pushed food around on her plate.

"But where would we go? Called Bethany earlier and asked if we could go there, but she said to wait till Carlos deploys."

"Well, you're here now. Let's enjoy dinner." Worry melted away as Stacie's eyes drank in the beautiful sight of these two special ladies.

Bethany

After the kids were down for the night, Bethany sat on the edge of her bed watching Carlos. He had a few papers in one hand and a stapler in the other. He frowned as he stapled the pages together. "I hope you know how much I love you." He sat next to her. "Some of the guys were talking about what women have done with this."

"Oh?" She glanced at the top page. General Power of Attorney. *Duh.* What women *have done with this* was take care of things their deployed husbands couldn't. "Okay …?"

"Divorce the husband and sign over his rights to the house, kids, cars. Everything."

"That's terrible." She didn't think a power of attorney gave a spouse that much control.

Carlos tossed the papers in her lap with a huff. "Come back from deployment. They have nada." He snatched the pages before she could pick them up. "You could take everything."

She blinked and shook her head. He wasn't making sense. He jumped to his feet and waved the pages in her face. "What would make you do that?"

Bethany pulled her head back to avoid getting smacked by the papers. "I *wouldn't* do that." Sure, she was looking forward to the break. But she just wanted him to get some help.

His tone swung to heartbreaking sadness. "You can't leave me like that. I've worked hard to get everything. You can't do that to me. I love you." He slumped on the bed next to her.

Her emotions jumbled. She wanted to comfort him and defend herself at the same time. She hugged him. "I love you." It was her go-to phrase when she had no idea what to say.

He pulled away with a sigh and put the pages on the desk at the other end of the room. They settled into bed and Bethany turned off the lamp. Only a few seconds passed before Carlos spoke into the darkness. "You could take it all."

This was ridiculous. "I *wouldn't* take it all."

"Oh, but you would *leave?*"

"That's not what I'm saying."

"Are you planning on leaving me, Bethany? If you're ever with another man, I'll skin him alive and make you watch."

"I'm not going to be with another man." She sighed. "You're all the man I can handle."

Carlos laughed. At least now, they could finally get some sleep. Bethany rolled to her side and closed her eyes. Maybe she was getting better at handling his mood swings. The welcome quiet soothed her tired mind as she drifted into a dream. Gloria chased Maria around the kitchen island. They were laughing.

Carlos' voice brought her back to their dark bedroom. "You could take it all and leave—" he snapped his fingers, "just like that."

Instant irritation grated her sleepy nerves. *You've got to be kidding.* "I'm not taking anything from you, Carlos. Can we just go to sleep?"

"But you *could.* You have the papers now that give *you* the power."

Something inside Bethany snapped. She bolted out of bed and flew to the desk. "Then don't give me the power." She felt for the papers in the darkness. "I didn't ask for it and I don't want it." She snatched the pages off the desk and threw them, imagining them flying across the room and smacking Carlos in the face. "Keep the power!" They fluttered to the floor at her feet.

Carlos sounded dismayed as he turned on the lamp beside him. "What are you doing?" With the light on, Bethany saw that blasted Power of Attorney mocking her from the floor. Get rid of it. Get some sleep.

She snatched the pages up and ripped them into big pieces. Carlos' eyes bulged. He leaped over her side of the bed, getting tangled in the bedding. Some of the chunks dropped to the floor as she tore them. She tossed the rest into the air like giant confetti. *Issue resolved.* "There. Now you'll know. I won't take anything from you."

He wrenched the last bit of blanket away from his body as he stood. The furious look on his face and barely audible voice rumbled and made waves in her belly. "What. Have. You. Done?" New reaction. She wasn't sure what to expect or how to brace herself.

She bit her lip and backed away from the scattered pieces without taking her eyes off his slowly approaching form. Heat flooded her face.

Carlos didn't seem to know what to make of it as he stalked toward the scattered and torn papers. Each step Carlos took toward the papers, Bethany matched in the opposite direction, working her way around him. Her heart raced. She was ready to bolt. His voice rumbled low, and his tone said he'd finally solved a mystery as his eyes bulged at her. "You really *are* crazy."

Blood rushed to her hands and feet, warm and tingly. Her brain screamed at her to run. He charged and reached for her neck. She'd seen his hand in that position only twice before. But they were forever burned in her memory.

The first time was two months after Gloria was born. Bethany couldn't remember what the disagreement had been about. They'd been in the bathroom with Bethany holding their new baby. Carlos' hand had shot out in that same position. He'd pinned her neck to the wall with his open palm and held her there. She still remembered the way the towel bar dug into her back. She'd been unable to breathe or swallow as she'd wildly searched his eyes.

She couldn't push him away while holding the baby. She'd clung to Gloria, scared she would pass out and drop her. She'd never felt more helpless. When he'd finally let go, she'd coughed out something about holding the baby while he'd choked her. He'd snatched Gloria from her arms and walked out. Bethany had become frantic and tried to get her back. But Carlos had acted like she was out of control and couldn't be trusted to hold the baby. She had been furious, but Carlos refused to let Gloria go until Bethany had convinced him she was calm.

Now, seeing his hand shoot out in that same position, she knew she was in trouble. She stumbled sideways, scrambling to run without taking her eyes off Carlos. Her first thought was to get out of the bedroom. But then where would she go? She had to keep him away from the kids. She hurried to the bed and shook her head violently with her hands up. "Please, don't choke me." He closed the gap, hand flying toward her throat. She waved extended hands. Her words tumbled over each other as she begged without pause. "Don't choke me, don't choke me, don't choke me, don't choke me."

Carlos latched onto her neck. She grabbed his wrist as her airway closed. Her wide eyes pleaded with his narrow ones for what seemed like forever. She couldn't breathe and she couldn't get his hand to budge. Suddenly, he dropped his arm and gave his head a quick shake before plunking down next to her.

She tried to scoot away and flinched when he stopped her. His hands felt like hot coals as he grabbed her and forced her into his lap. With his arms locked around her, he buried his face in her hair. "You know I would never hurt you. Why did you do that?"

Bethany coughed and tried to wiggle away, but Carlos held her firmly and continued in a cooing voice, "You scared me, baby girl, but I would never really hurt you. I love you."

She shook so hard her teeth chattered. Confusion clouded her mind. One second, he looked like he wanted to kill her, and the next, he was babying her. He said he'd never hurt her, but she could still feel his fingers around her throat. Her brain hurt just trying to make sense of it.

After several minutes of rocking and cooing loving phrases against her hair, face, and neck, he got up and gathered the torn pages. "You need this power of attorney while I'm deployed." He smoothed the pieces and pulled tape from the desk drawer.

She couldn't stop shaking as she watched him. "I don't want it." Her chattering teeth made the words come out funny. She clenched her jaw and hugged her knees.

Carlos taped pieces together as he talked. "Now, I know you will not take everything and leave me. You will not use this for bad. I understand that now. I trust you." As the trembling lessened, tears flowed and dripped off her jaw. She hated that stupid document. She didn't want anything to do with it.

What if she *did* want to leave?

Just get through tonight. That's all she would worry about for now.

Survive this moment.

CHAPTER SIX

FELICIA   **Friday, May 27**

Felicia adjusted the grocery bag of lunch items in her lap as her mom turned the car into the parking lot of Grammy's little flower shop. She didn't want the clear tray of sushi to tip and smear pale orange sauce onto the lid. This was a surprise lunch date, and Felicia could hardly wait to see Grammy's face when they walked in. Only one truck in the parking lot, besides Grammy's car. *Awesome. This would be so fun!*

"Do you think she saw us?" Felicia hoped not.

Mom shrugged and shut her car door. "I parked away from the window. Stay low, and we'll sneak around the side."

Felicia ducked and giggled as she crept close to the shop. "Stealth mode."

Her mom's face lit up in the way that always made Felicia feel like something special was about to happen. They tiptoed up the two steps to the door. Mom turned the nob. "Shhhh." She smiled and winked.

Felicia wanted to jump into the shop with a squeal, so she pulled her lips between her teeth to keep it all in.

Her mom cracked open the door and wrapped a hand around the bells hanging from the doorknob, muffling their cheery tune.

A burst of faint laughter reached their ears. Mom pushed the door open enough for them both to walk in unheard. Happy voices floated through the doorway of the back room, where Grammy had tables and everything needed for putting together flower arrangements. Why would a customer be back there with Grammy? Felicia and her mom straightened. A man's voice. Grammy's laughter. Man laughter. *What the heck was going on?*

Felicia tapped her mom's arm. They locked eyes. Her mom shrugged and shook her head. "I don't know, sweetheart. Let's go see."

Who made Grammy so happy? They popped into the back room. An old man! Well, he had grey hair anyway. Both old faces turned toward them in surprise with wide smiles and lingering laughter. Felicia had never seen this old dude before and didn't like anything about him. Not his button-up plaid shirt. Not his Wrangler jeans with big belt buckle. Not his old boots. Not even his straight teeth sparkling behind his wide smile. And why did his wrinkled eyes look so happy? What did he have to be happy about? Besides hogging Grammy's attention and ruining their surprise lunch.

And then, Felicia noticed the thing that made her hate him even more. The picnic basket and paper plates with crumbs. Grammy already ate! With *him.* Felicia's eyes narrowed to show him how unwelcome he actually was.

Grammy's expression changed as she took in their faces and the grocery bag. "Come in!"

"Who's this?" The old man smiled at them as if they were friends. Felicia's face was hot. He didn't know her, and she planned to keep it that way.

Her mom stuck her hand out and smiled. But Felicia knew that smile. Her mom didn't like the old geezer either. Good. "Holly." She nodded toward Grammy. "Her daughter. You are?"

"Rich. Nice to meet you, Holly." They shook hands while Grammy watched with a funny look on her face.

Yeah, Grammy. We busted up your secret lunch date with your secret boyfriend. That's what you get for keeping secrets. Felicia was too mad to talk. What the heck was going on? They finally got rid of Danny, and now a new guy was in their lives? Not if Felicia had anything to do with it. She walked past Old Dude and plunked the bag down on the table in front of Grammy. Hopefully, the sushi sauce was all over the inside of the lid. "Brought you lunch, Grammy. Let's eat. I'm hungry."

There was an awkward moment when none of the adults talked and were probably all making faces over her head as she rummaged through the sack to find her sandwich and chips. She plopped into a chair and made as much noise as the chip bag would allow while she opened it. She shoved a chip in her mouth, chewed with her mouth open, and unwrapped the sandwich. After taking a giant, messy bite, she wasn't sure how she would swallow past the lump in her throat. But she'd rather choke on it than let Old Dude have the satisfaction of knowing he got to her.

Old Dude cleared his throat. "I better get back to work, Stacie." His voice sounded weird. Tender. Guys didn't sound like that. What was wrong with him? *Wuss.* "Was nice meeting you, Holly. Felicia." He gave a little wave and disappeared. How'd he know her name? She'd didn't want him to know anything about her. The bells jingled and he was gone.

Her mom walked to the bag. "Who was that?" She took the sushi to the little fridge in the corner. "You might get hungry again later." She held it up before putting it inside and coming back for her sandwich.

"Thanks, hun. Rich is a friend." Grammy sat beside Felicia and patted her knee.

"How good of a friend?" Holly pulled a folding chair from against the wall and opened it to sit facing Felicia and Grammy.

"A good friend. But just a friend."

Felicia dug for an unbroken chip. "We wanted to surprise you with lunch. Didn't know you already had a date."

"It wasn't a date, sweetie. Rich just knows it's sometimes hard for me to stop for lunch. I didn't know he was coming by. I'm glad he did. I was hungry and he's a good friend."

Felicia couldn't believe Grammy preferred Old Dude's lunch to theirs. "Glad? But we brought you lunch! We were excited to surprise you. He ruined it. Guys ruin everything."

Her mom's eyes bounced between Felicia and Grammy while chewing. What was she thinking?

"Thank you for bringing lunch. That was so thoughtful—" Bells jingled from the other room, making Grammy hop up and poke her head out. "Be right with you." She looked at Felicia and Holly with a smile. "I'm glad you came in. I've wanted you to meet Rich for a while now. Not exactly like that, but ..." Her eyebrows and shoulders rose in unison before she walked out.

Felicia rolled her eyes. "That sucked."

Her mom nodded. "Not exactly what we had in mind, huh, sugar?"

"Looks like Grammy has a boyfriend."

BETHANY

Bethany couldn't find Maria anywhere upstairs. She heard a noise from the kitchen as she reached the bottom of the stairs. Creeping in, she followed the sound of plastic crinkling from the other side of the island. What did Maria get into? She peeked around the corner and barely managed to stop the laugh that contracted her stomach.

There was Maria, crouched in front of a bag of fresh spinach. She pulled a leaf out and examined it before popping it in her mouth with a smile. Maria saw Bethany and jumped away from the bag with giant eyes. It was so comical that Bethany couldn't hold in her laughter. "I've been looking for you. Whatcha got?"

Those big brown eyes never left Bethany's face, and then chubby arms lifted the bag. "Leaves. I like leaves."

Bethany laughed and scooped Maria up. "Oh, you do? Wanna share?"

Maria smiled and nodded. After searching in the bag, she pulled out a big leaf and held it close to Bethany's mouth. Bethany opened her mouth and ate it right out of Maria's little hand, causing Maria to squeal.

The front door shut, and Kenny called, "Hey, Mom, I'm home!"

Maria wiggled until Bethany put her down. "Kenny home." She slammed into his legs when he turned the corner to the kitchen. "Want leaves?" She held up the spinach.

Kenny shook his head and wrinkled his nose. "Gee, thanks. Just what I was looking for." Maria nodded.

Gloria raced in with her arms stretched out to hug Kenny. Maria offered Gloria a leaf, but Gloria jerked her head away. "Ew! No."

Bethany exchanged the bag for a banana and put Maria in a chair at the kitchen table. "We'll have more leaves later."

As Maria and Gloria ate bananas, Kenny grabbed a box of crackers from a cupboard. "I sneezed on Jenna today."

Bethany cringed. "Is she still your friend?"

He sounded jokingly insulted. "Hey! Yes." He dumped crackers in his palm. "It *was* gross, though. It covered her whole arm and the side of her neck."

Bethany grimaced. Poor Jenna. "Gross."

"Yeah, but then I found out I got an A on my final biology test."

"Wow, that's awesome! Studying paid off."

Kenny nodded and smiled. "Yeah, and that was the last test of the year. I think I only got one B on my report card."

"I'm so proud of you. Still wanna be a doctor?"

Kenny nodded. "I talked with my guidance counselor at lunch, and she said I should add advanced chemistry to my senior schedule for next year."

"Wow." Bethany had been worried about Kenny and his grades a couple years before, but when he decided he wanted to be a doctor, his whole attitude about school had changed.

The doorbell rang and Bethany went to answer it. Gloria ran ahead and peeked through the glass panel beside the door. Maria hid behind Bethany's legs. Just a delivery man.

Bethany opened the door. Gloria stepped in front of her with a smile. "Hi."

The man stepped closer and handed a package to Bethany. "Here ya go."

Maria let out a long scream that made the man jump. She continued screaming as she turned and clawed her way up the stairs. She acted as if she were being chased. Bethany took a step toward the stairs, but then Kenny jogged around the corner. "I've got her."

Bethany relaxed, a little embarrassed, and turned back with a sigh.

He frowned. "I'm sorry. I didn't know I was so scary."

"No, it's not you. Well." She shrugged. "Sort of. You're a man." She gave him an apologetic smile before closing the door.

There was no denying it anymore. Kenny was the only guy who didn't make Maria either freeze or run away screaming in terror. Somehow, she had to convince Carlos to stop yelling and blowing up all the time. But she wasn't looking forward to *that* conversation.

Bethany dropped the package on the bottom step and flew up the stairs. Once she got to the girls' room, Kenny handed Maria to her. "See, Maria, everything's okay." He kissed the top of her head.

Bethany was thankful for Kenny. Always strong and helpful. She smiled. "Thanks."

He nodded. "Can I talk to you for a minute?"

Something in his expression pricked at Bethany's heart. She set Maria in front of the dollhouse. Gloria ran in and grabbed a doll, swinging it around as she talked in a high-pitched voice. Bethany followed Kenny into his bedroom. It was a large room. Rubber gym flooring went together like a puzzle and covered half of his carpet. He kept his weights neatly stacked on that side next to his bench press. The other side looked more like a typical bedroom with a twin bed, dresser, and small desk.

Kenny shut the door and sighed. He seemed to have a hard time making eye contact. "I think there's something wrong with me."

He was darn near perfect. "Like what?"

"Well ..." When he didn't continue, she put a hand on his arm and squeezed. He cleared his throat, and then the words tumbled out. "Sometimes, I want to cut myself. Like, I don't *want* to cut myself, and then, suddenly, I get this urge to do it. I want to, but I don't want to."

He searched her eyes, but she shook her head, completely baffled. "I don't understand. You want to cut yourself? Like, with a knife? When?"

"Not all the time. But when I do, it's hard not to."

"Okay. But you haven't actually *done* it. Have you?"

Kenny looked at the floor and nodded.

"Where?" Bethany bit her lip.

He pulled up his sleeve and showed her the inside of his forearm. There were multiple lines. Some pink as if the scabs had recently come off. Three still scabbed over. She gasped and grabbed his arm. "No! Why?" Seeing her son's arm covered in cuts made her furious at the one responsible. But *he* was the one responsible. Why would anyone intentionally cut themselves?

Kenny lifted his slumped shoulders and let them fall again. "I don't *know*. That's why I think there's something wrong with me. Why do I want to do it, and why can't I stop myself?"

"How long have you felt this way?"

"Maybe a couple months. But Mom, it's getting worse. First, it was light, but I keep wanting to go deeper."

Bethany locked eyes with Kenny for a moment, and neither of them spoke. Her mind searched for solutions. She felt helpless. "Want to talk to a counselor?"

Kenny shrugged. "Think it'll help?"

"Won't hurt."

He nodded and watched her face. Now what? She chewed on her bottom lip as she thought. Carlos would flip if she mentioned counseling again. But she refused to stand by and let it get worse. "Okay. But Carlos hates them. He thinks it's sharing our business with quacks. He won't allow it, *but* he's deploying." She let that thought hang in the air and took a deep breath.

He seemed to follow her train of thought and nodded. She would keep this from Carlos. He had enough against Kenny as it was. He wouldn't understand. Bethany gave a sharp nod. "I'll find you a counselor." She lifted one shoulder in a half shrug and tipped her head to that side. "I'll just set the first appointment for *after* Carlos deploys. It's only eleven days away."

Kenny nodded and examined his shoes.

"But, Kenny." She used the edge of her finger to nudge his chin up. "You have to stop this. Tell me you won't do it again before your appointment."

"Okay. That's why I told you anyway. So, you could help me stop.

Bethany nodded and gave him a long hug. Her kids were falling apart, and she couldn't do anything about it until Carlos got out of the way. Deployment couldn't come fast enough.

• • •

It had been an exhausting day. Bethany looked forward to crawling into bed. Carlos sat at the desk in their bedroom, trying to finish something for work on the laptop. Perfect. She wouldn't have to pretend to enjoy his groping before going to sleep. As she came out of the bathroom, he said, "Don't go to bed yet. I don't want you falling asleep before I'm ready." He wiggled his eyebrows and winked.

Seriously? "But, I'm tired." Her body ached for the soft warmth of the bed.

He swung his head towards her with a scowl and curled lip. "Don't you want me?"

"I'm just tired." A twinge of concern pricked her tired mind. "You're not coming to bed yet anyway."

"You don't want me. I can't believe it." He turned back to the laptop and jabbed the keys.

Bethany hesitated. *That was it?* She slid beneath the thick comforter and wiggled her toes against the fresh sheets, letting her face soften into a smile with a quiet sigh. *Ah.* She rolled to her side, back to Carlos, and floated into dreamland.

She wasn't sure how long she slept before a short burst of clicks tugged at her consciousness. She clung to sleep. The next time they registered, the clicks started close together but got further apart and stopped after a couple of seconds. As they came to an end the second time, they pulled the last wisps of sleep from her mind.

She groggily wondered whether what she'd heard was part of a dream or something in the house. She opened her eyes and lay still, listening. She only had to wait a few seconds before the series of clicks filled the silence. Whatever it was, it was close behind her. She gasped as she bolted to a sitting position and swung her head to see.

Startled fear turned into choking horror. Slouching in the desk chair and facing her, sat Carlos with his revolver in one hand, barrel pointed in her direction. His narrowed eyes inspected her face. He reached up and spun the cylinder, causing another series of clicks like those that had awakened her.

Her mouth dropped open but her lungs refused to work.

His eyes squinted while one corner of his mouth twitched as if he were enjoying her reaction. If living with Carlos for the past seven years had taught her anything, it was *not* to give him the reaction he was looking for.

She flopped back into the position she'd been in while sleeping—with her back to him. Terror froze her in place. She couldn't hear anything over the sound of her heart drumming in her ears. As she lay there with her eyes wide open, she imagined him creeping up behind her. She could almost feel the cold barrel level at the back of her head. What would he tell the children when they found out her brains had been splattered all over the headboard and wall?

Tears slipped from her eyes as she wondered what they would think. Who would raise them? *Don't let him kill me. Let me live. Please, God. Please.*

Bethany heard the latches on the revolver case snap shut. Carlos slid between the sheets and tugged her close. "I'm glad you understand, baby."

She quivered against him, and a fresh wave of tears rolled from her eyes as her earlier thought of victory taunted her memory. His warning against defiance succeeded. But as fear and humiliation threatened to smother her, something else stirred. The pain awakened a long-dormant reaction she barely recognized—rebellion and a furious resolve.

A thought rode the growing wave of courageous determination. She snatched it and nourished it before it could escape. Even with all her juggling and hard work, things kept getting worse. Her survival and the survival of her children depended on her. But she had to be smart about it.

They would be free. They would be safe. She had to make it happen.

The days of passively praying that God would miraculously change Carlos were over. She finally understood. All the times she'd begged God to make Carlos safe seemed silly to her now. Foolish. God was fair. He wouldn't take away anyone's choices. Carlos made his own choices. She had to do the same. Why would Carlos change when he was getting everything he wanted? If Bethany wanted safety for her and her kids, *she* was responsible for taking steps in that direction.

Her silent prayer shifted from Carlos. *God, change* me. *I'm scared. I don't think you want me and my kids to suffer like this. I need your help. Give me the strength, wisdom, and opportunity to change.*

CHAPTER SEVEN

Bethany didn't sleep much, but that didn't stop her from sneaking out of bed early the next morning. The sun had taken the edge off the darkness so that she could grab the laptop without waking Carlos.

Since he liked to sleep in on Saturdays, she figured she could get the laptop back in place before he woke up. She crept downstairs, avoiding the creaky spot. The formal dining room was the most private. They didn't use it often. There was a good chance no one would even look there. If they did, she'd be able to hear them coming. There were two ways in—the kitchen and the front room.

She positioned herself so that she could see both entrances. Her stomach rumbled, and her mouth was sticky, but she wanted to finish before anyone else woke up. She stared at a painting on the wall across from her as she waited for the laptop to load. She imagined herself climbing the painted mountain and watching the sunrise from the top.

The screen came to life. Bethany opened a browser window and went straight to her email. As she clicked the button to create a new email, her hands shook with the growing knot in her belly. *Don't think about it. Just do it.*

Still, she hesitated, fingers hovering over the keys as she considered how to start. So many years of ingrained secrecy. But somehow, she had to break the silence. Just a baby step for now. She wanted to connect her brother with her pastor's wife. Someone from back home, in Texas, with someone nearby, in North Carolina. She didn't want her mom to worry. And her sister … Well, Bethany couldn't admit her situation to Holly. Not yet, anyway.

She decided a simple introduction was best. She typed, "Hello Nate and Trudy, I want to introduce you to each other in case something happens to me." Did she sound crazy? They didn't even know what had been going on.

"Nate, Trudy is my pastor's wife and a friend. Trudy, Nate is my younger brother, stationed at Fort Hood, Texas." There. Introductions were over. Now for the hard part. Admitting to both of them that Carlos was scaring her and that he might be dangerous. *Might be.*

But he hadn't hurt her. Why was she so scared of him? Doubt played at the edges of last night's resolve, but she managed to ride a piece of the determination she'd felt so strongly the night before. She had to crack the door of silent secrecy

"I know I'll have to talk with each of you to explain, but for now, I have to tell you both before I change my mind. Carlos has been doing things that scare the kids and me more and more lately."

Bethany wasn't sure what else to say. If she sent this, there was no going back. She couldn't pretend everything was wonderful anymore. Someone from her family and someone from church would both know. She glanced at the corner of the screen to see what time it was. She needed to finish and put the laptop back.

"Nate, don't call me while Carlos is home. Trudy, I'll see you at church tomorrow. Love you both, Bethany." Her hands shook as she pulled them away from the keyboard and read what she'd written. She was glad she hadn't eaten yet. It would've all come back up the moment she hit *Send*.

With one deep breath, she did it. No going back. Even if they didn't understand her confusing message, they wouldn't ignore it. Tears pricked her eyes as she packed up fear, doubt, and dread, and stuffed them somewhere deep inside. She closed the laptop and hugged it in her shaking arms and then hurried upstairs on the balls of her feet, almost running Kenny over halfway up.

"Oh! Good morning." She wrapped an arm around his waist and squeezed but didn't wait for a response before charging the rest of the way up to get the laptop back on the desk before Carlos woke up.

FELICIA

The sun was already fighting to break through the blinds when Felicia woke up. She smiled when she looked at her mom, still sleeping next to her. Staying at Grammy's meant they had to share a room and bed, but Felicia welcomed the closeness. She soaked up the attention Mom was now able to shower her with. She'd never admit it to her friends at school, but she'd snuggled close to her mom to fall asleep each night since they'd arrived. Her mom stroked her hair and back as they talked. She wished it could always be like this.

As Felicia watched her mom sleep, she thought about how pretty Holly was. Did Felicia look anything like her? She hoped she did. But then, she realized that might be one of the reasons her mom usually had a boyfriend. She was sweet and pretty. Her smile made the sun shine, and Felicia was sure it only rained when her mom was sad.

Felicia's stomach growled. Mom moved and cracked her eyes open. When she saw Felicia watching her, she smiled. "Morning, beautiful. Sleep good?"

"Sure." Felicia shrugged. "I smell bacon." She grinned, and her stomach told them both she was ready to find out what delicious surprises waited for them in the kitchen. She grabbed her mom's arm with a tug. "Let's go see."

They padded in together. "I smell breakfast, Grammy." Grammy was missing from the kitchen. The patio door was wide open. A fresh breeze fluttered the napkins in their holder on the counter.

Grammy stepped inside with a smile. "Just in time." She grabbed two full plates off the counter. Bacon and pancakes. "Holly, would you bring the eggs? Felicia can grab the salt and pepper shakers. We're eating outside this morning." She disappeared through the patio door.

Felicia and her mom exchanged glances and giggled. What a perfect Saturday morning.

Grammy's yard was small but green. In Texas, that took work. When Felicia and her mom deposited their items on the table, Grammy glanced at their feet. "Good. No shoes." She smiled like she had a secret. Felicia was cool with being barefoot. She hated wearing shoes.

Mom rolled her eyes with a smirk. "You're still into that?"

"If you mean earthing, yes. Let's pray so we can eat while the food's still warm."

Felicia hadn't paid much attention but remembered hearing Grammy talk about earthing before. Whatever made her happy.

After Grammy had blessed their food, Mom chuckled. "You know you sound like a hippie, right?"

"It's not hippie stuff. We need to have regular contact with the earth." She wagged a finger at Mom with a smile. "You're not allowed to make fun of me until you've seen the science behind it."

Mom yawned the word "science" and patted her open mouth. "Maybe I'll look into it at night." She smirked. "When I'm having trouble sleeping."

Grammy rolled her eyes and shook her head. Breakfast was good, and it didn't take them long to devour every bit of it.

Grammy ran a napkin over her lips. "We'll stay out a bit longer. *Barefoot.* Would you rather help me pull weeds or play croquet?"

Mom tapped a finger on her lips. "Hmm."

Felicia laughed. "Croquet, of course. I'll get it." Felicia was happy to set up the game. The cool grass felt good as she made a path with the wire arches.

Everything would be okay. It didn't matter that Danny had taken her phone and that she hardly had any clothes and no room to call her own. They were safe at Grammy's house. And that's all that mattered.

STACIE

Stacie enjoyed the game of croquet with her daughter and granddaughter. She couldn't remember the last time she'd had such a pleasant Saturday morning. Felicia won the game and celebrated by rolling in the grass while giggling. "I won. I won. I won."

Holly rolled her eyes and laughed with Stacie. "She likes to win."

"Clearly."

Felicia jumped up and ran to join them. "Can I make cookies?"

Stacie nodded. "Please do! Need help?"

Felicia shook her head. "Lemme surprise you." She skipped inside.

As they trailed after her, Stacie wrapped an arm around Holly and pulled her close. Holly leaned her head on Stacie's shoulder. "Gotta figure out what to do. Can't take up your spare room forever. Felicia needs her own room anyway."

Stacie nodded, trying not to let the idea of them leaving put a cloud over their sunny day. She wanted to be supportive of Holly's desires. But it was such a relief to know they were safe. "Could get a place closer to me or the shop. Felicia can help out at the shop. I could even pay her a little."

"That would be nice." They'd walked into the living room. Holly plopped down on the couch. "Could find a job closer to you. Got fired when Danny came in drunk on Thursday. That's what started it this time." She sighed and stretched out on the couch, putting an arm across her forehead.

Good, Holly was finally talking about it. "Did he hit you?"

"Don't remember much." Holly's voice was quiet. Stacie dragged the rocking chair close so they could talk without being overheard.

"Pulled my hair." Holly rolled to her side and tipped her head toward Stacie, face down, letting her auburn hair fall forward. She felt around and parted it in the back. There was a completely bald spot, almost the size of a quarter.

Stacie gasped. "He did this? Pulled a whole chunk out?"

Holly put her head back on the couch and curled up on her side. A tear slid out the inside corner of her eye and over the bridge of her nose to join the tears spilling from the other eye onto the couch pillow. "It hurt."

Stacie's eyes blurred. "Oh, I'm sure it did, honey." She pushed a lock of hair behind Holly's ear. "I'm glad you left. You do *not* deserve to be treated that way."

Holly sniffed. "Sometimes I make him mad. My fault." She rubbed her eyes with the palms of her hands. "Don't know what I'd do without you."

Stacie was weighed down by regrets from her past. No one deserved to be abused. Her kids had grown up with it and had learned to keep abusive secrets. Abusers used isolation tactics to keep their victims from talking with each other. An effective form of control. If they shared, they might band together. Abuse relied on isolation and secrecy.

Stacie's church ran a domestic violence support group for women in the community. Church attendance was not required. Stacie had co-led the group for the past few months. Two of the women in the group were still with their abusers. Most had recently left. A few women had been free for years but still suffered from depression, anxiety, or even PTSD.

Tomorrow, Stacie would introduce Holly to Zalika, the program director. The group had quickly outgrown the classroom they normally met in. Zalika planned to start a closed group. Stacie preferred to stay with the open group where she could continue to help women as they came in. She didn't care which group Holly joined, as long as she joined one.

Holly's breathing became heavy and rhythmic. Stacie's phone vibrated. Nate. She quickly stole away to her bedroom. "Hey, handsome!"

"Just got a weird email from Bethany. Very short. Sent it to me and someone named Trudy. Introduced us. Said Carlos scares her. Wanted us to know in case anything happened."

"What's he been doing?"

"Didn't say. Said not to call while he's home. How am I supposed to know when he's home? Could be on pre-deployment leave."

Stacie's heart thumped. Her gut had been right. *How bad was it?*

Nate sighed. "Sounded like she don't want me doing nothing. Wants me to wait till she calls. You were right."

"I'll try calling later."

"What's goin' on with my sisters? Where do they find these losers?"

Stacy shook her head. Guys like that seemed to have a sixth sense about which women would put up with their crap. It all made Stacie sick.

CHAPTER EIGHT

Bethany pulled their truck into the driveway after church. Carlos was halfway up a ladder next to the tree in the middle of their front yard, pruning shears at his side. Stray twigs were scattered on the ground. Kenny jumped out and unstrapped Maria from her booster seat. She clung to him as he carried her inside. Gloria ran to the bottom of the ladder as soon as Bethany set her down.

Trudy had cornered her after service to ask about her email from the morning before. Bethany didn't want Carlos to get suspicious, so she couldn't stay and chat for long. But she did tell Trudy about Friday night's scare. Trudy seemed to think it was a little strange but didn't read anything malicious into it. Maybe Bethany was overreacting and needed to work harder at seeing the good in Carlos.

The warm air smelled like freshly cut grass. It looked so inviting that Bethany had to slip out of her heels as she stepped off the driveway. Nothing like cool grass under her bare feet. Gloria looked up at Carlos. "What you doing, Daddy?"

"Making our yard the prettiest on the block."

Gloria laughed when a butterfly tickled her cheek and flew past her. She followed it, trying to touch the delicate wings as it fluttered from one flower to the next.

Carlos hopped from the ladder and slumped onto the grass, pulling Bethany down with him. His arms held her against his chest as the warm sunshine bathed them. What a beautiful time of the year.

"Daddy!" Gloria broke in with a squeal and jumped on Carlos' back. "Ride, Daddy." Bethany gave them room as she drew her knees close and wrapped her arms around them.

Carlos roared playfully and got onto all fours with Gloria clinging to his thick neck. She squealed and scrambled to stay on his back while he walked away on his hands and knees, tipping from side to side. He turned and lumbered toward Bethany. "In a couple of days, Papá can give you rides."

Bethany was surprised. "Your parents are coming?"

"Sí. Tuesday. They want to spend my last week here." He broke into a four-legged run, charging toward Bethany with a laugh. She fell onto her back as he ran over the top of her and stopped with his face inches above hers. "Hungry bear." He leaned down and pretended to snack on Bethany's neck. "Nom, nom, nom, nom."

She shrieked and laughed while his lips tickled her neck and gave her goosebumps. Gloria climbed off Carlos' back and giggled as she pushed against his side. "My mommy!" Carlos fell beside Bethany and kissed her. Gloria wiggled between them with a smile.

Bethany sighed, enjoying this playful side of him. "I love you."

"I love you *more*."

Gloria giggled. "Me too."

As Bethany looked at Carlos, she couldn't help the nagging feeling that she had been wrong to send that email. Wrong to be afraid of him. She felt guilty and needed to stop being so sensitive. She looked forward to his parents' visit. They always had a great time when Antonio and Luciana were visiting, even though Luciana never seemed to fully accept Bethany.

But Antonio made it all worthwhile. Bethany couldn't have asked for a more caring father-in-law. And the kids loved him. They'd be there in two days. Great way to spend that last week.

STACIE

Stacie took Holly's arm once they were dismissed from service. "There's someone I want you to meet."

"Mom. I'm not ready for another relationship."

Stacie chuckled and squeezed Holly's arm. "Glad to hear it. I'm sure we'll find Zalika by the coffee." She was easy to spot, tall and elegant with shiny, dark curls cascading over midnight shoulders. She was one of the most beautiful women Stacie had ever known. Inside and out. Stacie walked with her arm locked in Holly's. The plan would only work if she could get Holly to meet Zalika face to face. She wasn't letting go of that arm.

Zalika lit up when she spotted Stacie. Dark eyes roamed over Holly with an equally warm smile. "Who is this auburn beauty you've dragged over here to meet me against her will?" She winked at Holly.

Stacie admired Zalika's tender transparency. Rarely did her blunt observations offend. It was as if pure love poured from her eyes and tone, so no matter what her words said, there was no doubt they were spoken from a loving heart.

Holly stuck out her hand. "Holly." She side nodded at her mom. "Stacie's daughter."

Zalika smiled and dipped her chin. "Ah, darling, a handshake will not do."

Stacie released Holly's arm to make room for Zalika's warm embrace. She smiled as Zalika held her daughter. When Zalika pulled away, her hands slid down Holly's arms and caught Holly's hands. Zalika searched her eyes for a moment. It was no surprise that Holly's eyes brimmed with unshed tears. Zalika had that effect on hurting souls—drawn to a depth of love few people seemed to possess, but everyone desired. "I am Zalika. Tomorrow night I will be here with an amazing group of brave women. I can see you are one of us. Would you be my guest? I will save you the seat next to me if you will, please, say yes."

Holly turned to Stacie. Stacie nodded encouragingly. Holly hesitated. "What time?"

"Seven. Will you say yes?"

Holly scrunched one side of her face, then nodded. "Yes."

Zalika smiled as if Holly had just given her a gift. "I am happy. Your mother can answer any questions." She folded her hands against her chest with a content smile. "Thank you."

They turned and took a few steps when Stacie spotted Rich heading toward them. A hesitant smile lit his face when their eyes met. Holly squinted at Stacie's responsive smile.

Rich held out an arm.

Stacie stepped into a quick side hug. "You remember Holly."

Rich shook Holly's reluctant hand with a smile. "It's great to see you again."

Holly shot Stacie an unappreciative glance. "Yeah. You're friends, huh?" Her one lifted eyebrow seemed to call their relationship status into question.

Stacie nudged Holly. "Rich and I have served in some of the same areas here at the church. Hang out in some of the same friend groups and events."

"The more time I spend with your mom, the more intrigued I am with her. Over the past few years, I've come to consider her one of my dearest friends."

Stacie blushed and couldn't find the right words to respond with her daughter standing there staring at them. She wondered what it would be like to date Rich. Scary and exciting at the same time. Was she ready for something more than friendship? It had been so many years since she'd put that wall up. She wasn't sure if she was ready to take it down, but something about Rich made her want to try.

"Thank you, Rich. I feel the same." Stacie smiled while Holly cleared her throat.

Suddenly, a beaming Felicia bounded toward them from a hallway. "Made a new friend."

Stacie grinned at her. "Great!" She extended an arm toward Rich. "We were just chatting with Rich, but we're about to head out. Nate's meeting us at Mouton's for lunch."

Felicia darted a scowl at Rich before stepping between him and Stacie. "Is that Nate's favorite restaurant?"

Irritation at Felicia's rudeness dulled Stacie's tone. "Might be." Looking over Felicia's head, Stacie smiled at Rich. "I'll call you later."

He nodded. "Enjoy lunch, ladies."

What would lunch be like if Stacie had invited Rich to join them? He popped into her mind more and more lately. Maybe next time.

Felicia was chatty on the fifteen-minute drive. She'd hit it off with a girl named Olivia. Apparently, they were both a bit mischievous.

Once they got to the restaurant, they had to wait for a table. Sitting close to Holly gave them a chance to talk without Felicia overhearing. "So, tell me about this thing I agreed to." Holly looked nervous.

Stacie patted her hand and chose her words carefully. "You can't back out. Zalika will save a seat for you. She's a woman of her word and she expects the same from others."

"Great. What'd I get myself into?"

Stacie told her about the domestic violence support group and why she should go with an open mind. She could tell Holly was having second thoughts, but she was proud of her response.

"It scares me. But maybe it will be good for me. I'll check it out this one time."

"Sounds good. If you like it, they meet twice a week."

Holly nodded. "Felt like she cared about me even though she's never met me."

"She's like that. Incredible woman."

Nate arrived as they were being seated. Holly took Felicia to the bathroom to wash their hands. Nate leaned over the table. "Talk to Bethany?"

Stacie shook her head. "She texted me. Said it wasn't a good time to talk. They're getting ready for Carlos' parents to visit before he deploys. Asked her to call me when she has a minute, but she hasn't replied."

Nate leaned back with a huff. "Hardly slept last night. Must've read her email a dozen times. I'm just gonna call her."

"After she asked you not to?"

"Is she safe?"

Stacie shrugged. Letting Nate see her uneasiness would only make things worse. "If she's not safe, you won't help the situation by forcing her to talk about it in front of Carlos."

"You're not worried?"

"Course I am. But his parents will be there soon. He'll behave."

"I don't like it. You gonna tell Holly?"

"She's got enough to think about right now."

A moment later, Holly and Felicia slid into the booth. Felicia insisted on sitting next to Uncle Nate. Holly smirked at Nate. "Guess what Mom roped me into for tomorrow night?" He lifted an eyebrow. "A domestic violence support group."

Nate smiled. "Good for her. Wanna hear all about it afterward."

"Sure. Should be fun to talk about." Holly rolled her eyes.

Felicia's delicate brows knit together. "What's a domestic violence support group?" She looked more like Holly every day. But how would Felicia handle her budding beauty?

Would she resist the male attention better than her mom did?

Holly gave Stacie a pointed look. "Grammy'll tell ya."

Stacie shook her head and looked at the ceiling with a sigh. Maybe it was time for Felicia to hear what "domestic violence" meant. If she understood it, she might avoid the trap.

CHAPTER NINE

On Monday, Felicia and her mom joined Grammy in her shop. Grammy had promised to take them to get new phones after they closed. Felicia couldn't wait. She'd finally be able to text her friends again. Let them know where she was spending her summer break. There were only two who really mattered to her. But they mattered a lot.

Helping Grammy in the shop was fun all morning. They were busy. How did Grammy manage this all by herself? The phone rang with random questions and flower orders. The bells kept jingling as customers came in empty-handed and walked out with flower arrangements or an order to be picked up later.

Felicia was proud to be earning her cell phone. And it was all good until they skipped lunch. Skipping lunch should be a crime. Illegal. Outlawed. Completely forbidden. What should have been lunch was the busiest time of all. There was actually a line. More than once, she eyeballed the open/closed sign and considered flipping it when Grammy wasn't looking.

By one o'clock, Felicia was sure her belly was about to cave in and leave a gaping hole in her midsection. "When's lunch? I'm starved."

Her mom shushed her as the bells jingled again. Where were these people coming from? *Leave!* The roses looked tasty.

The next time the bells jingled, Felicia rolled her eyes and made a big show of doubling over while holding her stomach. Grammy came close and whispered in her ear. "I know. We're all hungry."

"How do you do this all by yourself?"

"It's not this busy very often. Some days hardly anyone shows up. I'm sorry, sweetie."

Felicia rolled her eyes. "Had to be busy *today*."

"Hey, now. You're not afraid of a little hard work, are you?"

"Nope. Just afraid of starving to death."

Grammy chuckled. "Soon, dear."

But soon didn't come soon enough. Sure, the time flew by while they were busy, but Felicia thought she was about to die. Her stomach had already caved in on itself, and if she didn't put something in it immediately, the rest of her would cave in with it. This must be where black holes came from. Well, earth was about to get sucked into a big one.

Stacie

It had been a very productive day at the shop. Since they hadn't been able to take a lunch break, Stacie closed a couple of hours early. She was determined to get Holly and Felicia new cell phones. She'd lose a leg before she'd let Danny control their contact again. They'd all worked until their hunger demanded attention. Stacie's stomach growled so loud it embarrassed her. "Freddy's Frozen Custard & Steakburgers is right by the cell phone store. Sound good?"

"Sounds weird." Felicia wrinkled her nose.

Yeah, it did. But it was a cute little fast food joint in a great location. "If you don't like it, there are lots of options in the area. Asian food, burgers, chicken, tacos, bagels, sandwiches ..." Someone was bowling in Stacie's stomach and had just gotten a strike.

"I'm not picky. Just need food. Now." Holly's laugh sounded forced.

They all ordered off Freddy's menu. Once they'd walked in and were hit with the fast-food aroma, no one wanted to wait another minute.

By the time empty wrappers littered the table, Felicia sat back with a smile and declared Freddy's to be her new favorite restaurant.

Holly covered a burp with her hand. "Excuse me. I'm stuffed."

"No kidding. I'm thinking something light for dinner." Stacie put a hand on her belly.

Holly laughed. "Dinner hadn't even crossed my mind." She sighed. "More worried about this meeting I'm going to tonight."

Felicia scooted close to her mom. "Want me to go with you?"

"Aw. Thanks for the offer." She wrapped her arm around Felicia's shoulders and kissed her temple. "Probably best to stay with Grammy tonight. I'll be okay."

Once they'd cleared their table, they strolled next door to pick out cell phones. "None of the newer models, now." Stacie wasn't excited to increase her monthly bill, but it did give her peace of mind to know they'd be able to reach each other again.

Phone shopping went smoothly, and soon, they were all set up. Talk was scarce on the way home as Holly and Felicia focused on their new phones. Once they got home, Felicia seemed eager to disappear into the guestroom and reconnect with friends. Holly curled up in the recliner.

Stacie's phone chirped. Her heart warmed at Holly's simple text, "Thanks, Mom." After saving the new number with Holly's picture, she replied, "Anything for my princess."

She wandered into the kitchen for a cup of tea and let her mind drift to her other princess. Would Bethany pick up if she called now? Worth a try. Bethany's phone rang three times, and then her breathless voice came on the line. "Hi, Mom!" She sounded happy.

"Hey, beautiful! How you been?"

"Good. Getting ready for Carlos' parents to arrive tomorrow. Always a good time."

"Sounds fun. Was a little worried after the way our last call ended."

"Oh, yeah."

Stacie turned the burner on under the teapot. "What happened that day?"

Bethany was quiet. After a moment, her muffled voice sounded like she was talking with one of the kids before she spoke into the phone again. "So, the in-laws are renting a minivan when they fly in. Only way we can all get around together."

Stacie's heavy lunch churned uncomfortably in her belly. "That'll be nice. Big plans?"

"Just fun, family stuff."

"I didn't get a chance to say goodbye last week."

Carlos' voice floated over the line. "Who's that?"

"Mom." Into the phone, "I'm about to put dinner on the table. Can I call you back later?"

"Would love that." They hung up. Stacie placed a teabag in her favorite mug while mulling over their conversation. Nothing particularly alarming. Carlos was home and Bethany was still able to talk. Other than avoiding her questions, Bethany seemed okay.

Stacie poured steaming water over the teabag and watched it catch bubbles and float to the top. Taking it to the living room, she noticed Holly had leaned back in the recliner and appeared to be napping. What was she going to do with her girls? If only she could take everything she'd learned from what happened with their dad, and dump it in their brains. Maybe they'd make better choices than she had. Or at least make them sooner. Hopefully, Holly would benefit from the meeting tonight.

Stacie turned and headed for her bedroom. She curled up in a chair by the window and drank in the backyard flowers. Sipping the hot tea was relaxing. Her eyelids drooped. She set the mug down, leaned her head back, and rested her eyes.

Her vibrating phone lifted her from a drowsy fog. Rich's picture lit the screen along with her heart. She tried not to sound too eager when she answered. The sound of his voice brought more warmth to her core than the tea.

"Just wanted to check-in and see how things are going with Holly and Felicia."

She filled him in. They shared a few laughs at some of the comical things Felicia had said while working in the shop. Was it her imagination or had his feelings for her been growing the way hers had been for him? She tried to figure out when his interest in her seemed to change. It was over a year ago when he first called just to check in on her. The frequency and length of their phone calls had increased so gradually, she'd hardly noticed.

Rich cleared his throat. "I've been thinking. Before Holly came to stay with you, I wanted to talk with you about something. Now, I'm not sure it's a good time. You've got your hands full. I don't want to take your attention away from your daughter and granddaughter."

"What did you want to talk about?" She held her breath and leaned forward.

"I— Well, I—" He sighed. "Why is this so hard?" Nervous laugh.

Stacie felt like a 16-year-old girl.

"Maybe it would be easier in person. I can't read you over the phone like this. I need to see your face. Would it be too hard for you to get away for dinner? With me. Alone. Well, not alone. Out. Just out. Not tonight. Our own table. Wow. I'm making a mess of this."

Stacie's grin stretched her lips. "Yes." It was barely more than a whisper, but that's all she could manage when it felt that oxygen was in such short supply.

"Oh, good. Wait. Yes, it would be too hard? Or yes, you'll have dinner with me?"

Her cheeks hurt from smiling so big. "Yes, I'll have dinner with you. Does Friday work?"

"Seven?"

"How about 6:30?"

Rich chuckled. "I'll be there to pick you up at 6:30 on Friday."

Stacie was still smiling when she hung up. What did he want to talk about? Why was it too hard over the phone? She felt like a giddy school girl asked out on her first date. But was it a date? She didn't care what they called it. Stacie leaned her head back and closed her eyes. Dinner with Rich. Just the two of them. Well, sort of. Out. Their own table. She couldn't stop the laugh as she replayed his voice, tripping over his words. She'd never heard him sound so nervous before.

CHAPTER TEN

Carlos' parents had arrived earlier and he wanted to make dinner. He'd put Bethany in charge of the salad and pasta. Salad was done. She dumped the uncooked pasta into boiling water and set the timer. Carlos leaned over the oven door with a meat thermometer and growled. He straightened and shut the door. "Go check on my parents. Dinner will be a little longer."

Bethany gave him a quick nod and hurried out. Antonio's cheerful voice floated from the family room. He was kind, still handsome, even for being in his sixties, and his silver hair looked sophisticated against his bronze skin. He seemed comfortable sitting on the floor in front of the couch. Gloria sat on one of his outstretched legs while he held a book.

Luciana was perched on the edge of the loveseat. *Where were Kenny and Maria?* Bethany pushed down the twinge of frustration that they weren't entertaining Luciana. She may be difficult, but she was still their guest and family. When Bethany walked in, Luciana's eyebrows rose as quickly as she stood. Bethany was gripped by the same nervous urgency to please her as she always felt with Carlos. "Sorry. Dinner's almost ready."

"The military send my son to danger, and he spend his last days cooking." She pressed her lips together and brushed past Bethany, disappearing around the corner. Bethany bit her lip.

Antonio moved Gloria off his lap and pulled Bethany out of her daze with a light touch on her shoulder. "Luciana is tired. Is worried for deployment of Carlos." His unexpected tenderness stung Bethany's eyes. She blinked and nodded before returning to the kitchen.

When she walked in, Luciana glanced at her and gripped Carlos' arm. She spoke in an exaggerated whisper. "Why *you* cook? Bethany get a job?" Bethany pretended not to hear as she drained the water from the pasta.

Carlos shook his head. "No, Mamá."

Luciana let out an exaggerated sigh, left the kitchen, muttering in Spanish, and talking with her hands. Carlos set the garlic powder aside and stirred sauce in a pot. He tasted the sauce and wrinkled his nose while Bethany added oil to the pasta. After stirring, she covered the pot with a lid. Carlos dipped a spoon into the sauce and held it out to her. "Try this."

Close. Maybe a little more salt would do the trick. She pulled her lips to one side. "Almost." She wanted to jump in and help but sensed his mood shifting.

"Should've been done by now. Mamá is hungry."

Bethany nodded. "Want me to tweak it?"

He shook his head and nudged her aside. "I know how to cook."

She smiled and kissed his cheek. "True." He'd been in a playful mood since Sunday, and she desperately wanted to keep it that way. Maybe if she was playful now. She chuckled. "But you better get it right, or your mom will have both our heads."

Carlos dropped the spoon. Sauce splattered on the stove. He swung around. Color flooded his face. His eyes were huge. A vein had popped out near his temple. "It's funny to you?" *Oh, no.* Tingly warmth spun from her chest to her arms and out her fingertips. He grabbed her upper arms, forcing her elbows to stick out on either side, and raced her toward the dining room.

Bethany stumbled as she tried to keep up while being propelled backward. Carlos' fingers dug into her upper arms, which helped keep her upright until they reached the doorway. But then, her right arm smashed against the doorframe, snapping her head back while her feet swung forward. Ripped from his grasp, she slammed to the dining room floor. Before she could catch her breath, Carlos rushed over and snatched her up by one arm.

He forced her into a dining chair and leaned over her with a low growl. "What's wrong with you?" Bethany trembled. Tears blurred her vision. His hot breath choked her. "Nothing is going right, Mamá is upset, and you're making *jokes?*" He gave her a little shake.

Her voice squeaked. "Trying to play with you." A sob caught in her throat. "Have fun."

"Fun? Look what you made me do." He held his hands out. "Go get cleaned up." His lip curled. "You are a mess and it's time for dinner." He turned and stormed to the kitchen.

She stood on shaky legs and steadied herself on the furniture, making her way to the doorway closest to the staircase and away from the family room. The other hand covered her mouth to muffle the sobs she was helpless to stop. Her body ached, but she didn't know what hurt more. Her arms, head, backside, or her heart. Joining him for dinner, as if nothing had happened, made her dizzy, but she didn't see any other choice. Somehow, she'd have to pull off normal in only a few minutes.

Bethany stumbled into their bathroom and cringed when she saw her reflection. Mascara streaked her cheeks with big smudges under her eyes. She washed her face. The tears wouldn't stop flowing as her mind raced over what had just happened. If she was going to get cleaned up enough to join the family for dinner, she'd have to force her thoughts somewhere else.

Antonio was visiting. That was a good start. Bethany loved her father-in-law. He always made her feel valued and loved. They were all going to have a great week together. What else? The toilet needed cleaned. She grabbed the toilet brush and ran it around the bowl. A minute of focused toilet scrubbing helped. New tears had finally stopped forming, making it possible to apply fresh mascara over damp eyelashes. Defeated eyes stared back at her as she applied a second layer.

The back of her right arm throbbed. She lifted her arm to inspect the area in the mirror. The spot that hit the doorframe was discolored and already swelling. *Great.* She threw on a light sweater. As she flew down the stairs, she heard chatter coming from the dining room.

She pasted on a smile and stepped in as Carlos carried a steamy dish past the same doorway she'd flown backward through only a few minutes before. She pushed the new memory from her mind before fresh tears could ruin her makeup again. He placed the dish on a hot pad near the rest of the meal. His proud smile held no hint of their recent trouble.

Antonio and Bethany sat at one side of the table with Maria in a booster seat between them. Carlos was at the head of the table, to Bethany's right, with his mom across from him. Bethany was in a fog while the food was passed around. The constant pain in her arm as she passed each dish haunted her heart. She wasn't sure she'd be able to eat anything on her plate.

Kenny gave her a concerned look from across the table, so she forced a bite of tasteless pasta into her mouth. Swallowing proved harder than she'd thought, but she managed to drive the lump down her throat.

Maria stiffly held her spoon. She faced forward, but her eyes kept turning toward Antonio. He seemed somewhat amused and curious at her odd behavior.

Luciana broke the silence. "Muy Bien, Carlos."

He smiled. "I'm glad you like it."

Antonio nodded. "Sí, is good, Bethany."

"Thank you, but Carlos did most of the work."

"Sí, but Luciana no teach this."

Carlos darted a piercing look at Bethany before he smiled at his dad. "No. I taught *myself*." He smacked his chest. "I'm the best cook at this table."

Luciana smiled proudly at him and nodded. "I believe it."

Antonio turned to Maria with a smile. "You like your dinner?" Maria froze, face forward, eyes strained sideways toward Antonio. She'd always loved her grandpa before. She was still okay with Kenny. Bethany had just assumed she would also be fine with Antonio. Now, she wasn't so sure. Antonio chuckled and leaned close to Maria. "I see you watching me."

Maria's shrill scream made everyone jump. Suddenly, she was out of her booster seat and in Bethany's lap, screaming and bouncing as if she wanted Bethany to run her to safety. The tears Bethany had fought so hard to control instantly filled her eyes. She scooted her chair back, ready to take Maria from the room, but Carlos raised his voice above the screams. "Maria! That's enough. Back in your seat."

Maria clutched Bethany and whimpered in her ear. Maria's tears made Bethany's neck wet, which only caused Bethany's own tears to spill. *So much for fresh mascara.* She held Maria's trembling body tight. Carlos looked furious. His lips twitched as if holding back his typical outburst took all of his restraint. Kenny jumped from his chair. "Want me to take her?"

Carlos snapped at him. "Mind your own business. She needs to obey." Kenny glared at Carlos but took his seat.

Bethany was afraid to look at her in-laws as she peeled Maria off and put her in her booster seat, showering her with gentle strokes, kisses, and soothing sounds in her ear. With one hand on Maria, she addressed the others in a low tone. "Just pretend you don't see her." She pleaded around the table with her eyes. Luciana tucked her chin and frowned. Antonio's eyes were moist as he nodded. After a moment of awkward silence, Bethany cleared her throat. "Thanks for dinner, honey. It's amazing."

Carlos grunted but seemed to relax. Antonio put his fork down and gave Carlos a steady look. "We cannot stay a whole week." He shook his head.

Luciana's eyebrows rose. She opened her mouth as if she had something to say but then slammed it shut and pursed her lips.

Carlos shook his head. "Stay until I ship."

Luciana and Carlos exchanged a look, but Antonio was firm. "No. We go in three days. Friday." One solid nod of his head and his word was final.

A swirl of emotions raced through Bethany. Relief at only having to put on a show for a few days. Fear of upsetting Carlos. Anxiety that Antonio could obviously tell something was up. Hope that someone understood the stress. She forced the overwhelming emotions down and concentrated on getting through dinner.

CHAPTER ELEVEN

Wednesday, June 1

Holly had made dinner by the time Stacie got home from work. How did garlic smell so amazing in the pan but so bad on the breath? Didn't matter because it made Stacie's mouth water. She followed the glorious aroma to the kitchen, where her heart overflowed.

Felicia looked adorable wearing one of Stacie's aprons. Strings wrapped all the way around and tied in the front. The apron was wearing plenty of powder with a chocolate smudge that matched the one on Felicia's cheek. "What do we have here?"

"Mom made dinner and I made dessert." Felicia beamed. If only Stacie had one more bedroom, they could just move in. Maybe she should find a bigger place.

Holly smiled. "It's the first day of my favorite month and I wanted it to feel special."

"It's working."

Felicia put a pan in the oven. "Why's June your favorite month, Mom?"

"Lots of reasons." Holly set a steaming dish on the table. "I guess it started when I was a kid. First month of summer break." They took their seats and Stacie prayed over their meal.

Felicia heaped brown rice on her plate and plopped a giant hunk of butter on top. "Okay. But why is it *still* your favorite month?" She swirled the butter through the rice, watching it melt.

Holly looked thoughtful. "Hm. Well, everything seems to wake up. Flowers bloom. Grass is still green. People don't give up on that till after the 4th of July." They all laughed. "It's not too hot yet. Just enough to swim and play outside, but not so much to stay indoors. And then there's the best reason of all." She shrugged and put a heaping bite of food in her mouth, chewing as if she hadn't a care in the world.

Dinner was amazing—roasted veggies, brown rice, and grilled lemon chicken. When had Holly become such a great cook? Stacie enjoyed hearing her share, and it seemed Felicia was hanging on her words as well.

"What?" Felicia watched her mom chew.

Holly swallowed. Her eyebrows lifted as if she'd already forgotten what they were talking about. "Hm?"

Felicia rolled her eyes. "Mom! The best reason …?" Her voice trailed off expectantly.

Holly smiled and reached for Felicia's cheek. "The reason it will *always* be my favorite month is *you*. The best thing that has ever come into my life arrived in June."

Felicia's mouth dropped open and her eyes filled with tears that spilled when she blinked. She flew from her chair and flung her arms around Holly. "I love you, Mom."

"Oh, sweetheart. I love you too. So much."

Pleasant conversation flowed for the rest of the meal with frequent buzzing from a vibrating phone.

By the time they moved onto dessert, Stacie's curiosity got the best of her. "All right. Whose phone is blowing up?"

One side of Holly's mouth lifted. "Sorry."

"No. It's fine. Who is it?"

Holly glanced at Felicia. "Danny."

Dinner grew heavy in Stacie's stomach. Felicia's eyes flew from her plate to Holly. "How'd he get your new number?"

"A friend. He's been calling and texting all day. Haven't answered yet."

"What's he want?"

"Wants us to come home. Says he's sorry."

Felicia slammed her fork onto her plate. "He's said that before. Don't believe him, Mom."

Holly sighed. "He wants to talk. Has something to tell me. Something *new*."

Stacie wanted to shake her. *They'll say anything to get you to come back.* "What do you think?" It was hard to ask. She wanted to *tell* Holly what to think. But that never worked.

"I don't know. He loves me. I miss him." Holly looked surprised at her words and shook her head. "Not the mean, drunk side." She sighed. "I guess I'll just have to tell him."

Felicia's eyes were thin slits as she watched Holly. "Tell him what? I don't wanna go back." She turned to Stacie. "Grammy, can I just stay here? It's summer break, anyway." Stacie didn't want to be put in the middle, but she was about to say yes.

Holly stood and rinsed dishes before placing them in the dishwasher. "He has to stop drinking. That's the only way we can go back."

Felicia's worried eyes found Stacie's. The idea of them going back made Stacie sick. "Are you going to the support group tomorrow night?"

Holly wiped her hands on a towel and met Stacie's gaze. "Yeah. I'll go. It was actually really good. I'll keep going. You know, a couple of the women there still live with their guy. They're just learning how to set boundaries."

Stacie nodded. Some of the women in the group tried that. It was still working for one of them. But most of them eventually either left their partner or left the group. Everyone had to make their own choices, and one of the things the group was big on was not judging each other's choices.

Judging only drives people away and these women needed each other too much for that.

Stacie went to Holly and hugged her. "I want what's best for you. Stay in the group, no matter what. I'd rather you stay here than go back. I care about you. Want you safe. Happy. Danny's not the only one who loves you. I love you. Felicia loves you, and she *needs* you."

Holly nodded and waved a hand at Felicia. "Come join our hug. We're still here. I didn't say we're going back."

FELICIA

Felicia had no energy. The day had been pretty good, but she hadn't expected her mom to turn her heart to mush during dinner only to strike fear into it before dessert. Why was she even talking to Danny again anyway? This was the worst news ever. Felicia wanted to punch something.

Later that night, she climbed under the covers and waited for her mom. Emotions she couldn't name tumbled around in her chest. It was hard to breathe. Her stomach didn't feel good either. She wished she hadn't eaten so much.

When her mom finally crawled in on the other side of the bed, Felicia didn't know if she wanted to snuggle. After a few minutes, her mom turned toward her in the dark. "Ya mad at me?"

Felicia sighed. She didn't know. *Mad? Yes. At Mom? Maybe.* "You can't talk to Danny. Don't even talk to him, Mom."

"No harm in talking."

"Yes, there is! That's how we end up back with him. He'll be all sorry and you'll go back. Just don't talk to him. *Please.*"

Her mom rubbed Felicia's arm. "Sweetie. If I hear what he has to say, that doesn't mean we'll live together again. Part of me is curious about this new thing he wants to tell me."

She scooted close and kissed Felicia's forehead. "Was there ever a time you liked having Danny around?"

Felicia snorted. "Yeah, that *one* day he wasn't drinking." She knew she was being rough on him. She didn't want to give him another chance.

"What if every day was like that *one* day? Would you be okay with him then?"

It was impossible. Would never happen. "Sure, Mom."

Felicia snuggled against her mom, wondering if these nights were almost over. Tears pricked her eyes. She longed to freeze time and stay here with her mom forever. Her pillow was damp by the time sleep transported her to dreamland.

CHAPTER TWELVE

Bethany examined her arm in the bathroom mirror while getting ready to go to bowling. Carlos' parents were flying out the next morning. They were trying to cram as much fun as possible into the little time they had left. It was supposed to be warm and she didn't want to add a layer over the tank top she had on. But if anyone saw her arm, they'd surely ask what had happened. A giant bruise covered her elbow and extended at least six inches above it. The entire area was tender and swollen, a dark contrast to her pale skin. She couldn't even make out any of the bones in that elbow. It was just a big, soft, ugly mass. There was also a small, oval bruise on the front inside of each upper arm. She didn't know what those were from until she lifted her arms to throw her hair into a ponytail.

On the back of each arm was an uneven row of four round bruises, the lowest ones in the rows were a much lighter color and smaller. After a moment of confusion, she recognized them. As if Carlos had left fingerprints. She sighed in frustration. Memories from *that night* threatened her emotions, so she shoved them down with the welcome reminder that Carlos was deploying in only five days. *Five days!*

In the walk-in-closet, Bethany stared up at her long-sleeved hoodies as a shirtless Carlos strutted in and pulled a muscle shirt off a hanger behind her. She reached up, touching the soft material while searching for the thinnest one.

From behind, Carlos wrapped his arms around her waist. "What are you doing?" He kissed her neck.

"I think I should wear something over this."

Carlos moved in front of her and visually devoured her with a hungry smile. "Why cover all this beautiful skin?" His fingertips traced up her side, toward her underarm. Bethany rolled her eyes and pulled a light hoodie off its hanger. Carlos' eyes followed his fingers to her arm. He stopped at the bruise and gasped. She tried to drop her arm but he grabbed her wrist on its way down. "What's this?" He pulled her wrist up and looked angry.

"From when my arm hit the wall." *Duh.*

"When?"

"When you pushed me into the dining room."

"I didn't know you hit the wall."

Bethany crinkled one side of her face. "What did you think happened when I suddenly flew out of your hands and landed on the floor?"

"I thought you got away from me."

That was the most ridiculous thing Bethany had ever heard. Her eyebrows flew up, and a disbelieving laugh burst from her lungs. "Seriously? How could I? Look!" She pointed to her upper arm. "You squeezed so hard your *fingers* even left bruises. I couldn't get out of that."

Carlos' mouth hung open. Bethany stared at him, wondering how he could be so stupid. Carlos pulled the hoodie out of Bethany's hand and helped her put it on. His hands and voice were gentle. "I'm so sorry, baby girl. You're right. You should cover-up." He hugged her for a moment and stroked her hair. She squeezed her eyes shut and tried not to enjoy his warm embrace. She didn't want this yo-yo life. His tender words confused her. "I didn't mean to do that. I would never hurt you. I feel so bad."

"Your parents are waitin' on us."

"I don't care about anyone else right now. I just want to make sure you're okay." He leaned back and searched her eyes. "I'm so sorry. You know I did not mean for that to happen, right?"

Bethany shrugged.

"Sweetie. You *cannot* tell anyone."

As if she could. He'd already told her what he'd do if she called the cops on him. "I wasn't planning to." She wanted to scream at him. She wanted to shake him and force him to care about *her*. "That's why I'm wearing a hoodie on a hot day."

"It would ruin my military career. Adiós, steady income. We'd lose everything."

Bethany nodded as a numbness took hold of her emotions. It was getting difficult to be the submissive wife she was supposed to be. "I won't say anything. Let's go."

He looked satisfied with her response and grabbed her hand. After a quick peck on the temple, he led her out. "I love bowling." One last glance in the mirror made her pause. She saw an intensity in her eyes that she hadn't seen there before. As they reached the top of the stairs, he hollered. "I'm going to crush you all. I hope everyone is ready!" He let out an evil laugh and pounded his chest.

Everything looked different. He was a fraud. She was a fraud. Their whole life was one big deceptive game that she was tired of playing.

• • •

Dragon Lanes was the perfect place to bowl and grab lunch. Being a Thursday afternoon, only about a quarter of the lanes were occupied. Aside from the two groups in military uniform, the place looked pretty much like any other bowling alley. Bethany tried not to be irritated when Carlos assigned Kenny to the lane where bumpers were set up for Gloria and Maria. Didn't being sixteen qualify him to bowl with the grown-ups? But Kenny was a good sport. The only indication that he was unhappy with the arrangement was the discreet eye roll he threw Bethany. At least their lanes shared the same ball return.

Kenny was busy, repeatedly setting up the bowling ball ramp for his sisters and then moving it out of the way when it was his turn. She'd make sure he got plenty of nachos and soda to help make up for it. Bethany held Maria on one hip as she ordered lunch from the scrawny teenage boy behind the counter. He grimaced and pulled his focus from Maria to take the payment. A quick look at Maria told Bethany she needed to wipe Maria's nose.

He handed the card back, darted one last look at Maria, and shuddered before turning away to get their order. *Seriously?* Bethany rolled her eyes and spotted a napkin holder nearby. As she scooted toward the napkins, she saw the problem. Maria had plunged her first two fingers deep into her snotty nose. Then, she sucked them clean with a satisfied look on her chubby face. Bethany snatched a wad of napkins from the holder. "Ew! Stop." She cleaned Maria's hand before wiping her nose. "Don't do that. It's icky."

The boy pushed two loaded trays toward her as Antonio came to her rescue. He scooped up both trays with a smile and a wink. "Your turn."

By the time the food was nearly gone, the adults were halfway through their second game. Antonio picked up a ball and placed it in Gloria's outstretched arms on the other side of the ball return. Carlos called to Kenny, "Why aren't you helping your sister? We shouldn't have to manage your lane."

Kenny hopped up and moved the ball ramp in front of the kids' lane as Antonio positioned himself to take his turn.

Carlos stood and lifted his hands at Kenny. "What are you doing?" He gestured toward his dad. "It's rude to go when the person in the next lane is about to roll their ball." Kenny sighed and pulled the ramp back, but Antonio motioned for him to continue. While Kenny pushed the ramp in place, Antonio drank water and watched Gloria take her turn. When she was done, he stepped up and threw a gutter ball.

Carlos laughed. "Another perfect throw."

Antonio shrugged and winked at Bethany. A surprised laugh shot up and snorted out her nose. She ducked forward and pretended to check on Maria. She appreciated the way Antonio kept Carlos happily distracted. He was a pro.

When Gloria finished her turn, Kenny moved the ball ramp. Carlos grabbed his ball just as Kenny was coming to get his. Carlos stepped into position but stopped. After a short pause, Kenny walked forward and tossed his ball down the lane with bumpers.

Carlos dropped his ball on the ball ramp with a loud thud and raised his voice. "What did I just tell you?" Kenny shook his head. Carlos charged at him and grabbed a fistful of his shirt. He shoved Kenny toward the seats. "It's rude to take your turn when the person next to you is about to go."

Kenny tripped but caught himself and thrust his chin in the air. "You were just standing there."

Carlos shoved Kenny into the seat next to Gloria and held him down with his palm on Kenny's chest. Kenny struggled to get out from under Carlos' hand, but Carlos leaned in.

Bethany rushed to Carlos' side. "He didn't know. Stop."

Carlos shoved Bethany away with his free hand. Spit flew from his mouth into Kenny's face as he yelled. "You never think of anyone but yourself!"

Bethany took in the bulging eyes of nearby bowlers. Maria's soft whimper behind her. The plump woman rushing to the shoe counter while pointing at them. Gloria's sudden distraction with the hem of her shirt. Antonio's gaping mouth. Luciana's abrupt obsession with the remaining nachos. And the barely contained explosion clearly brewing in Kenny's eyes.

It felt like someone sucked all of the air out of the room. A heavy weight landed on her shoulders as she felt solely responsible for bringing the chaos back into order.

Bethany snapped into action when she saw the bowling alley manager fix his eyes on their group and reach for the phone. "We have to go." She didn't know if it was her tone or the words that caught Carlos' attention. Either way, he finally looked around.

Most of the bowlers faced them. A woman nearby brought her phone up and aimed the camera at Carlos and Kenny. His hand shot back from Kenny's chest as if he'd been stung. His voice was low and urgent. "Change shoes." He plopped down next to Kenny and reached for his shoes. "Now."

Bethany was already out of her bowling shoes and moving. Each sock received a quick tug before being stuffed in the pocket of her hoodie. Thankful she'd worn flip-flops, she slid her feet into them and rushed to Gloria and Maria. By the time she'd pulled their little bowling shoes off and turned around, all the bowling shoes were empty. She gathered them up and rushed to return them. She didn't care about organization when she dropped them on the counter and turned, intent on scooping her girls up and getting her kids away from the curious stares. Antonio intercepted her. He must have wanted to talk with her away from the others because he only wore one shoe. "Why is Carlos so angry?"

Bethany was frustrated and didn't have time to answer his question. Her voice came out shaky and high pitched, "I can't do this anymore. He needs help. He needs counseling, something."

"How can I help?" Antonio's face was creased with concern. He touched her arm.

"You can't help." She spat the words but immediately regretted the harsh tone. He cared. Not just about his son, but about all of them. She paused and grasped at the fleeting speck of hope Antonio's question had dripped into her mind. But one look at Maria's stiff body, and it was gone.

This was taking too long. She was furious with Carlos and needed to get rid of Antonio so she could get her kids out of there. "Maria's scared. I have to go." She rushed back, caught Kenny's eye, and nodded toward Gloria as she reached for Maria. Kenny dropped his shoelaces and swooped up Gloria. Bethany and Kenny sped to the front doors without looking back, leaving Carlos and his parents to finish with their shoes and pay.

As they strapped the girls into the minivan, a military police car pulled into the parking lot. Kenny nodded toward the car. "Why not just tell them?"

Shocked, Bethany shook her head. She didn't want to ruin Carlos' career. He loved being in the military. Retiring from the military was his dream. She wouldn't take that from him. She didn't want to hurt him. She just wanted him to deploy so they could get a break and she could convince him to get help and change.

Bethany jumped into the front passenger seat. Carlos and his parents came out of the bowling alley and passed the MPs heading toward the front door. Carlos paused to tell them something as he pointed inside. They nodded and disappeared inside. Carlos jogged to the van. He hopped into the driver's seat and started it, punching the buttons to open the side doors as his parents reached them and climbed in.

They drove through the parking lot with a short pause before getting on the road. Bethany held her breath, eyes glued to the bowling alley door. Their van pulled onto the road as the MPs rushed outside. Too late. They ran to their car but disappeared from sight as Carlos turned the corner. Bethany didn't see the MP car again until Carlos drove through the gate, taking them off post.

Bethany finally faced forward and leaned her head against the headrest as Carlos matched the flow of traffic on the freeway. She hoped no one talked to her because she didn't think she could hear a thing over her racing thoughts. She was shaken and embarrassed at what his parents must think of them.

Gone were the last scraps of the careful façade they had tried to weave about their family and marriage.

What was wrong with her? Why did she pick cruel men? Or worse, did she cause them to become cruel? Was it her fault? She wanted to be loved and cherished.

Cherished.

A word for fairy tales.

CHAPTER THIRTEEN

Holly strolled into the kitchen Friday morning, looking happily sleep deprived. Stacie sipped her coffee and watched her daughter pour a cup and join her at the table. The domestic violence support group had gone well the evening before. A smooth transition. They all agreed Holly should join the closed group Zalika led. Stacie didn't want Holly holding back because her mom was in the room.

Holly had been quiet on the way home and called it a night shortly after walking in the door. This morning, she rubbed the sleep from her eyes and yawned. "Stayed up too late talking with Danny."

Stacie sipped coffee to avoid commenting as Holly stretched.

"He hasn't had a drop of alcohol since the day after we left. One week sober." Holly smiled and took a dreamy sip from her cup.

"Nice. Is he quitting for good?"

"Think so. He said he quit for me. And if I come back, he won't touch the stuff again. I could actually help him get sober."

Was there any way to make her daughter see the dysfunction in that? She kept her tone casual as she gauged Holly's response. "Quitting's great. What are his other reasons for quitting? Not that quitting for you isn't good. It's just that if he hangs it all on you ... Well, sweetie, that's a lot of weight on your shoulders. You're not responsible for his drinking. Or not drinking. Does that make sense?" She held her breath.

Holly shook her head. "Oh, I know I'm not responsible for his drinking." She waved a hand with a smile. "But it does feel good to know that he'd quit for me."

Stacie rocked her head in a slow nod and licked her lips. "Yeah. That would feel good." She got up and busied herself with a bagel and cream cheese. When she set it on the table in front of Holly, she was ready to continue. "You should give him at least a month. Three would be better. See if he can be responsible for his own sobriety."

Stacie suspected Holly stole her trick of coffee-sipping to avoid commenting. The cup stayed against Holly's lips an extra second. As soon as she pulled it away, she brought the bagel to her mouth with the other hand. *May as well get to the point.* "What are you going to do?"

Holly traced an eyebrow with her fingertips. "Would you mind taking Felicia with you to the shop today?"

"She's welcome anytime. What are you going to do today?"

Holly sighed and looked Stacie in the eyes as if she'd just come to a decision. "I'll go talk to Danny in person. If he's serious about not drinking, maybe this could work."

With everything in her, Stacie wished it were that easy. But habits were tough to break, and Danny had more bad habits than there were brands of beer. Holly was a grown woman, and Stacie would respect her decisions even if she didn't agree with them.

"I think this is it. He loves me. He'll be better now that he's sober." She smiled with so much hope that it crushed Stacie's heart.

They say without hope, a person can't survive. But sometimes, surviving was not enough.

Sometimes, hope had to die before things could get better. She'd seen hope and fear keep too many women in the cycle of abuse. But fear would only hold them for so long. Fear alone was never enough.

But hope …

A person would stay in an abusive relationship forever if even a drop of hope for change remained.

The only chance was to rediscover hope somewhere *outside* of the relationship. Hope was a powerful emotion. Stacie had seen women successfully leave domestic violence by shifting their hope and focus. Could be a new career, school, job training, relationships developed in the group, or simply hope for freedom and independence.

The heart would always follow hope.

That's why it was important to let the women in group talk about their experiences and hear each other's. Stacie believed this was the first step to letting false hope die. It was equally important to educate the group on abusive relationships so they could begin to recognize the pattern in their own lives. Past or current. Recognize red flags in future potential relationships.

But it would all be for nothing if they neglected boundaries. They talked about how to set them and how to enforce them. That was the toughest part for many women. Sometimes it was a completely new concept. Stacie enjoyed hearing about the boundaries her friends in the group were setting. The empowerment on a woman's face after setting a new boundary, and actually *enforcing* it, was one of the most beautiful things Stacie witnessed. It thrilled her every time she saw the look of wonder from the others who had yet to try it.

The birth of new hope.

And *that* was what she wanted for Holly. It wasn't something she could nag or lecture into her. It was something Holly would have to experience within her group. If only Holly had been ready to start group sooner. Unfortunately, there was no rushing that part without risking pushing a loved one away. Stacie had seen that happen too. The timing had to be right. For Holly, it was finally the right time. She just wished Danny would back off long enough for Holly to redirect her hope.

Felicia

Felicia couldn't believe her mom was going to meet with Danny. If she were a fire breathing dragon, Grammy's house would be in ashes by now. Anger was the only emotion she could let her mom see. Inside, she was terrified. She didn't want to go back to tip-toeing around the house to avoid setting Danny off. Listening to him yell at her mom and accuse her of stupid crap that didn't even make sense. Feeling trapped in her room when he was home. He'd only gotten worse the longer they'd all lived together. Couldn't her mom see that he wasn't happy with them?

Maybe her mom would just talk. Maybe she wouldn't actually go back. Maybe Felicia wouldn't have to move back in with them if her mom did go back. Grammy had room for her. She could stay where she was. Why couldn't Felicia decide where she wanted to be? She was almost a teenager. It wasn't fair. She couldn't wait to be an adult and make her own choices. She was angry enough to smash everything in her room. But it wasn't really her room. It was Grammy's spare room. Grammy's house. And besides, if she did that, she'd be just as bad as Danny. No way. She was better than that. Better than him.

Stacie

Stacie was trying to decide what to do about dinner with Rich that night. Holly might not be back from talking with Danny in time. Stacie couldn't leave Felicia alone to worry about her mom. Holly was being selfish. Didn't she realize her decisions affected more people than just herself? It would be time to close up shop soon, so Stacie needed to figure this out.

She called Holly. Voicemail. "Just wondering what time you'll be back. I had dinner plans with Rich, but I don't want to leave Felicia alone. Call me." Stacie sighed and sent Holly a text with the same message. When she looked up, Felicia stood in the doorway to the back room.

"You're going out with the old guy tonight?"

"That was the plan. Please use his name, sweetie. It's Rich."

Felicia brushed past and flopped into a chair.

"Let's close up a little early." Stacie went to flip the sign before any other customers came in and then headed to the back. She pulled a chair close to Felicia and took her hand. "Talk to me. What's on your mind?"

Stacie studied Felicia's face with a frown. *Was it Holly or Rich she was more upset about?*

"You worried about your mom?"

Felicia shrugged. "You ditching me tonight?"

Stacie shook her head. "Wanna come to dinner with Rich and me?"

"Why do you want a boyfriend, Grammy? Guys are nothing but trouble."

Stacie sighed. "Sure seems that way, huh? But I think Rich is different. I've known him many years now. He's … Well, I think he's one of the good ones."

Felicia looked up. "Like Uncle Nate?"

Stacie nodded. "Yeah. Kinda like that."

A comfortable silence hugged them for a few minutes before Stacie squeezed Felicia's hand. "How about dinner with us?"

Felicia searched Stacie's face and then nodded.

"Guess I better let Rich know." Stacie winked and pulled out her phone. This should be interesting. Not exactly what she had in mind. She sure hoped Rich would be okay with the change of plans.

CHAPTER FOURTEEN

Saturday night, Bethany and Carlos had dinner at the home of Mike and Melissa. They only lived six blocks away. Mike was deploying in the same company as Carlos, different platoon. He and his pretty wife had invited them over along with another young couple Bethany didn't know. Carlos was thrilled when they said he could smoke inside. He downed mixed drinks while telling stories that kept everyone entertained. Bethany was exhausted from pretending to enjoy herself. Dinner was fine. Sitting around drinking with people she didn't know, not so much.

The smoke gave her a stuffy nose and headache, and she'd heard all of Carlos' stories before. Some of them used to be her stories. He had a way of morphing others' most entertaining experiences into his own to share with a new crowd. She didn't know how much longer she could make her laughs and smiles sound genuine. When the others were distracted, she pulled Carlos aside and lowered her voice. "I'm ready to go." She smiled, hoping he'd agree.

"It's just starting to get fun."

"I know. But my head hurts and I'm worried about the kids."

"Aww." He leaned into her with a sloppy kiss. "My baby girl doesn't feel good." His warm breath poured over her face, a revolting combination of cigarettes and fruity alcohol. "You can go. I'll walk home when I'm ready." He stroked her cheek.

Really? His proposal made her giddy. She could go home. Alone and guilt-free. Hang out with the kids and tuck her girls in. She kept her face as neutral as possible and nodded. "If you're sure …" She let her voice hang on the last word as if hesitating.

"Of course." He smiled and walked her to the door, calling over his shoulder. "Bethany is worried about the kids." Their beautiful, young hostess nodded with a sympathetic look and joined them at the door.

Bethany thanked her for dinner and received a warm goodbye from everyone. Carlos wrapped an arm around Bethany in a quick hug and gave her a gentle push out the door with a wave. "See you soon, babe!"

When the door shut, Bethany giggled and strolled to the truck looking for stars in the clear sky. A breeze brushed her face and neck and stopped her halfway down the driveway. The heavy scent of gardenias rode a warm gust to delight her senses and brought an instant smile to her face. She followed her nose to the large flowers under the front window. Their white petals seemed to glow from the street lights. She resisted the urge to take one home with her and settled for burying her nose in the glorious blossoms. She drank in the sweet aroma with her eyes closed. Crickets played her a symphony while her headache floated away on the breeze.

The two-minute drive brought her home, eager to sneak up and surprise the kids. She let herself in and stood in the entryway listening to a competitive game of Hungry Hungry Hippo©. A smile stretched across her face as she crept close to the family room and peeked around the corner. They were on the floor around the game with only a few marbles left in the middle. Gloria seemed determined for her hippo to eat them. Maria spotted Bethany and ran with arms wide open. "Mommy!"

Gloria wasn't budging from getting that last marble but did look up with a grin. "I'm gonna win, Mommy!"

Kenny sprang up and looked past her. "Where's Carlos? Thought you were going to be out late?"

"Yeah, but I missed you guys and wanted to come back in time to put the girls to bed." She buried her nose in Maria's neck. Maria squealed and laughed and wiggled in Bethany's arms. She set Maria down and squatted next to Gloria. "How'd you do?"

Gloria swished her finger through the marbles in her tray. "Look. So many."

"You get the most?"

Gloria nodded proudly.

"Nice job!" Bethany stood up. "Okay, girls, time to run upstairs and get your jammies on." Bethany sat on the couch as the girls raced noisily up the stairs. Kenny plopped down, almost on her leg. She loved it when he sat this close, squished up against her side. It had gradually taken the place of cuddling as he grew older.

"When's Carlos coming home?"

Bethany shrugged. "No idea. So much alcohol. I wasn't comfortable. Just wanted to be home with you guys." She nudged his shoulder with hers.

"Oh. You kinda stink."

Bethany laughed. "I'm sure. Only three days left. I think Carlos wants to socialize and drink while he still can."

Kenny nodded. "Glad you came home early."

"Yeah. Now you don't have to put her sisters to bed." She winked and nudged him. Kenny chuckled and nodded with an eye roll. "Yup, Mom. You got me all figured out."

She laughed. Deployment was going to be so sweet. For now, she just wanted everyone to be in bed before Carlos came home.

• • •

Bethany woke to the sound of Carlos stumbling up the stairs and cracked her eyes to peek at the clock. The blue numbers read 3:24. Wow, he'd stayed out late. She cringed at the noise he was making as he lumbered toward their bedroom. The door opened. She pretended to sleep as he bumped through.

Their room was dimly lit by the streetlight that poured between the gap in their curtains. Bethany watched him sway clumsily toward the bed. Hopefully, he'd just pass out. Tomorrow was church and she didn't want to be tired all day. Carlos flopped onto the bed and poked her ribs. "Sleeping?"

"Was." She rolled toward him but jerked her head back to avoid the stench. "Smells like you had fun."

"Maybe drank too much." Carlos slurred and chuckled. His head wobbled toward Bethany with a sloppy kiss. "So beautiful." He slid closer and stroked her face.

Her stomach turned. The odor was almost too much. "I love you."

"Love you *more*." Carlos jerked his arm dramatically. His slurred words became tender. "Enough to die for you." He dropped a hand to Bethany's face and pushed hair from her ear and neck. "Do you love me that much? Enough to *die* for me?"

No. He was cruel, selfish, and right now, repulsive.

He stroked her neck. "So tiny." His touch gave her chills. Fear laced icy fingers around her heart. She strained to see his eyes, desperate to read him. "Fragile compared to my big, strong hand." He wrapped his hand around the front of her neck. The fear grew and fought for space in her rational thoughts. With fingers touching one side and thumb on the other, he applied gentle pressure to her throat as he stroked up and down.

Bethany braced her palms against his wrist and forearm as if she could stop him if he chose to choke her.

His words came slow, and the tone of his voice dripped with affection. "I could squeeze and crush your throat. Easy. I'm so strong." Horror grew and clawed its way up her throat.

But he wasn't hurting her. He wasn't squeezing. Just clumsily, drunkenly stroking. She was terrified of provoking him. His wretched breath poured over her face. "Do you love me, baby girl?"

"Yes. I love you." *You're sick.*

"Enough to die for me?"

Never! Stay away from me. With the light behind him, his eyes looked like black pits. She was dizzy. Lost in those pits and unable to form the expected words.

"Enough to die and let me raise the kids?" The kids! She didn't want this lunatic anywhere near her children. His question trapped her. If she said yes, he'd kill her right there. If she said no, he'd kill her for not loving him enough. But she didn't want to die.

His stroking hand became heavier, making it harder to swallow. "Do you?" Her mind raced to come up with a safe answer.

"Love me enough to let me kill you right now? Let me raise the kids?" Inside she screamed. *Where are you, God? Help me! I need you. And my babies need me.*

Her mouth was so dry it was hard to get the words out. Her voice croaked from the pressure of his hand. "They need their mom."

The sweetness evaporated from his tone. His frustration intensified the slurring and stuttering. "No. Asking if y-you *love* me enough to let me k-*kill* you. Raise kids my*self*?"

Bethany pushed against his arm, but it wouldn't budge. Her sweaty body shook. She managed to rasp through the increased burden on her throat. "You're. Scaring. Me." Admitting her fear out loud caused tears to flood and slide out, wetting the hair at her temples. His hand relaxed a bit. "Don't want to die." Her voice cracked, and a sob escaped her lips.

His tone changed. Discouraged. Broken but still slurred. "Oh, no. People always fear me." He slid his hand from her neck to her waist and dropped his head on her chest. "Never thought you would. My p-power is too strong. Scares people."

Tension lifted so fast the room began to spin. She was confused. Every muscle still flexed. *Was it over?* She placed one shaky hand on the back of his head, hoping to keep him calm, and laid the other over her mouth to muffle fresh sobs. She was afraid to move. Carlos grew heavier on her chest and stomach as his breathing became deep and steady. Her back cramped.

When she couldn't stand the pain any longer, she gently turned her body, prompting him to roll off and resettle in the middle of the bed. She would send another email to Nate and Trudy before he woke up. Keep them in the loop in case anything happened to her. If Carlos killed her before he deployed, Bethany would not let him get away with it.

She wasn't sure if she'd be able to relax enough to sleep. So many questions and fears rolled around in her head. What would he say when he woke up? Would he apologize? Would he still be upset with her? Would he kill her? He was crazy. Absolutely nuts.

CHAPTER FIFTEEN

Before the sun was up the next morning, Bethany sent an email to both Nate and Trudy about what had happened. She'd barely sneaked the laptop back onto the desk when her phone vibrated. A text from Nate. "Call me right NOW." Her stomach tightened.

The only place she knew she wouldn't be overheard was the garage. Her phone vibrated another text. Nate was impatient. In the garage, she sat where she could see the door to the kitchen and then called. He must've been staring at the phone because he answered before she heard it ring. "Yer freaking me out."

"What you doing up? It's like four in the morning over there."

"Been worried about you all week and ya never called. Got yer email a few minutes ago. Figured you didn't send *that* while Carlos was around, so it's a good time to talk."

Bethany nodded. "I told you what happened in the email."

"Ya'll need to get outta there today. Why ya still there? I'm looking at flights. Gonna let Carlos know he's not as tough as he thinks he is. I'll bring a U-Haul and get you and the kids. Reckon my commander'll give me emergency leave for this. Was gonna make a call to *his* commander and report him, b—"

"No!" He'd kill her for sure. He'd kill Nate. "He's deploying in two days anyway."

"By the sounds of it, ya'll might not last that long. He's crazy, sis! Let me getcha outta there."

"I'm not leaving—"

"Yer not stayin—"

"You don't understand. He was *drunk*. He's not always like that. I just wanted to make sure— well, just in case— I don't know!" Frustrated, she waved her free hand. "He can't know I talked and I don't want to mess up his career. When he deploys, I'll have a year to convince him to get help. Then things'll be better." Bethany couldn't tell by the long silence if she'd convinced Nate or not.

She felt like she was lying to her brother. Maybe she was lying to herself. She was losing control despite all that she had poured into maintaining the delicate balance.

"Don't feel good about this, sis. Lot can happen in two days."

"I know, but I've got this. You have to trust me."

"Not *you* I don't trust. Ya shoulda told me about him sooner. Mom said she thought something wasn't right and I blew her off."

"Mom knows?"

"She don't know nothin' but she suspects. Ya shouldn't keep her in the dark. Look what happened with Dad. She's stronger than ya give her credit for."

Bethany chewed her lip. "Still ..."

He sighed. "If anything else happens before deployment, *call me*. I'll be on the next flight to whoop his butt."

"It'll be fine."

"When you gonna tell Mom and Holly?"

Bethany shook her head and rubbed her face. After Nate's reaction, not until Carlos deployed. She sighed. "Nate?"

"Yeah?"

"Thanks for being there for me. And for keeping quiet."

"Nothin' better happen to ya." His voice cracked. Hearing him choke up touched a part of her heart that hadn't been touched in a long time. He loved her. She hadn't done anything at all to deserve it. She'd been dishonest with him but he loved her anyway. Pure, fierce, sweet love. Without expectations or demands. Loved despite disagreements or disappointments. Just loved.

Bethany hung up. She cried over the deep ache that left a hole in her heart. She wanted someone to protect her. Wrap her up in strong arms and make everything okay again. But understanding was beginning to dawn. This was no fairy tale where a wave of the wand would make everything better. Reality was much less forgiving.

She allowed a few minutes to feel sorry for herself before drying her face on her sleeve. Stuffing the phone in her pocket, Bethany grabbed a jug of milk from the extra fridge in the garage. She jumped when the house door opened to a pink-eyed Carlos. "I've been looking for you." He eyed the milk in her hand. "What are you doing?"

How long had he been looking? She played dumb and held up the milk with a wide smile. "Didn't expect to see you up so early. Ready for breakfast?"

FELICIA

Felicia missed her mom as she rolled out of bed. She was too depressed to get dressed and dragged her feet all the way to the kitchen. Grammy cracked eggs into a hot pan. Felicia opened the fridge to get the apple juice. Her mouth felt like she'd been sucking on her tee-shirt all night.

Grammy greeted her with a smile. "Good morning."

"Is it? Mom spent the night with the jerk and there was no emergency." She sighed as she pulled a glass from the cupboard. "Why'd she hafta go back?"

"You wanted an emergency?"

"No. Well, kinda." Felicia shrugged. "Means we're going there after church, right?"

Grammy nodded.

Felicia's lip curled as she poured juice. She couldn't help it. She'd trusted her mom to stay away this time. She felt betrayed. She loved it with all three of them at Grammy's. Why would her mom show her how wonderful life could be and then strip it away so fast? "And you're going to leave me there." Felicia met Grammy's gaze. "Right?"

Grammy sighed and slid the pan of eggs to a cold burner. She stepped close to Felicia. With her hands on Felicia's shoulders, she searched her eyes. "I don't want to. But it's not entirely up to me, sweetie."

Felicia leaned into Grammy and wrapped her arms around Grammy's waist. "It's not fair. Why can't I choose where I want to live?" She felt tears welling up in her eyes, which irritated her even more. She missed the mornings of laughter.

"You don't want to live with your mom?"

"Only Mom. And you. Guys suck. I'm never gonna get one. Wish they'd all die."

Stacie jerked. "You want Uncle Nate to die?"

"Never!" Not Uncle Nate! Felicia took one step back and looked up into her grandmother's face. Grammy's lips were pressed together but there was a tenderness in her eyes. Grammy understood. Felicia didn't know how Grammy could possibly know where she was coming from, but somehow, Grammy knew.

"Not all guys suck, sweetie. Uncle Nate doesn't suck. Rich doesn't suck. And your cousin, Kenny, seems like a pretty cool guy too."

"They're probably the only ones on the planet." Felicia's tone and body language were both dramatic as she flung herself into a chair.

Grammy smiled and shook her head. "I hear that you don't want to live with Danny. And you've been around too many jerks in your twelve years."

"Almost thirteen."

"Yes, almost thirteen years old, and you've had more experience with jerks than some women have in a lifetime. I'm so sorry it's been that way. Your mom wants to give Danny another chance. If anything happens that you don't like, call me and I'll come get you. Have I ever left you there when you've called?"

Felicia mumbled from her slouched position. "No." She hated to admit that Grammy had a point. But still—

"Okay, then. We'll put on a smile, enjoy our breakfast together, and go to church. I'll take you to lunch before I take you home."

Felicia straightened in her chair with a sigh. "But, what if I—"

Grammy's phone rang from the counter beside her. She glanced at it and frowned. "Nate."

"You gonna answer it?"

Grammy looked up with a stiff smile. "I'll call him back. You were saying, what if you...?"

"What if I don't wanna stay once we get there?"

"Then, I'll talk to your mom and see if you can stay here longer." She smiled. "Deal?"

Felicia rolled her eyes with a half-smile. "Fine. I'm starving. Let's eat."

"Fine. You get the plates and forks."

BETHANY

Carlos took in Bethany holding the jug of milk and grunted. When he stepped aside to let her pass, Bethany let out the breath she hadn't realized she'd been holding. He must have only just started looking for her. He was up hours earlier than she expected. What a relief she'd already hung up with Nate.

Keeping with her mock casual attitude, she pecked his rough cheek as she squeezed past.

"We have bacon?" His hangover morning breath almost gagged her.

"Yup."

He followed her to the kitchen. She poured coffee beans into the grinder. Her mouth watered from the rich aroma.

Carlos sat on a kitchen stool and watched until the grinder stopped. "No church today."

"There is." Confusion lined her face.

"No. I mean, you won't be going." His eyes bored into hers.

"Why?" *Because of last night?*

"I deploy day after tomorrow. Want to spend time with you and the kids." He shrugged and rubbed his eyes.

Understandable. "Okay."

As she lined a pan with raw bacon, the ache to hear tender words of regret and remorse grew. It was almost unbearable. She chewed her bottom lip. Dull silence pushed against the walls of the kitchen as she worked.

Didn't he care? Wasn't he sorry?

"Going out for a smoke. Bring coffee when it's ready." He disappeared out the back door.

The coffee was done by the time Gloria and Maria bounced down the stairs together. They entered the kitchen, chatting and laughing. Distracted by disappointment, Bethany hardly noticed how adorable they were. She poured a cup of coffee and sent Gloria to deliver it, watching long enough to make sure she succeeded.

Carlos leaned back on one of the patio chairs with a cigarette dangling from his fingers. His other arm was over his eyes. Gloria balanced the coffee and kept it from spilling as she set it on the table in front of him. He gave her a surprised smile before pulling her onto his lap.

Bethany grabbed the egg carton and a skillet. Kenny rounded the corner and gave her a good morning nudge with his shoulder. "Making breakfast?"

Bethany nodded. "Hungry?"

She laughed at his raised eyebrows and *are you crazy* expression. When breakfast was nearly made, she sent him out with a stack of plates and forks.

She started to put Maria in the seat next to Carlos, but as soon as Maria saw where she was heading, she fussed and drew her legs up.

Bethany quickly shifted her to the next chair, hoping Carlos hadn't noticed. "Such a gorgeous day! Hope everyone's hungry."

Carlos watched Maria throughout the meal, causing uneasiness to grow in Bethany's middle. By the time they were done, his lips were pressed into a thin line. "Maria." Maria's eyes dropped to the bow on her shirt. "Come inside and play with me."

Maria tugged on the bow. Carlos stood and held out a hand. "Come."

The bow was at risk of being ripped from her shirt as she twisted it in her fingers until her shirt bunched up around it. Bethany broke the stretch of silence. "Want me to go with you?"

"No. I'll take her." Carlos dismissed Bethany with an irritated shake of his head.

Bethany's heart pounded. She hoped Maria just went along with Carlos. But Maria wasn't as compliant as the rest of them. She'd always been more stubborn and reserved.

"Maria." His voice was firm. Too firm. He'd never convince her like that.

Kenny stood. "Want me to—"

"Help your mom take all this inside." Carlos waved a hand toward the dirty dishes on the patio table. Bethany felt as if she were abandoning her daughter with her little girl's worst fear.

The best way to protect Maria was to keep Carlos calm. The best way to do that was to go along with what he wanted. Although what he wanted put Maria at risk, which didn't feel like protecting her.

But Carlos loved Maria. He wouldn't hurt her. He was always talking about his "bloodline" and how strong and superior Gloria and Maria were because they had his blood. Bethany weighed Maria's emotional well-being against her physical well-being. Maria may be scared, but she would be okay if she complied with what Carlos wanted. Bethany would stay close in case Maria needed her.

She leaned over Maria and kissed her head while she whispered in her ear. "It's okay, sweet pea. Daddy wants to play with you. It'll be fun." She tried to sound happy.

The look Kenny threw her didn't help. She stacked dirty plates as fast as she could.

Carlos came around and lifted a stiff Maria out of her seat and carried her inside. She didn't freak out. Good start.

Kenny filled his hands with dishes. He shook his head as soon as they disappeared. "Mom. She's scared of him."

"I know. But he's her dad. Let's just hurry."

They got it all in one trip. Gloria trailed behind with a couple of empty mugs. Kenny looked over his shoulder. "I'll do the dishes. Just go to her."

Gratitude washed over Bethany's exposed nerves as she left her stack of dishes on the counter.

STACIE

Stacie downed her breakfast faster than normal, but Felicia didn't seem to notice. "I'm off to finish getting ready." She smiled and patted Felicia's shoulder on her way out.

Once in the bedroom, she dialed Nate and waited for him to pick up. "Missed a call from you," she said as soon as he answered.

"I'm worried about Bethany."

Stacie froze, staring at a piece of lint on the rug beside her bed. She was afraid to ask as a herd of elephants ran over her chest.

"Mom?"

"I'm here. What's going on with Bethy?"

"I think she'll want to tell you. But I will tell ya this. I don't like Carlos, and if I ever see him again, I'm gonna let him feel it right on his stubby jaw."

Alarm rose to Stacie's throat. "Is she okay? Should I be there?"

"Says she's fine and he deploys in a couple days anyway. She don't want no one coming while he's there. Already asked. Probably shouldn't have said anything, but I was so upset when we hung up, and I know I can tell ya anything. Just be praying, Mom."

Stacie nodded. "Will do." Great. First Holly going back to Danny and now Carlos was doing God-only-knew-what to Bethany.

BETHANY

Maria stood with her backside nearly touching the couch. Carlos sat on the floor at her side and glared at Bethany when she walked in. "Look." Carlos put his arms around Maria. "Hug Daddy." Maria remained motionless. Carlos leaned away with a huff.

Bethany knelt beside Maria. "Daddy wants a hug." Maria was like a little mannequin, stiff and unyielding.

Suddenly, Carlos sounded heartbroken. "Why won't you hug Daddy?" He wrapped his arms around her frozen body and waited a second before dropping them. He looked on the verge of tears. "Don't you love Daddy? Daddy just wants a hug."

Bethany smiled at Maria. "It's okay, princess. He just wants a hug."

His voice dropped and sounded like he had a secret. "Daddy buys you toys and food and all the nice clothes you have. Hug Daddy."

It looked different when it wasn't happening to her. Bethany could easily see the shift in tactics. Demanding. Then sad. Now guilt. She knew what came next. This had to stop. She tried sounding logical as she spoke close to his ear. "Should we force her to hug? Giving and receiving affection should be a choice, right?"

"I'm her dad. She doesn't have a choice." His face was set when he turned to Maria. Tone demanding. "Hug Daddy."

The Maria statue barely appeared to be breathing.

Carlos grabbed her tiny arms and jerked her close to him. "Hug Daddy."

Bethany was transported to her own childhood. Scoffed at, made fun of, criticized, or abused when rejecting uncomfortable touches and affection. Years of conditioning. Knowing that the terms of love were dependent on her compliance. She didn't want the same for her daughter.

Carlos smacked Maria's bottom twice, so hard that Maria had to shift her feet to maintain her balance.

"Stop!" Fierce protectiveness and rage at past injustice rocked Bethany's emotions. "This isn't going to work on her."

"Oh. She'll learn to love her daddy." He raised his voice. "Give Daddy a hug."

Bethany took a step toward them, fists clenched.

Gloria came from nowhere and jumped on Carlos' lap. "I'll hug you, Daddy."

Carlos gave Gloria a quick hug and set her aside. "You love your daddy. Why doesn't your sister?"

Gloria leaned against his arm. "Play with me, Daddy."

"I'm busy right now. Later." He leaned close to Maria. "Your sister hugged Daddy. Now you hug Daddy."

Maria didn't even twitch.

When Carlos reached for Maria, Bethany moved between them. "Gloria wants to play with you."

"I told her. I'm busy." His eyebrows rose as he looked between Gloria, Bethany, and Maria. His voice took on a sing-song whine. "Maria needs her sister and Mommy to come save her. You need your *mommy*, Maria?"

"This will not work on her."

"Won't work? Fine." Carlos snatched her up and carried her out. He shoved against Kenny, who blocked the doorway with arms crossed, and stormed upstairs. Bethany was on his heels.

Carlos took Maria to her room and plunked her down in the middle of the floor. He closed the blinds, picked up a heavy blanket, and hung it from the curtain rod, plunging the room into darkness. He pushed Bethany out and shut the door. "She doesn't come out until *I say* she comes out. No one goes in there."

He grabbed her elbow. Pain throbbed from the bruise that still covered most of her upper arm. Cringing, she jerked away. "Ouch."

He moved as if to charge her but stopped with his nose close to hers. Hangover, coffee, cigarette, need-to-brush-your-teeth breath spewed all over her face. "Don't. Open. That. Door."

Bethany trembled as she fought to keep her fists at her sides. She wanted to scream in his face and pound his chest. But if she lost control, she was sure he would too.

Carlos stomped away while Bethany watched his back disappear around the corner. Her shoulders slumped as she turned to the bedroom door and placed one palm against it. She longed to open it and scoop her daughter into her arms, but she didn't want to bring his wrath down on Maria again. For now, Maria was in the safest place in the house. Bethany leaned her forehead on the cool wood of the door and wondered what her little daughter must be feeling.

With Carlos out of sight and the crisis on its downward swing, Bethany's emotions refused to remain caged another second. She managed to choke down the first two sobs but they came hard and fast. She ran for the privacy of her room before Maria heard her.

In her bathroom, she shut the door and crumpled to the floor. As she curled into a ball, she cried. The flood of tears made her face slide on the cold tiles with every sob that shook her body. She wept for Maria. For Gloria. For her own stolen childhood. Helpless tears. Then, angry tears. And finally, tears of resolve and growing courage. This would not go on. *Could* not go on.

If only she knew how to stop it.

After her sobs subsided, she lay there while the involuntary gasps for breath grew further apart. Her shoulder hurt from the hard floor, and she couldn't feel that arm. She rolled to her back and flexed her fingers to bring the blood and feeling back to her hand.

Her runny nose needed attention so she pushed herself up and crawled to the counter for tissues. She slid the box off the counter and onto her lap and then dropped back to the floor with the cabinets supporting her back. It took half the box to empty her nose. She took a deep breath and stood to survey the damage in the mirror.

Matted hair was glued to her face with dried tears. Bethany peeled strands of hair from her cheek and splashed cool water on her face. She was eager to get to Maria. She was a horrible mother for leaving her in that dark room by herself all this time. No matter what Carlos had said, she should have been strong enough to go in there.

She dried her face and was struck by the hardness in her eyes. She was changing. She could feel it and now she saw it in her reflection. Carlos thought his grip on her was tighter than ever. He was blind. Bethany opened her bedroom door to see Kenny on the other side, about to knock. "Carlos just left. Said he's going to the store."

She nodded and gave him a brief hug before hurrying to Maria.

Light from the cracked door poured over her baby, curled up on the floor, right where her dad had put her. Bethany sat beside her and pulled Maria into her lap. They rocked and hugged for several minutes. This would not happen again. Bethany would die before she saw a child punished for refusing physical affection.

● ● ●

Carlos had been gone a couple of hours. A much-needed break for Bethany and the kids. A cartoon played on the TV. Bethany and Kenny sat on the couch with Maria and Gloria on their laps. Empty hot chocolate mugs littered the coffee table. When the front door closed, Bethany tensed and watched for Carlos to come around the corner.

His teeth showed behind a wide smile. "Come look what I got."

Gloria scrambled down and ran to Carlos, giggling and bouncing with her hands clasped. "What'd you get, Daddy?"

Bethany nudged Kenny. "Here we go. Smile." She plastered on a fake smile and stood with Maria wrapped around her. Kenny followed, but without a smile.

Like Santa pulling gifts from his sack, Carlos made a big show of rummaging through the paper shopping bag in his hand. He slid out an adorable stuffed puppy. "Gloria's new puppy!"

Gloria squealed and reached for it while Carlos laughed. "See how much Daddy loves you?" She nodded and hugged it close. "Do you love your Daddy?" He held out his empty arm.

She ran into it and hugged him tightly. "Yes! I love you, Daddy!" She plopped down on the floor to watch the rest of her daddy's show.

Carlos rustled around in the bag with a grin. "Who's next?"

Maria buried her face in Bethany's neck. *Yeah, sweetheart, I'm not impressed either.* Bethany rubbed her back and kissed her head.

Carlos pulled out a canister. "What's this?" He feigned confusion and turned it to read the front. "Protein powder? Who'd want something like this?"

Kenny shifted his feet.

Carlos looked at him. "Want this?"

The canister shot the short distance to Kenny, thumping into his chest. He fumbled to catch it before it hit the floor. "Thanks." He looked hurt and confused.

"See, I love you too, Kenny." Carlos glared at Kenny until he made eye contact and then pulled his lips back in what almost looked like a smile.

Carlos went back to pretending to dig in the bag before he pulled out a pink teddy bear holding a heart.

Gloria gasped. Maria twitched as if she wanted to look but changed her mind. Gloria was excited enough for them both. "Look what Daddy got you." She stood and tugged on Maria's ankle. "See how much Daddy loves you?"

Maria pulled her leg loose with a grunt. Bethany peeled Maria back and turned her toward Carlos. "For you." She pointed to the bear.

Carlos held it closer to her and turned his wrist back and forth, making the bear wave. Maria held out a chubby hand.

Carlos bent with a smile, trying to get her to look at him, but she would only look at the bear. "Daddy got you a teddy bear. See, it even has a heart. You have Daddy's heart." He let her touch it but didn't let go. "Do you love your daddy?" She buried her fingers in the bear's fur and pulled on it. He held out his other arm. "Give daddy a hug, and you can have it." His expression was soft and inviting.

Maria leaned toward him. He lifted her out of Bethany's arms and close to his chest. "That's better. Do you know Daddy loves you more than anything in the world?"

Maria wiggled to get the bear in front of her and wrapped her arms around it. Carlos didn't seem to care that she ignored him. He tipped his face close to her ear and talked in an exaggerated whisper. "There's one more thing in this bag. What could it be? Who is it for?"

Maria reached toward the bag and opened and closed her hand. He opened it under her chin. Her face lit up, and she pulled out a beautiful metal butterfly. It had smooth, flat stones in the wings, and was firmly attached to a hairclip.

Bethany's jaw dropped. She'd never seen anything like it. "So pretty."

Carlos smiled. "For a pretty girl. *My* girl." He took it and gently clipped some of her hair back with it. His fingers stroked her face as his hand left the clip. Why couldn't he always be so sweet? Her aching heart soaked up the attention as fully as her kids had.

They were all his puppets. He'd probably always known that, playing them constantly. But did he know that she was finally starting to see it too?

CHAPTER SIXTEEN

BETHANY   **Monday, June 6**

Carlos was full of energy the next morning. Lots to do before his last wake-up at home. At the top of his list was shopping for his first care package.

Gloria and Maria were excited to go. It was a rare treat to go shopping. Whenever Carlos was coming, Kenny stayed home and watched his sisters.

Carlos was loud. Bethany had to admit it was embarrassing. Sometimes shocking. His rude comments and observations turned heads everywhere they went. Bethany didn't fault Kenny for avoiding public with Carlos. But her girls didn't know his critical statements and insults were inappropriate. Yet.

Today, she matched their enthusiasm as she braided Gloria's hair. The ride was filled with chatter. Carlos named items he didn't want to forget. "… and jerky."

Gloria tried to help. "Don't forget animal crackers and bananas, Daddy." Carlos and Bethany exchanged an amused look. "And Goldfish crackers. The cupcake ones! Yummy. Mommy, can we get some too?"

"Don't let me forget."

Once inside, Carlos grabbed a shopping cart. "Does anyone want a ride?" Gloria ran to the other end and jumped onto the bar. Maria tightened her grip on Bethany. But Bethany wasn't about to carry her the whole time.

Even little ones like to have choices. Bethany gave her two that didn't involve being carried. "Do you want to ride here in the seat," Bethany pointed to the seat by the handle-bar, "or in the basket by Gloria?" Maria pointed to the basket and settled down close to her sister.

Carlos pushed the cart, dropping items in the basket. Bethany walked beside him and listened to him talk, nodding at all of the appropriate times.

"I want to take lots of pictures with me."

"Okay."

"We can take them tonight. It'll be fun."

It took a moment for his implication to sink in. Did he mean …? She searched his face.

He wiggled his eyebrows and nodded. "Those kind."

Bethany shook her head. "What if someone else saw them?"

"I'll just put them on my laptop."

"I don't think so."

"I have to have something to look at."

"I don't want those kinds of pictures out there."

"I'll hide them on my laptop. No one could find them."

Bethany shook her head while her mind raced, searching for any excuse he might accept.

He shrugged. "You should be thankful."

"Thankful?" How would she get out of this without a big fight? Her mind flashed back to just over a week ago when he woke her up by spinning the chamber on his revolver. The threat had felt real.

"I could just look at other women. But I want pictures of you."

Bethany's stomach quivered. He knew her tender spot. When she was pregnant with Maria, she'd found out he was looking at porn online and contacting local escorts.

She hated being sneaky, but she hadn't felt that she had a choice. So, she'd purchased spyware and hidden it on his computer. What she saw had made her sick. She'd suffered in silence for months. Unable to tell him, helpless to stop him, hopeful that he'd just quit on his own. He hadn't. The secrecy consumed her until she'd finally told him. His reaction shocked her.

"What? You don't trust me! If you don't trust me, how can I trust you? I can't even trust you to leave my computer alone." He'd stormed out of the house.

When he'd come back, his tone had been completely different. Sincere and kind. "Sorry you felt like you had to install it. I won't go to those websites again. I never enjoyed it anyway. It was just something to pass time and laugh at. Besides, you're much hotter than those girls."

Turned out, something happened with one of the guys he worked with. Army Criminal Investigations Department (CID) took the guy's laptop. He was looking at charges. Carlos hadn't wanted her reporting him to his command, so he'd promised never to look at sites like that again. And he hadn't. At least, not that she could track.

Now, she was sure he was purposely touching on the pain from that experience. She made one last argument to get out of what he was asking. "But what if we both die and the kids go through our stuff and find that?" The thought had nagged at her last time she'd given in.

He stopped pushing the shopping cart and faced her. "You're overreacting. Just like yesterday with Maria. You made her not even want to hug me."

What? Bethany glanced at the girls. They chatted while Gloria's arms hung over the side of the cart, stretching toward the snacks that Maria kept just out of reach. "I didn't make her not want to hug you."

"I told her to hug me. She was about to when you came in and tried to take her. Then, you made me put her in her room. Why do you always get between me and the kids?"

Her mind reeled. How did they go from pictures to over-reacting to his twisted version of what had happened the day before? She didn't even know which topic to respond to. They were stopped at the end of the cookie aisle, their cart poking out into the main aisle. Other shoppers had to go out of their way to get around them.

"She didn't look like she was about to hug you."

"You scared her when you came in. She was fine until then." His voice rose, and shoppers shot curious glances their way.

I scared her?

Gloria stepped off the end of the cart. Maria passed a package of crackers to her before she handed it back to exchange for something else. Bethany was glad they were distracted.

"I'm sorry, Carlos." Maybe she had misread the situation the day before. She wanted to get home. "Can we finish shopping?"

Carlos grunted. "This mean you'll let me have the pictures I need?" His eyes challenged her as he grabbed the cart and shoved it forward, slamming it into Gloria. She fell. One of the wheels ran over her foot and ankle as she cried out and burst into tears.

Bethany gasped and ran to her daughter, sprawled out in front of their shopping cart. Scooping Gloria up, Bethany glared at Carlos. He exploded. "Why didn't you listen, Gloria? I told you to move." Gloria looked confused as fresh tears rolled from her eyes. Baffled, Bethany replayed it in her head.

Carlos took Gloria out of Bethany's arms and cuddled her while smiling at onlooking shoppers. His lecture was loud and syrupy sweet. "Baby girl, this is why you *listen* to Daddy. Daddy tells you things for a *reason*. See what happens? You did not listen, and you got hurt. Next time listen to Daddy, okay?"

Gloria nodded and rubbed her eyes.

He shrugged and dipped his head at a woman passing by. "Tell Daddy you're sorry for not listening."

Bethany was beside herself. She didn't want Gloria taking the blame. But which was worse, Gloria thinking she messed up or knowing her daddy lied to her? She could just hear Carlos claim Bethany was trying to get between him and the kids. Again.

Gloria did as she was told. "Sorry, Daddy."

He patted her back. "It is okay. Just make sure you listen to your daddy next time." Gloria nodded. He put her back on the cart and they continued shopping.

But Bethany's churning thoughts wouldn't let up. She kept her voice low. "You didn't tell her anything before you ran her over with the cart."

"Your version."

The churning moved to her stomach. "What do you mean? You were looking at *me* and talking to *me,* and then you ran her over."

"I remember it the way I want to remember it. You remember it the way you want. And now, Gloria remembers it my way." Bethany's cheeks grew hot. "It was your fault anyway." He shot her a knowing look. "For making me so upset." He smiled and shrugged while her mouth went dry in disbelief. "And it was her fault. For not being on the cart when I was ready to go. Don't try to blame me."

Carlos wrapped an arm around her waist and pulled her close. "I'm just glad you finally agreed to let me take those pictures tonight." He chuckled in her ear.

• • •

By the time the girls were in bed for the night, Bethany had worked herself into an emotional frenzy. She absolutely did not want to give Carlos what he wanted. But she was terrified to refuse. At this point, she couldn't even feel excited about the deployment. Dread had been tumbling around in her stomach all day. She needed help.

She made up an excuse to leave Carlos in the bedroom. "I'm thirsty. Be right back."

"Okay." He sat on the foot of the bed and fiddled with the camera.

She had to be quick. It wasn't the first time she'd snuck downstairs before going to bed with him. Rushing into the kitchen, she snatched a glass from the cupboard and set it on the counter. She ignored the tug in her heart that warned against becoming dependent as she reached for the stool tucked away in the cabinet next to the fridge. She pushed it against the refrigerator and jumped up to reach the cupboards over the freezer.

She heard Carlos' footsteps above the kitchen as he headed for their bathroom. Probably brushing his teeth. That should give her a few minutes. She opened the left cupboard door to reveal their stash of hard liquors. They used to keep them in the freezer until Kenny got old enough to rummage for his own snacks.

Alcohol lasted a long time in their house since it usually only came out when they had company. But it had started going faster in the last few weeks or so. Carlos hadn't noticed.

Physical intimacy with him had just gotten too difficult for her to stomach. Just the thought made her queasy. She'd found a way to deal with it. Chugging a glass of spiked juice before bed.

Terrified of becoming an alcoholic, she was glad he was leaving soon. Her kids needed her too much to go down that road. If only she could stand up to him. If only he hadn't turned into a monster. If only— What a waste of time.

His voice floated to her. "Baby girl. I'm waiting."

"Coming." She rinsed the glass and threw it in the dishwasher.

CHAPTER SEVENTEEN

BETHANY   **Tuesday, June 7**

Had the sun already been up for over an hour? The day seemed to be holding its breath. Two long, green Army duffle bags rested near the front door. Bethany sat beside Carlos on the couch and watched him tighten the laces on his tan combat boot. She was numb and oblivious to the morning chill despite her bare arms and thin nightgown. The day had finally arrived.

She must be dreaming. It couldn't be real. He'd be home tonight. The phone would ring any minute to tell him he wasn't going anywhere.

Boots tied, laces tucked inside the top, Carlos straightened and put a hand on her thigh. His penetrating gaze cut to her soul. Could he see it? Did he know she'd been longing for this day? She wanted to talk but the only thing she could think to say would give away her eagerness for him to walk out that door. She pulled her bottom lip between her teeth and waited.

He studied her face as the sound of little feet waking up and running over their heads broke the silence. Bethany mentally begged her girls to come and distract them. Jump in Carlos' lap and brighten his face. As if hearing her, light footsteps flew down the stairs. They both turned as Gloria's dark and crazy bed-head raced in.

"Mommy! Maria pooped in her Pull-Up again. It's all over her blanket. Come quick!"

She'd been rescued. She jumped up and took one step before Carlos snagged her wrist and jerked her down beside him. He tipped his head back and raised his voice. "Kenny! Clean your sister up." Turning to Gloria. "Go tell your brother to clean it up."

Gloria nodded as she ran out. Bethany sighed. "I can do it."

Carlos grunted. "We're talking. Almost time to go and I'm worried."

She settled against the cushions and rubbed her wrist while waiting.

"This deployment has me stressed." He took her hand and kissed it. His lips touched her wrist. The inside of her forearm. Gentle. Like a butterfly. Carlos lifted her arm and kissed up to her elbow. The swelling was nearly gone, but the discoloration from her run-in with the door frame was still vivid against her light skin. His finger traced the edge of the large bruise. "This was an accident. We were going into the dining room to talk. You were angry and banged your arm on the wall."

"You were angry." Had he forgotten?

"No. *I* was only stressed. My parents were here. Dinner wasn't working. I wanted to sit down and talk. When you overreacted, this happened." He tapped the ugly mark. "I would *never* hurt you."

Bethany stared at the lacey edge of her nightgown. She hadn't overreacted. Her brain clouded as she strained to remember exactly what had happened.

Carlos pushed her chin up with his finger. His eyes prompting her to believe him. Agree with him. "I would never hurt you. I love you too much."

Her brain hurt from the constant contradictions. She just wanted him to leave. "Maybe this deployment will be good for all of us."

The finger under her jaw hardened while his thumb clamped down on her chin. "What does that mean? You don't love me? You won't miss me?"

"Of course, I will." The temperature dropped. Chills swept over her arms and legs.

"I work hard. Do all this for you and those kids. Make a better life for us. I cannot do that if you go behind my back and make me look bad."

Bethany pulled her chin from his grip and shook her head with a frown.

His shoulders sagged and his voice grew sad. "It doesn't matter to you, does it? What are you going to do? Take pictures of the bruises? Show someone and blame me for what you did?"

"What?" *Pictures? Who would care? What was the point?*

His eyes popped open and he drew his head back. "Oh my gosh. *That* is what you are planning to do? Did you already take the pictures? Where are they?"

"I haven't taken any pictures. I'm not planning anything like that." Exhaustion from trying to keep up with his accusations crept into her shoulders and pricked her eyes.

"Sure. We'll see." His words said he didn't believe her. But his body relaxed.

She needed this deployment. "I love you. Just make sure you come back safe." Did she sound convincing? She had a whole year to persuade him to get help. To fix the damage he'd done to them all.

He smiled. "I love you *more*. I'll be back. No one can stop this." He flexed his bicep.

Bethany sighed in relief. Carlos was fine. She was fine. He jumped up, fueled from the energy he'd just sucked out of her. She followed him to the door and wiped her palms on the sides of her nightgown.

Carlos swung a stuffed duffle bag over one shoulder and looked up the stairs. "Time to say goodbye."

• • •

Bethany watched out the window as Carlos swung his duffle bags over the side of the pickup bed. At least she didn't have to drive him on post. The couple that Carlos had gotten drunk with the other night had offered to give him a ride. She watched him smile and talk. A different person. Maybe she wasn't good for him. He looked so much happier when she and the kids weren't around.

Bethany watched him hop in the backseat of his friend's truck with a lump in her throat. Would he be the same the next time he walked through their door? Would the time away make him want to treat them better? Or, would it make him even more angry?

Suddenly, they were gone. Bethany continued to stare at the quiet street. He was on his way to another country. A year. Seemed forever. Pulling her gaze from the window, she turned. The wall clock ticked louder than usual. The house was so quiet.

He was gone.

A strange stirring started in her stomach and expanded to her chest. Joy. Excitement. Hope. Elation. Her face stretched into a smile that grew as fast as the spreading warmth. *Carlos was gone.*

She wanted to laugh hysterically. *Well, why not?* There was no one to glare at her. Criticize her. Smother her. She let out a giggle that seemed to open the floodgates. She laughed. Louder. Harder. It was freeing. Her hands found her knees for balance.

She laughed so hard that her abs hurt.

She snorted as she sucked in air for the next round, which made her laugh even more. Tears rolled down her tight cheeks. Her sides hurt. Kenny appeared over the rail at the top of the stairs. He smiled and bounded down the steps. "He's gone?"

Bethany tried to answer but couldn't form words as she gasped for breath. She nodded, snorted, and laughed harder. Her legs felt weak, but she couldn't stop. Didn't even try.

It was contagious. Kenny was soon doubled over with her. They kept each other from falling, clinging to each other's arms and howling.

Gloria and Maria squealed as they ran downstairs. They weren't about to miss out on the fun. They slammed into Bethany and Kenny, making them all tumble into a crazy laughing pile on the floor.

When they caught their breath, Bethany cranked up some music. She sang to the first song she heard and danced her way into the kitchen to pour cereal for her girls. While Gloria and Maria ate, Kenny joined Bethany by the stove, where she cracked eggs into a pan. She looked at his arms. "Don't forget. Tomorrow I'm taking you to counseling. You still wanna go, right?"

He lifted his forearms and nodded. "Nothing new, Mom. And, yeah, I still wanna go." He put an arm around her shoulders. "Almost doesn't feel real."

She could relate. "Right? But we have a *one-year* break." Her eyes stung with happy tears. "Peace. No yelling. A year." She sighed.

He nodded, face troubled. "How long do you think it'll take before they figure out he's not that easy to live with?"

Bethany gasped. She hadn't even thought of that. "Oh, wow. I don't know." She shook her head, eyes round. "But I'm sure we'll find out."

Just the thought of all those soldiers seeing the real Carlos seemed insanely funny. They burst into another peel of laughter.

STACIE

Stacie flipped the sign on her florist shop to "closed." She leaned against the front counter with a sigh. She'd called Holly twice with no answer. A mix of concern and frustration churned in her belly as she recalled Holly's promise to keep attending the support group. She'd been a no-show the night before and Stacie wanted to know why.

Should she drive out to Holly's? This was where that fine line stretched before her. She didn't want to be the overbearing mother who kept intruding into her daughter's personal life, uninvited. But she also didn't want to be the mother who wasn't there for her daughter when she needed her. If Holly'd just answer and tell her *something*.

Stacie tapped the screen on her phone and found Felicia's number. Felicia's cheerful voice came over the line, accompanied by a crowd of voices in the background. Relief washed over Stacie. "Hey, beautiful. Where you at?" She tried to speak over the noise.

"Can barely hear you, Grammy. This restaurant is so loud!"

"You with your mom?"

"Mom's here. Danny took us out to eat."

"Fun! Wanna call me later?"

"That's mine." Felicia giggled.

"I'll let you go, but can you call me later?"

"Oh, food's here, Grammy. Gotta go! Love you."

"Love you, too."

Why hadn't Holly been answering? Things sounded like they were going well. She sighed and stuffed the phone in her purse. Holly's lack of communication stung. She wanted to be there for her kids, but when they only spoke to her when they needed help, it hurt. She shook it off. She was glad they came to her. Now it was time to go home and relax.

• • •

After dinner, Stacie's thoughts drifted to Bethany. Was today the day Carlos deployed? The thought made her jump to look at the calendar. It was! Bethany should have no reason not to answer or talk to her now. She was giddy with excitement as she tapped the call button on her phone. It only rang twice before she was rewarded with her oldest daughter's sweet voice.

"Hi, Mom!" She sounded happy. Carefree. Different.

"Hey, sweetie! Whatcha up to?"

Bethany's soft laugh floated through the speaker like music. "Whatever I want." She said it with a gentle sigh at the end.

Immediately, Stacie understood. "Carlos deployed today?"

"This morning."

Stacie tried teasing her. "Don't miss him yet?"

There was a pause. When Bethany spoke again, her voice sounded guarded. "Well. He just left this morning. I've been busy with the kids. I'm sure I'll miss him soon. Just doesn't feel real yet, ya know?"

Stacie nodded. "Yup. So, everyone good?"

"Yeah. We're just hanging out and taking it easy today. I'm getting ready to make dinner so I can't really talk much right now. Wanna chat with the kids?"

Stacie tried to hide her disappointment. "Love that."

Kenny came on the line next. "Grandma?" His voice sounded so deep. Grown-up.

"Hello, handsome! How's it feel being the man of the house again?"

He chuckled. "Amazing."

Stacie got to catch up with Kenny. He didn't seem in a hurry to get off the phone. It warmed her heart that he didn't tire of her questions. He talked about school and his career goals. What a great young man he was turning out to be. She was proud of him.

She didn't talk with Gloria or Maria very long because dinner was ready, and Bethany wanted everyone to sit at the table together. Nothing was holding Stacie back from visiting Bethany now. She'd look at the calendar and flights during a slow time at the shop the next day. Her heart longed to see and hug her growing grandkids. She missed Bethany. It would be great to reconnect while Carlos was gone.

BETHANY

While Bethany made dinner, she caught pieces of the conversation Kenny was having with her mom. She felt a little guilty for passing the phone off so quickly, but her mom's question about missing Carlos alarmed her. She realized most of the other wives in her husband's unit were probably struggling and heartbroken on this first night. She had a hard time imagining what it must feel like to miss him and wish he were home. *Nope.* She shook her head as she gave up. Her imagination just wasn't that good.

Bethany made a simple dinner.

Because she could.

Chicken nuggets and instant mashed potatoes with gravy. The kids would be thrilled. When dinner was ready, Bethany considered putting her mom on speaker in the middle of the table while they ate. But she was selfish and wanted to relish every moment with her kids during their first dinner of freedom.

Besides, she didn't want her mom to hear how happy they all were when they should be missing Carlos. She wasn't quite ready to drop the careful façade she'd created over the last several years. But since she longed for the openness she used to share with her mom. The curtain would be pulled back sometime this year. Just not today.

Bethany smiled as she set candles up on the table between two platters of chicken nuggets. Once the candles were lit, and the lights dimmed, she called the kids to the table. Her heart swelled when they exclaimed delight over the glorious dinner set before them. Joyful chatter and laughter danced between the flickering candles.

And there was no one to spoil it.

CHAPTER EIGHTEEN

BETHANY   **Wednesday, June 8**

Bethany was nervous as she sat in one of the chairs sprinkled between plants, book racks, and toy shelves. She'd only spoken to Kenny's new counselor, Dr. Davis, for a few minutes before watching Kenny disappear into his office. Never having been to a professional counselor herself, she wasn't sure what to expect. What were they talking about in there?

Bethany chewed her lip as she watched Gloria and Maria play. What if Carlos found out she'd brought Kenny in for counseling? He'd be angry. She was doing something she knew he was against. But he was a world away. By the time he returned, Dr. Davis would have helped Kenny, and there would be nothing to tell. She took a shaky breath and checked the clock.

The office door finally opened. She jumped from her chair. Kenny dipped his head and smiled at her as he dropped to the rug beside his sisters. "What you playing?"

Dr. Davis stepped into his doorway. His black slacks and white button-up shirt perfectly pressed. The top two buttons of his shirt were undone, showing a few gray hairs that matched the graying at his temples. "Mrs. Garcia. Would you please join me in my office?"

Bethany nodded, eager to find out what Dr. Davis had to say but terrified at the same time.

His office was furnished in browns and yellows. The back wall had a large window with the shades pulled halfway up.

One entire wall was filled with brown bookshelves. Books filled the higher shelves. The lower shelves were home to games and miniature toys. People. Animals. Furniture. She sat on the edge of a plush armchair and waited. He cleared his throat as he rolled his office chair closer to her. The room shrunk.

"What do you know about Kenny's relationship with your husband?" Why was he asking her? Kenny was just in there.

"It's not good. Carlos is hard on Kenny." When he didn't respond, she filled the silence. "Kenny doesn't like Carlos. He talked about moving out a couple weeks ago. Changed his mind." She shrugged. Why wasn't he telling her what Kenny said? How to help him stop cutting himself? That's why they were there.

"You said your husband is hard on Kenny. Tell me more about that."

"He expects a lot out of him."

"What happens if Kenny disappoints him?"

Flashes of Carlos pushing Kenny and pinning him to the wall, in a chair, at the bowling alley ... Her mind was full of them. Her tongue felt thick. She was the worst mother in the world. But she'd stopped Carlos each time. That was good. Right? "Carlos sometimes pushes Kenny." Her heart clenched.

Dr. Davis nodded and looked concerned. "What else?"

Her tense muscles screamed at her. She couldn't move. "Mostly just pushing ..."

He waited.

"Hard." She dropped her stinging eyes to her clenched hands, blurred with unshed tears. "There are dents in the walls where he's pushed Kenny." She blinked making the tears spill. A box of Kleenex appeared across her knees. "He pins Kenny to the wall or whatever he pushes him against."

"Have you ever called the police?"

Was he crazy? Her eyes shot to Dr. Davis while her mouth dropped open. *I'm trying to keep us all alive.* Dr. Davis waited for her response, but she had a hard time finding her voice.

Bethany finally shook her head.

"Have you ever seen your husband choke Kenny?"

"No!" *Choke Kenny?* She shook her head. *Never!* He only choked her. If he'd choked Kenny … Fury boiled inside Bethany. "Has he?" Carlos wouldn't do that. Dr. Davis studied her face.

He gave her one curt nod with raised eyebrows.

"He never told me." Bethany felt sick. Her heart ached and there was no stopping the tears. "Why didn't he tell me?"

"Said he was scared to tell anyone." Dr. Davis' eyes remained focused on her face.

"Is that why he's been cutting himself?"

He sighed and looked at the window over Bethany's shoulder. "Hard to say."

She pulled handfuls of Kleenex from the box to mop up her face. "I never saw the choking." He had to know she wouldn't have let it happen if she'd seen it—she protected her kids. "And I always stopped Carlos when he pushed Kenny."

"Mrs. Garcia." Dr. Davis leaned forward and rested his elbows on his knees. "This. Is. Abuse. By law, I have to report it to Child Protective Services."

Was she in trouble? "Then what happens? Carlos is deployed."

"The real question is, will he ever have access to Kenny again?"

"I don't know what to do. Carlos needs help. Counseling."

"Has your husband ever been physical with you or your daughters?"

"Wha—" Bethany had never been asked that before. She wanted to deny it. "No, he—" She started to shake her head, but images bombarded her brain. The screaming, shoving, bruises, choking, threats. This wasn't why she came here.

What was happening? How could she tell this strange man intimate details about her home life? She'd learned from a young age to keep what happened at home a secret. Her father had taught her well.

A tsunami of memories consumed her vision. In horror, she watched them roll one after another. Her hands came to her face and she cried. Words wouldn't come. Only sobs. She pressed clutched hands against her belly as she wept. She had just wanted Kenny to get help for his cutting. Carlos wasn't even home.

When she was finally able to see past the mental barrage, she pulled several Kleenex from the box. Why'd she even bother putting mascara on that morning? Now, the Kleenex was wearing it.

Dr. Davis had leaned back in his chair with his hands folded over his flat stomach. His face was kind but intense. "I know it's hard to talk about. But I do need you to tell me. Has your husband ever been physical with you or your daughters?"

Bethany took a shaky breath. "The only thing he's done to the girls is spankings. But a couple of times, there were bruises afterward." She blew her nose. "Mostly, he yells all the time."

"And what has he done to you?"

Chills swept over Bethany as tremors pulsed her stomach. "He doesn't get physical very often." Her jaw tightened so that she had to answer through clenched teeth. "He's grabbed my throat." That sounded worse than it was, so she quickly justified it. "But he only squeezes enough to scare me." The tremors intensified until they shook her entire body. "He shoves, pushes, and—" She pulled her lower lip between her teeth.

Should she show him? She was afraid to. But she desperately wanted someone to understand. Someone to confide in. She needed to *see* someone recognize what Carlos had done to her. It was suddenly important to know whether her fears were grounded or if she really was overreacting. Or crazy.

Dr. Davis prompted her to continue. "And what?"

She tugged her arm out of the sleeve of her hoodie. Even with the swelling gone, the fading bruise still clearly covered a good portion of her upper arm and elbow. "He pushed me through a doorway, but my arm didn't clear it."

Dr. Davis nodded and sighed. "Tell you what. Since your husband just deployed, you've got some time. I won't report it because it's *currently* a non-issue. He's not even in the same country."

Bethany wasn't sure what to feel. Relief? Disappointment? She nodded.

"But listen carefully." He walked his chair a step closer and leaned forward. She met his hard gaze. "If he comes back home to you, *all* of this will be *immediately* reported to CPS. I won't have a choice. He'll face charges and you could lose your children."

"I'll lose my children?"

"If you fail to protect them from your husband. Possibly." He pushed back to the desk. "You cannot let him back into the home. Do you understand?"

She nodded, feeling sick.

"He's deployed for a year?"

She nodded.

"Good. I need to see Kenny again on Monday."

Bethany blew her nose.

"I'd like to make an appointment to see you next week too. Are you up for that?"

"Okay." Her mind spun. *What would happen when Carlos' deployment was up?* How was she going to convince him to get help too? No way she could tell him what she'd done. He'd be furious if he found out anyone said he couldn't come home.

She needed to talk more *now*. Next week wouldn't come fast enough. Something was set in motion that she didn't fully understand. She needed her mom. Guilt at the way she'd brushed her off the night before filled her with doubt. Her sister would be easier to start with. Maybe it was time for that visit. She'd call Holly as soon as she got home.

Stacie

The shop had been bustling all morning. A steady stream of customers came and went until after two that afternoon. Stacie pulled a sandwich and sparkling water from her mini-fridge in the back room and settled down to devour her lunch. As she savored the last bite of sandwich, her mind drifted to Friday's dinner with Rich and Felicia.

He'd been such a gentleman, taking the change of plans in stride. Not missing a beat, he'd treated Felicia like the princess she was. He'd even brought each of them a pink carnation. It hadn't happened instantly, but by the end of the evening, he'd seemed to at least put a crack in Felicia's resistant wall.

Stacie was ready to hear whatever it had been that Rich had wanted to talk with her about. Should she call him and ask him to dinner this time? Should she wait for him to make the first … err, second-first move? Maybe she could call to say hi and give him easy access to asking her out again. *Oh, please. How juvenile.* She was a grown woman. She could come right out and ask him what he'd wanted to say.

She wasn't sure how she went from thinking the thoughts to listening to his phone ring. Voicemail. She hung up and made herself busy creating bouquets and straightening up the little shop. A couple hours later, there wasn't much left to do. It seemed she'd reached the end of her customer flow for the day and her mind was right back on Rich.

He called her back just as she flipped the sign over and locked up. After all of the thoughts bouncing around in her head all afternoon, she was tempted not to answer. She took a deep breath and rubbed her temple. "Hey, Rich."

"Not sure what your dinner plans are but thought maybe I could spare you from having to cook tonight."

She smiled. "Sounds tempting. Can I meet you there?"

"Sure thing."

• • •

Stacie pulled into her garage two hours later. It had been a pleasant and casual dinner. Friends meeting after work on a weeknight. Nothing special. But somehow, it was special because it was Rich. He said he wanted to pick her up on Saturday for dinner, where he planned to talk with her about what had been on his mind. Their date back on, Stacy could wait.

CHAPTER NINETEEN

Thursday, June 9

Bethany stretched as she woke up. The cold sheets on the other side of the bed made her heart skip a happy beat. Peace for the second morning in a row. No dreadful anticipation about what awaited her. Incredible.

Her thoughts bounced to the only thing left to worry about—counseling and the gruesomeness of working through that mess. She needed to talk with someone before she met with Dr. Davis again. He'd really freaked her out. Why hadn't her sister called back? She'd called and sent text messages asking Holly to call her. *Bah. Annoying.*

Bethany threw the covers back and headed for the shower. Her mind drifted to the day's activities and her heart sang. No Carlos to worry about. Her cheeks were getting quite the workout since smiles came more easily and seemed to last longer.

She'd just finished rinsing the soap from her body when her phone played Holly's ringtone. She shut the water off and jumped from the shower, dripping a path to the counter. Holly wanted to video chat. *Perfect.* Bethany slid her finger across the screen.

Holly's delicate face appeared as Bethany rushed to grab a towel. "Impressive display of lights over your mirror, but I was actually calling to talk with my sister."

Bethany poked her dripping face in front of the camera and smiled before covering her face and hair with the towel.

"You get to finish your shower?"

"Yeah, was just rinsing off." She wrapped the towel around her body and took the phone into the closet.

"Sorry I couldn't call back sooner. Danny took a couple days off work to spend time together. Didn't want to upset him." Bethany's lip curled. At least she didn't have to worry about *that* for a year. "He's at work now. What'd ya want to talk about?"

Where to start. "Have you ever been to counseling?" Bethany stared at the clothes hanging in her closet but only saw the inside of Dr. Davis' office.

Holly laughed. "Nope. Why? Think I need it?"

"That's not it." Bethany shook her head and smiled. "Kenny wanted to go, but Carlos has something against counselors, so I set the appointment for after he deployed. Couple days ag—"

"Oh yeah! He's gone already?"

"Yup. Left Tuesday." Joy bubbled inside. Bethany pulled a tee-shirt off the hanger and scooped up a pair of jeans from the floor on her way to the dresser in her bedroom.

"Miss him?"

Bethany was tired of pretending. "No. It's been amazing." She set the phone on her dresser and pulled out undergarments.

"What? I thought *he* was amazing."

While getting dressed, she said, "I haven't exactly been open about things." She could only imagine what Holly must be thinking. Confused eyes penetrated the phone screen. Bethany's heartbeat sped up. Her insides felt jittery. "Carlos," she swallowed, "did things." She'd shared with Dr. Davis. Why was it so hard to tell her sister? She plucked the phone from the dresser and sprawled out on her bed. "Anyway, I took Kenny to counseling yesterday and ended up telling the counselor some things about Carlos."

She thought Holly would say something. But her face hadn't changed and her lips were pressed together. The jittering spread to her limbs. She had to set the phone on the bed to keep it from shaking. Rolling to her side, she leaned over the camera. "Counselor told me it was abuse and he had to report it to Child Protective Services." That got Holly's attention. Her eyebrows shot up as her eyes widened. "Later, he changed his mind and said he wouldn't because the kids are not at risk while Carlos is deployed. *But* he'll report it if I let Carlos come back home."

Holly's mouth dropped open. "Are you serious?"

Bethany nodded.

"What'd you tell Carlos?"

Bethany squeezed her eyes shut and covered half of her face, pressing on that eyebrow. "Haven't talked to him yet." She sighed and dropped her hand. "He'll contact me once he's set up there."

Holly nodded.

"But I can't tell him about *any* of it. I can't even tell him we talked to a counselor."

"Why? How you plan on keeping it from him? That's pretty big."

"Well. I don't *have* to tell him if I convince him to go to counseling and *change*. Besides, I can't tell him. He said he'd kill the kids and me if I told anyone."

"What?" Holly shook her head and scrunched up her face, looking completely confused. How could Holly's face look so perfect even all scrunched up like that? "How long's this been going on? Thought you found a great guy." Maybe if Bethany were as hot as her little sister, Carlos would have been able to love her enough to be faithful and treat her right. "Why didn't you tell me? I thought we were close."

Bethany's heart was heavy. Hurt was all over Holly's face. "I'm sorry. I wanted a great marriage. Fake it till you make it." She tried to push out a laugh but it fell flat. A great marriage could still happen. She had to believe it. Christians weren't supposed to get divorced. If he got some help, he really could be the great guy she saw deep down inside. He had potential. And he loved her. He loved the kids. He just needed counseling.

Bethany shook her head and smiled. "Anyway, I was wondering if you still wanted to come stay with me for a while? With Carlos deployed …" She smiled. "We can catch up."

Holly shook her head. "Can't come. Danny's doing better. Stopped drinking." She dipped her head with a smile. "He really loves me. He'd be hurt if I ditched him now. He didn't drink at all last weekend. Took some time off work and never touched a drink the whole time. Just hung out with Felicia and me. Was great. I love him so much when he's like this."

Disappointment hit Bethany but she didn't want Holly to see it. She understood not wanting to leave and feeling responsible for his behavior. Not wanting to trigger the bad times. "How's Felicia?"

"She's great!" Holly went on to brag about how smart Felicia was while Bethany tried to follow along. She smiled but she was scared. She was alone with the weight of her family's future pressing on her shoulders. Was she doing the right thing?

Maybe it was time to open up to Mom. Her cheeks filled with color at the thought of admitting her deception. How had she gotten here? For the first time, she felt a twinge of understanding for her mother and the tough choices she'd had to make. Suddenly, confessing to her mom actually sounded like a good idea. Bethany realized she had full access to a woman who'd already walked in her shoes.

Stacie

Stacie pulled into her shop's little parking area as her phone rang. Bethany! She smiled. "Hey, gorgeous lady!"

She could hear the smile in Bethany's voice. "I love you, Mom. Whatcha doing?"

"Love you too. Perfect timing. Was about to open up the shop, but I think it's going to open a little late today. What's up?"

"Oh. Thinking of you. Haven't really talked in a while."

Stacie grabbed her purse and stepped out of the car. "True." She unlocked the shop door only long enough to let herself in. Bethany was so quiet that Stacie pulled her phone away to see if they were still connected. "Everything okay?"

"I don't know where to start. Talked with Nate lately? Or Holly this morning?"

"Haven't talked with Holly for a couple days. Nate calls often. Why?"

"Talk about me?"

"What's going on, Bethy?"

"Just trying to figure out where to start and what you already know."

Stacie wanted to hear it from Bethany herself, so she remained silent while straightening up the counter and shelves.

Bethany sighed. "Okay, fine. Carlos deployed on Tuesday and I took Kenny to counseling yesterday." Her words picked up pace. Stacie found a chair so she could focus. "Kenny was cutting his arm. He told Dr. Davis that Carlos sometimes choked him."

Goosebumps raced down Stacie's arms, her heart pounded, and the air in the room seemed to thin. She was ashamed of herself for not knowing, not helping. Her mouth went dry.

Bethany continued, "I didn't know he'd ever choked Kenny. Carlos pushed him into the walls or furniture sometimes. But I always stopped him. I didn't know about the choking." Her voice cracked. "If I knew, I wouldn't have just *let* it happen. He choked my baby." Bethany's voice dissolved into tears.

Each broken sob clutched Stacie's heart tighter than the one before it. Her eyes were full, but she fought the tears and concentrated to make out Bethany's words as they picked back up with a thick slur.

"Counselor said he was going to call CPS and I might lose the kids!" She sniffed and cleared her throat. "Carlos can't come back, but I can't *tell* him that. He needs counseling. Maybe anger management. I don't know. He grabbed my throat a couple of times but didn't actually hurt me. Just scares me and the kids. Maria doesn't even like him anymore. I don't know what's wrong with him. He needs help. He'll be calling any day now. I don't know what to tell him, but I hate lying, so I don't know what to *do*." She practically wailed that last line. Stacie recognized the desperation in her oldest child's voice.

Tears streamed from the outside edges of Stacie's eyes as she tipped her face to the ceiling and listened to Bethany break off and cry. She didn't trust her voice, but she had to say something. Her eyes scanned the room as if searching the walls for the right words. There were no right words. Her voice was thick and raspy. "Oh, honey." Tears poured down her face and neck. She longed to hold her sobbing daughter. "I'm so sorry. I wish I was there." She sniffed. "Listen to me, sweet pea." She adopted a lovingly stern tone. "I *know* it doesn't seem like it now, but this is the turning point that leads to good things. Baby, I know it hurts. I know it's scary. Don't try to do this alone, sweetie."

Bethany sniffed. "I don't know what I'm doing." Urgency crept into her voice. "Carlos can't know I told anyone." She sighed. "And I don't want to ruin his career. I'm going back to the counselor on Monday. When Carlos gets back, we could go to marriage counseling and fix things. I've got one year to convince Carlos it's a good idea. Anyway, just needed my mom. I hear the girls looking for me. Need to get them breakfast. Gotta go."

Stacie had failed. She'd failed as a mother when her children were young, and she'd failed as a mother now that they were grown. She ached to be with her daughter. Bethany made it sound simple. Some marriage counseling and they'd all live happily ever after. Stacie used to think that was one solution until she saw firsthand how dangerous an abuser could become afterward. It gave the abused a false sense of security where they opened up only to be punished for it after they left. Carlos needed a very different sort of help.

CHAPTER TWENTY

Friday, June 10

Felicia stood in front of the bathroom mirror and examined a pimple on her cheek that was competing with her nose for space. She huffed and yanked open a cabinet door. "Mom! Did you get me face cleaner? Told you I was out *yesterday*!" She knocked cleaning bottles over as her hands searched for anything that would stop the birth of an elephant on her face. Where was her mom? This was an emergency.

Fine. She'd just stay home for the next six months since that's about how long this thing would take to go away. Her summer was ruined. She could just fall back and die right there on the bathroom floor. Her mom probably wouldn't even discover her body until she wanted her to do the dishes. Felicia flopped onto the pink bathmat and rolled her eyes back. The end was near. And no one was there to witness it.

From her bedroom drifted the sound of an alien space ship, the ringtone she'd given her best friend. Pimple catastrophe forgotten, Felicia jumped off the floor and raced to her room.

Jasmine squealed when Felicia answered. Felicia yanked the phone from her ear with a big smile. "Now that my ear's bleeding, what's up?"

"Where in the world have you *been*? Thought you *died*."

It felt good to be missed. "Mom didn't want me using my phone much this week. Danny wanted to hang out. All about what Danny wants. Guys are totally lame."

"That sucks. Wanna hang out at the mall? Mom said she'd take us."

Danny was back at work today, so maybe Mom would let Felicia go. But she hadn't gotten to spend any time alone with her mom since they'd left Grammy's house a whole week ago. "Can we go tomorrow?" Danny had Saturday off. If Jasmine could wait, she'd get to hang out with her mom today *and* miss Saturday with Danny. She held a hopeful breath while Jasmine went to ask.

It took so long that Felicia finally went looking for her mom. She found her in the kitchen, making grilled cheese sandwiches. "Hey, Mom, can I go to the mall with Jasmine? Hopefully tomorrow?"

Her mom flipped the sandwiches. "Tomorrow? But it's Danny's day off."

Exactly. Duh. "I know. But I thought maybe you and Danny wanted some time alone together." Maybe she should have waited and asked Danny. He was usually happy to get rid of her.

Jasmine spoke into her ear. "Can't you come *today*?"

Felicia was torn. But being alone in the kitchen with her mom, knowing Danny was gone for several more hours, reminded her of how much she'd been looking forward to this day all week. "Can't today. Asking about tomorrow." She lifted her eyebrows at her mom and pulled the phone away. "*Please.*"

Mom nodded. "What time and how long?"

After Felicia worked out the details with Jasmine, she hung up and sat at the table with a steamy grilled cheese sandwich. "Thanks!"

Her mom sat across the table and took a bite. She smiled with crumbs stuck to her lips. Her eyes looked different. Tired. Happy. Sad. Mom took a sip of water from a tall glass beside her plate. "Sounded like she wanted to go today."

Mom's knowing eyes made Felicia squirm, but she nodded.

"You didn't ask to go today. Just tomorrow. Why?"

Felicia wasn't sure how to answer. "It's just us today. Rather go when Danny's here."

Mom folded her hands on the table and squinted. Felicia's throat felt constricted, so she put her sandwich down and waited. "Didn't you have fun with Danny this week?"

"Sure."

"Don't you like Danny? He's been better all week. Right?"

Felicia wasn't sure which question to answer, so she went with the one that felt safest. "Sure. He was better." She nodded. Inside she begged her mom. *Please drop the subject. Please don't make me talk about things I don't understand. I don't like him. I'm trying to like him for you, Mom, but I just can't do it. I'm not good enough. Not like you. You always see the best. Believe the best. I can't trust him. And I don't want to. There must be something wrong with me. I still don't trust him after he's been nice all week. Why can't I like him?*

What would her mom think if she told her? Felicia plastered on a smile and picked up her sandwich. Her mom would never know what a horrible daughter she had. She forced herself to take a bite and chew through the fake smile she struggled to keep.

Her mom licked her lips and nodded. "I'm glad you didn't try to ditch me today." She smiled and hooked her foot around Felicia's ankle, pulling it up under the table. "Kinda like hanging out with my favorite girl."

Felicia relaxed and smiled. A thought flashed through her mind and washed her in shame. If only Danny were dead.

BETHANY

Bethany had taken the kids to get ice cream. It was a warm day, and she gave in to the temptation to get a double scoop in a waffle cone. One scoop of coffee and the other salted caramel. Kenny copied her. Who could blame him?

Gloria and Maria were delighted when each of them received an ice cream cone filled with cookies n' cream. Bethany had them all in the truck with the AC blasting as quickly as she could. She made sure Kenny kept checking on his sisters in the backseat. "Have them lick before they drip." They would never have gotten away with this when Carlos was with them. The thought made her smirk as she slid the truck into a parking spot at the park.

As they happily piled out, her phone rang from inside her purse. Nothing was more important than the fun she was having with her kids. She stuffed her purse into the giant glove box and locked it. Handing the keys to Kenny, she winked. "You have bigger pockets than me."

He rolled his eyes with a smile and dropped them in his pocket. "Wear baggier clothes."

She skipped and nudged him on the way by. "Stop complaining and eat your ice cream."

He laughed and jogged past her while Gloria and Maria squealed and ran after them.

Time raced until they realized the sun had dropped low in the sky. They were suddenly famished. As they walked toward the parking lot, Kenny offered his elbow to Bethany. She was happy to lock arms with him and allowed him to escort her back to the truck. She took a deep breath of the cooling air and let it out with a joyful sigh.

Kenny turned with a smile. "It was a good day."

"Yes. It was amazing."

As soon as she opened the truck door, she heard the faint ring of her phone from the glovebox. It stopped ringing, so she started the truck and turned the AC down low before fishing it out. She had thirty-six missed calls. Her heart pounded as fear crept across her chest. All from a number she didn't recognize. Her eyes were glued to the phone as her mind raced.

Kenny leaned over to see. His eyes shot to hers. "Who's that?"

Bethany shook her head. "I don't know the number." She didn't want to say his name out loud. The person who was going to be calling any day. The person no one missed. He'd be furious by now. What was she going to say?

How had she thought his deployment would make everything better? She turned the ringer off and set the phone in her lap. The vibration would be more than enough to get her attention.

She drove in a dreadful fog. Either the kids were worn out, or they sensed something had changed. They were too quiet. Like Carlos was in the truck with them. She could feel the joy from their perfect day fall away as quickly as if someone had pulled the plug on a drain.

She didn't have the energy to cook, so she hit a drive-through on the way home. Her phone vibrated as the teen girl handed bags of food through the window. Bethany passed the bags to Kenny. Should she answer while she was driving or wait until they got home? No. She wouldn't put the kids through listening to it. Her mind was so tormented that she barely remembered getting to the house. They ate in relative silence. Kenny shot concerned looks her way, but she didn't know how to reassure him. She dreaded the next time the phone vibrated. She didn't have to wait long.

"When they're done, get them ready for bed."

Kenny nodded and watched her disappear.

Carlos' voice sprang from the phone as soon as she tapped the screen to answer. He was laughing and talking with someone else. It took a couple seconds for him to realize it wasn't ringing anymore. His tone instantly changed. Angry. "Hey. Anyone there?"

"Hi, honey." She tried to sound sweet.

"You finally leave your boyfriend's house so you could answer your phone?"

The fear melted and annoyance rose in its place. "My boyfriend?"

"Only reason you could have for avoiding my calls all day. I thought you would be waiting to hear from me. You know, miss me. But you already forgot about me."

"I haven't forgotten about you. I was at the park with the kids."

"And?"

"Just me and the kids. I mean, there were other people at the park but not with us."

Carlos grunted. "I can't talk long *now*. You've wasted all my time and I have to go. Tomorrow we can do a video chat online. Don't leave the house. I'll call you when I'm ready to get online. I don't know what time yet."

"Okay. Love you."

Carlos snorted. "Love you *more*."

Bethany hung up, feeling sick. A video talk with Carlos. And he was already mad at her. Great start.

CHAPTER TWENTY-ONE

STACIE   Saturday, June 11

Stacie stood in front of her bedroom mirror. Again. She couldn't believe she hadn't thought to buy a new dress or top for this occasion. She was sure between church and all of the activities they'd done together, Rich must have seen every piece of clothing she owned by now. Oh, well. He'd be there any minute. She'd finally settled on black slacks, a red satin top, and comfortable pumps. She had to get away from the mirror before she found a reason to change again. The last thing she wanted was to be between outfits when he arrived.

As if on cue, the doorbell sounded down the hall. She dropped her phone in a little black evening bag.

When she opened the door, the familiar scent of his cologne greeted her. She thought she detected a hint of nervousness in his face before being replaced by a warm smile when their eyes met. He wore a black suit jacket over a pale blue, button-up shirt, tucked into a dark pair of Wranglers with a big belt buckle. But not too big. He even wore his Sunday boots for the occasion. "Evening, Stacie." His husky voice somehow caressed her name on the way out. The lines around his eyes deepened with his smile.

At that moment, she realized she was no longer content to be single the rest of her life. Rich had become one of the best friends she had. If that's all they ever were, she'd take it. But, God Almighty, please let there be more.

Rich extended a single red rose with a chuckle. "Felt a little guilty buying a flower from someone else."

"As you should," Stacie admonished and winked at him. "It's beautiful. Thank you. Let me put it in water real quick before we go."

He was shaking his head with a smile as he followed her to the kitchen. "Can't say it'll be the last time. A man's gotta be able to surprise a special lady every now and again."

As Stacie made a new home for the rose, she shook her head and clicked her tongue in mock disapproval. "I suppose I can forgive that."

The rose smiled at them from its slim vase on the counter. Stacie gave it one last admiring look and turned her attention to Rich. "Ready?"

His extended elbow answered her question.

BETHANY

Bethany loaded the dishwasher after dinner and fumed inside. She'd been carrying the phone around with her all day. Why had he told her to stay home if he wasn't going to call until late? If he called at all.

Immediately, she felt guilty. He was deployed. What if something had happened to him? Well, if something happened to him, she'd be free. *Stop it,* she scolded herself.

Once the kitchen was cleaned for the night, Bethany climbed the stairs to see what her children were up to. Kenny was sprawled out on his bed, watching a YouTube video with his bedroom door open. She waved when he looked up. Backtracking four steps, she walked into Gloria and Maria's room. They played with their stuffed animals and Bethany sank onto Maria's bed to watch and think. It might be better to put them to bed early in case Carlos called at bedtime. She didn't know how long he'd be able to talk, and she didn't want them staying up too late.

Her eyes burned and scratched every time she blinked. Waiting on Carlos and not knowing what to expect had been like a slow drain on her energy all day. What if he didn't call after she got the kids down for the night? Did she wait up or just go to bed? She was pulled from her thoughts by Gloria's loud voice. Her stuffed dog was yelling at Maria's stuffed monkey.

"Time to brush your teeth." Bethany smiled and motioned for Gloria and Maria to follow her. Apparently, the angry dog wasn't about to be pulled away so easily. When Maria set the monkey down and ran to Bethany, Gloria raised her voice even more. "Come back here! I not done with you yet."

"Oh, ho, little princess. You're done. Let's go get those teeth brushed."

Gloria sighed and stood on the bed. She bounced twice and then launched to the floor, tossing the stuffed dog in the air. "Not you, Mommy. *Monkey* was da mommy."

Bethany pulled the little stool from the bathroom cabinet and placed it in front of the sink. She absently pushed a dab of sparkly toothpaste from a bright tube onto two small toothbrushes and handed one to each of her girls. Why hadn't Carlos called yet?

Going through the motions automatically, Bethany kissed each girl goodnight as she tucked the covers up under their chins. "Goodnight, sweet peas." She switched off the light and stepped out.

"Mommy." Gloria sat up.

Bethany poked her head in.

"I'm thirsty."

Bethany nodded. "I'll bring a glass of water, but you stay in bed."

"Me too." Maria kicked her covers off.

"I'll bring two. Stay in bed."

After kissing them goodnight and tucking them in a second time, Bethany shut the door with a sigh. She poked her head through Kenny's doorway. He'd fallen asleep with his phone in hand. Bethany smiled. He was a heavy sleeper so she figured she could sneak in. She leaned over his beautifully peaceful face and placed a hand over the hairline at the top of his forehead. Her heart swelled. She pushed his blond curls against the top of his head and kissed his forehead while drinking in her son's scent. Still her precious baby boy, no matter how big he got. Once again, she was thankful for the break from Carlos. Countless times a day, she had the same feeling rush through her. The surge had yet to diminish of the immense appreciation for the peace that Carlos' absence had brought to the house. She didn't know if it was possible to miss him.

Bethany slid Kenny's phone from his hand and placed it on his nightstand. She spoke softly so she wouldn't wake him. "Goodnight, my precious son. I love you. So much." She turned to tiptoe from the room.

"Goodnight, my precious mom. I love you too."

She spun to see his eyes half opened and a sleepy smile on one side of his mouth. She shook her head. "I wake you up?"

"Naw. Was getting tired and about to sleep. Glad you came in. G'night." He rolled to his side and pushed the pillow under his chin.

Bethany smiled as she closed the door. "Goodnight, sweetheart."

She strolled to her room, feeling lighter than she had all day. Three amazing kids. That's what she had. She brushed her teeth and got ready for bed, thinking she may not hear from Carlos after all. That was okay with her. Just annoying that she'd had to waste the whole day waiting.

The phone rang before she got a chance to crawl between the sheets. With a sinking heart and a forced, happy tone, she answered. He was online and ready. He wanted her to send him a video-chat invite once she had the laptop on.

Bethany pressed the power button. As soon as the screen came to life, she took a deep breath and sent the video-chat invite to Carlos. It took several seconds to connect before his smiling face filled the screen. "There's my baby girl."

She smiled. "You just missed the girls. I wasn't sure what time you'd be calling."

Carlos shook his head. "It's okay. Want you tonight. I've missed you."

She nodded.

"You miss me?"

"Of course."

"You better." He laughed and leaned close to his camera. "Don't have much time tonight, but I had to talk with you. I had this idea and I couldn't wait to share it. See what you think. I'm so excited."

She nodded. "What's up?"

His intense eyes seemed to bore into her soul. "I need a son to carry on my bloodline."

Not at all what she was expecting. Bethany wrinkled her nose and half-closed an eye. No way. She didn't even know what to say. He saved her from an immediate comment as he rushed on. "When I come home for mid-deployment leave, I want to get you pregnant again. That way, you'll be almost ready to have the baby by the time deployment is over. It's perfect." He sat back and folded his hands over his chest with a satisfied smile on his face.

She didn't know what to say but he'd flip if he knew what she was thinking. She couldn't tell him all that had happened in the five days since he'd left. Mid-deployment leave. When would that be? She'd forgotten all about it. "We have Gloria and Maria to carry on your bloodline."

"They're girls. I need a son." He nodded as if that settled it.

Bethany fiddled with the mouse and tried to hide the panic that rose in her chest.

Carlos lost his smile. "I want to hear the words."

She frowned. "What words?"

"Say you want to have my son."

Bethany studied the keyboard as if she'd never seen one before. She couldn't lie. She couldn't say it. She chewed her bottom lip as her mind raced.

"You don't want to have my son?"

She looked back at his video image on the screen.

His voice was stern. "I'm going to have a son."

"I can't say yes right now."

"That's not fair. You have a son. And I gave you the two daughters you wanted. Now, I want *my* son. Are you trying to deny me that?" Carlos tapped a cigarette on his desk.

"That's not it. I have to think about it."

He put the cigarette in his mouth. Took it out. Drew it under his nose and took a deep breath before he finally responded. "Okay. You have one week to decide. If you deny me a son, I'll make a few calls."

"Calls? For what?"

"To take you and your son off my insurance. No more TRICARE for you. I'll also start the paperwork to take the girls from you. My parents can come pick them up and care for them until I get back to the states."

Bethany shook her head. "Why do I have to decide this now?"

"Because baby. I calculate everything. I need time to put things in place. You've got the next move. One week, baby girl." He chuckled before the chat screen went blank.

Bethany tasted blood from the sore spot she'd chewed into her bottom lip. She couldn't bring another child into their dysfunctional home. What would she tell him? She crawled into bed, knowing sleep wasn't going to be her friend.

Stacie

Dinner had been wonderful. The conversation comfortably transitioned from casual to deep, with bouts of laugher thrown in at all the right places. Although there nagged, in the back of Stacie's mind, what Rich brought her there to talk about, it never seemed to come up during the meal. By the time the waitress brought the check, Stacie had begun to feel disappointed. What had he wanted to say and why hadn't he said it by now?

After Rich had paid for their dinner, he shifted in his chair. Color crept from the collar of his shirt, up his neck, and into his cheeks. Stacie had never seen him like that. "You okay?"

He cleared his throat and nodded. "Yeah. Do you have time for a walk? Weather's good for it." He gestured toward the window where the sky glowed with the sunset.

"Of course." Was he sick? Dinner not set right? An after-dinner walk sounded nice. She hoped it would bring the relaxed Rich back to wrap up their evening.

Outside, he offered his elbow, which she gladly took as they strolled down the sidewalk. A refreshing breeze bathed them and seemed to do the trick. The color in Rich's face returned to normal. He drank in a deep breath. Stacie smiled. "Feels nice, doesn't it?"

He grunted and nodded. "Sorry about that. It's just—" He sighed. "I've rehearsed this so many times in my mind. Can't believe I'm having trouble now. Truth is, last week, when Felicia joined us, I was relieved she got me outta sayin' what I been wantin' to say for months." He chuckled and shook his head.

Stacie forgot to exhale as she waited for him to finish.

"I didn't plan on feeling this way, Stacie. I wasn't looking for it, asking for it, or anything else. I've always enjoyed spending time with you. I admire you. You're strong, brave, Godly, and ..." He cleared his throat. "Beautiful."

It was Stacie's turn to feel flushed. Beautiful? Rich made her feel that way. Tonight, she felt about thirty years younger. She stepped over a wad of gum on the sidewalk and took a deep breath before she could look at his face again.

He didn't seem to mind that she couldn't find her voice. He steered them toward a bench along the sidewalk where they sat down.

"Stacie. You're one of my dearest friends. I don't want a girlfriend. I don't want someone to date. I'm not lonely."

She studied his face, trying to understand what he was saying.

"I've got friends, family, employees, and plenty of acquaintances."

Her cheeks burned as she searched her mind for a time she might have given him the impression she wanted more than friendship.

"I can call any number of people if I want to chat or spend time with others."

The thought came to mind recently but she didn't think she'd been so obvious. Did he bring her to dinner to tell her he never wanted more than friendship? What was the point in that? They could have just continued the way they were.

"I just want you to know that. Before we take this any further. I haven't been lonely or anything like that."

Another couple strolled their way. Stacie wanted Rich to shut up until the younger couple passed. How embarrassing. Rich giving her the "let's be friends" talk in public.

"But I find myself caring about you in different ways. I worry about you more than I think I should. I want to find out what all of your favorites are and then shower you with them. I found myself looking at your daughter and grand-daughter and finding joy in identifying the similarities they have with you. I love seeing you happy. When you're sad or worried, it affects me in unexpected ways. I want to be there when you're down. And then, there's the other side of it too. When something good happens, you're the first person I want to share it with."

He laughed, but she just stared at him, trying to wrap her mind around what he was saying. Just friends? More than friends?

"I feel like I'm rambling now. I want to give you a chance to respond." He took a deep breath and searched her eyes. She was so confused. His eyes bounced around on her face.

"I don't understand. I value your friendship and I never want to lose it. Are you saying you feel the same way?"

Rich chuckled. "I guess you could say that. It's true. I never want to lose your friendship either, so if this conversation jeopardizes that, we can change the topic and not bring it up again."

Something amazing was in the palm of Stacie's hand, and she was letting it slip away, but she didn't know how to take hold of it.

"I'll just say one last thing, and then, if you're happy with the friendship we have, I won't bring anything else up again." He cleared his throat. "The longer I know you, the more I start to doubt my decision to stay single." He gave a stiff nod, as if that settled it, and seemed to be waiting for a response to his confession.

"So. Uh. You're not lonely, but you might not want to be single?"

Rich laughed softly at first, but it grew louder as he shook his head. It looked like he wanted to say more, but each time he opened his mouth, he just laughed harder. It was contagious, and soon she was laughing too. He caught his breath and nodded. "When you put it like that, sounds like I completely botched up the point I wanted to make tonight."

Her heart soared. She smiled. "Just tell me the point, Rich."

He was serious. His eyes wouldn't let hers leave. "I love you, Stacie Newfield. I've loved you for a very long time. I will love you as a friend for the rest of my life. But I think I'd like to love you as a wife."

Stacie gasped as his words became electricity shooting through her veins.

"Now, I'm not asking you to marry me today. I'm asking if you could honor me with the opportunity to court you and maybe even become your best friend in the process. The opportunity to see if marriage is where we want our friendship to go. But no matter what," he pushed a stray strand of hair from her face, "I never want to lose your friendship."

Inside, she was screaming, *yes*! But she was still a little confused and wanted to understand before she agreed to anything. "You said you don't want a girlfriend or someone to date." She shook her head. "Help me understand."

His face lit and he nodded. "I'm sorry I made such a mess of things. Dating is about having romantic fun, which may or may not lead to marriage. That's not something I'm interested in with anyone. What I'm looking for is deeper. Girlfriends and boyfriends come and go. But you are my dear friend. If you allow me to court you, you can be sure I will be faithful to you. I will be open with you. I will be honest with you. I've known you many years now, and we've been close friends for a few of those. I think I already know." He tipped his forehead closer to hers. "But I want you to know too. So, I'd like to court you. And one day, if you decide you feel the same way, I'd like to marry you. But I want to do this thing right. You're worth it."

There was no stopping the tears that spilled onto her cheeks. Half of Rich's mouth lifted as he reached to dry them. "Oh, my dear, I hope that means yes."

All she could do was nod. He wrapped an arm around her shoulders and drew her close to silently watch the last trace of daylight make room for the night sky.

CHAPTER TWENTY-TWO

It was late afternoon when Felicia walked out of the movie theater with Grammy on one side and Uncle Nate on the other. They tossed empty popcorn buckets in the trash can on their way out. "I can't believe she died! How long till the next one comes out? I hate waiting." Felicia flung herself against Uncle Nate's arm.

Uncle Nate laughed. "Silly girl. Don't ya'll know? No one's ever *really* dead in Hollywood. Wouldn't be surprised if she miraculously survived somehow."

Felicia's eyes swung to his face. "Really? But *how*? No one could survive that. She was totally dead. Until that last second of the movie when she twitched."

"If I'm right, ya gonna wash my truck?" He nudged her shoulder.

"You're on! That means you'll have to bring me to watch the next one." Felicia let out an evil laugh.

Uncle Nate shrugged. "Why not? It's the least I can do for a good truck washing."

Felicia looked at Grammy, but it looked like Grammy's mind was somewhere else. She seemed happy, but not totally there with them. She hoped Grammy wasn't sick.

Felicia grabbed her grandma's hand and swung it high. "Whatchya think, Grammy?"

Grammy shook her head. "I'm with Felicia. If we're right, you gonna wash my car, Uncle Nate?" She winked at Felicia as they strolled through the parking lot.

Felicia laughed. They all climbed into Uncle Nate's truck. It would be cool if Mom were there, too, but her mom would rather spend time with the loser. "Grammy, can me and Uncle Nate spend the night at your house?"

Uncle Nate glanced in the rearview mirror at Felicia. "Where would I sleep? I hear you hog the guest room."

Felicia laughed. "You can have the couch."

Nate shook his head with a smile. "Can't anyway. Gotta work in the morning."

Bummer. Would've been so cool.

"Sides, I told your mom I'd have ya home tonight. I heard you were out with a friend all day yesterday, and now yer out with us today. Your mom probably misses you."

Felicia sighed and looked out the window. Danny would be home. But he had work in the morning so that was good. It was pretty cool that he'd kept his word and stopped drinking. He was really trying to be nice when they were all together, but she still felt like he didn't want her around. That was okay because she didn't want to be around him either.

• • •

When Felicia got home, her mom was alone on the couch. "Where's Danny?"

Mom patted the couch. "Said a friend needed his help replacing the engine in his truck."

Felicia tried not to let the smile spread too big across her face while her heart did happy flips. "Oh." She curled her legs up and leaned on her mom. Her mom wrapped an arm around Felicia and pressed a button on the remote, scrolling through movies and TV shows.

"Whatcha wanna watch?"

Felicia shrugged. She didn't care. She just hoped Danny would be out until after she went to bed. She didn't hate him. She just didn't like him.

CHAPTER TWENTY-THREE

Little feet running on the stairs dragged Bethany from sleep. With the sun sending a ray of blinding light through the gap between her curtains, she knew it was past time to be up. She opened scratchy eyes to check the time. It was almost 9 o'clock! She remembered seeing each hour of the night at least once until around six when her last thought was that she might as well get up for the day. She'd better grab coffee to help wake her up before their counseling appointment later.

She couldn't get Carlos' demand out of her head all day yesterday. The countdown pressed on her mind like a drill. What in the world was she supposed to tell him?

Skipping a shower, she threw on a pair of shorts and a tank top. One look in the mirror told her she'd better at least wash her face and put on a little mascara. Irritation still lingered in the eyes that looked back at her from the mirror. A brush through her hair and she was set.

A son. She already had a son. She couldn't imagine having another child. Especially with Carlos the way he was.

She hesitated in the kitchen entryway. She didn't know whether to laugh or cry. Maria and Gloria were on stools at the counter. Gloria had the bear-shaped honey bottle turned upside down as the girls watched it drown a slice of bread on the counter. She didn't appear to be in a hurry to turn the bottle right-side up. Instead, she created a trail to the slice of bread in front of Maria. Honey disappeared into the bread like water in a sponge. Maria licked her lips. "Mmm."

"Okay, that's enough, honey." Bethany stepped in and reached for the bottle. Gloria handed it over with a smile. Bethany regretted taking the sticky bottle as soon as it was in her hand.

They picked up their pieces of bread, sagging and loaded with honey. Maria's little tongue darted over her lips a couple times before the sweet bread reached them. Gloria's first bite disappeared behind a satisfied grin.

Maria smiled and talked with her mouth full. "Gowia make bweakfast."

Gloria dipped her head. "Want some, Mommy?"

"No, thank you." Bethany ran hot water over the outside of the bottle while rubbing the honey off with her fingers. Setting it aside, she grabbed a fresh dishrag and wiped the mess from the counter. "Next time, you need to ask before you make breakfast. Okay?"

Gloria nodded and licked her lips. She'd managed to get honey in her hair. It was down the front of Maria's pajamas as well.

"As soon as you're done eating, it's bath time."

Bethany got the coffee going while they finished eating. As soon as they were done, she stripped Maria down to her training pants before carrying her up the stairs. Gloria trailed behind them. "Keep your hands together and don't touch anything. You're sticky." At the top, she tossed Maria's dirty PJs in the laundry room on the way by.

Kenny raised his eyebrows as he approached, heading for the staircase.

Bethany smiled and blinked burning eyes. "Hey. Don't forget we have a counseling appointment in a couple hours."

He disappeared down the stairs.

An hour and a half later, the girls were bathed, dressed, and they'd all had a proper meal. Bethany was on her third cup of coffee when she realized it was time to get moving. She strapped little shoes to little feet as she called up the stairs, "Time to go, Kenny."

Maybe Kenny fell back to sleep or was playing his music because she didn't hear him coming. "Going to get your brother." She raced up the stairs to Kenny's room.

His door was open and he was spread out on the bed, staring at the ceiling, when she rushed in. He appeared deep in thought.

"Hey. Time to go."

He blinked.

"Kenny." She sat on the edge of the bed and touched his arm.

"What?" His eyes dropped to her face as if he'd just noticed her there.

She frowned. "Time to go. What you been doing?"

"Laying here."

"Okay." She stood and patted the side of his leg. "We gotta get going or we'll be late."

Gloria and Maria raced in, laughing, and jumped on Kenny's bed. Maria fell on Kenny's chest with a squeal.

Kenny scowled. "Ouch. You didn't knock."

Gloria bounced close to his face and tapped her little knuckles on his forehead with a smile. "Knock, knock."

He turned to slide away from them and off the bed. "Not funny." He walked from the room and slammed the bathroom door.

That was weird.

Gloria put on a pouty face. "What's wrong with Kenny?"

Maria held her arms up. Bethany scooped her up and shook her head. "Not sure."

• • •

Bethany had gone in first and talked with Dr. Davis about the video chat conversation. She'd shared her confusion about what to do or how to respond. Her concern about losing health insurance for Kenny and herself. She was surprised how much ground they'd actually covered. It felt good to share. He encouraged her to lean on some of the support people in her life. Her mom. Trudy. By the time she'd traded places with Kenny, she felt confident about what she'd say to Carlos during their next video chat. She sat in the waiting area and watched Gloria and Maria play while she mentally rehearsed her speech to Carlos.

When Kenny came out, Dr. Davis asked to speak with Bethany.

"I'd like to see Kenny again on Wednesday."

"So soon?"

His eyebrows drew together as he looked through his schedule. "I'm completely booked that day, but I think it's important that I have a little check-in with him anyway." He leaned back in his chair with a sigh. "Can you bring him by at noon? I'll squeeze him in during my lunch."

"Sounds like it's important. I'll make sure he's here."

"Great. Between now and then, I'd like you to keep an eye on him. Spend time with him. Make his favorite meal. Try to do something together that he usually loves. Don't mention I suggested these things. When you bring him back, let me know how all of that went."

Kenny didn't talk much on the way home. Bethany stopped by for ice cream, but he wasn't interested. She wasn't sure what to do to cheer him up. Maybe a movie night with popcorn would be just the thing for them all.

Stacie

Stacie pulled out of the church parking lot later than usual after group that night. She was tired but had a good talk with Zalika while cleaning up after their sessions. Zalika had asked about Holly. She hadn't attended since moving back in with Danny. Another broken promise. Zalika had encouraged Stacie to keep showing love and support.

Stacie had also opened up and told Zalika about Bethany's recent call. She was concerned about Kenny and glad Carlos was out of the picture for a year. She planned to fly over and spend time with Bethany's family soon. A visit was long overdue.

What would Rich say about her going? She'd miss him. Warmth filled her as she thought of him. She looked forward to introducing him to the rest of her kids. She needed to see what they all thought of him. But was it too soon?

CHAPTER TWENTY-FOUR

Bethany sat at the desk in her room as tears rolled down her face. She was tired. The two-hour video chat she was in with Carlos made her wonder why she thought it would be better when he deployed. She was trapped in a critical conversation that appeared to have no end.

About thirty minutes in, she'd pulled up an audio recording app on her phone and hit the record button for her own sanity. Then, she could go back and see if she really said things the way he told her she'd said them. She felt misunderstood and attacked. Didn't he have somewhere else to be? It hadn't even crossed her mind that he'd be able to do this to her from overseas.

No matter what they talked about tonight, it kept coming back around to him wanting a son and her trying to rob him of his greatest desire, to pass on his bloodline to a male child. At one point, she'd tried to get him to talk with Gloria. That lasted about three minutes before he told her he wanted to finish talking with Mommy. The only time she'd been able to convince him to give her a break was to put Gloria and Maria to bed. But she had better be right back in her seat as soon as they were down.

Carlos' scowl penetrated her heart through the screen of the laptop. "Clock's ticking. Four days before you tell me if you're going to let our girls grow up without their mother."

"They wouldn't grow up without me. I would never leave them."

Carlos laughed. He'd found a button and seemed intent on pushing it. "Oh, you would. That's your choice. If you won't give me a son, you're making the choice to leave them without a mother. Maybe even be raised by a step-mom. How would it feel to know they'd be calling some other woman 'mom'?"

"What are you talking about?"

A cruel smile lifted the corners of his mouth. "I calculate everything. Got all sorts of ways to get what I want." He chuckled as if thinking of some private joke. "I can't tell you all the ways. No one can know the way my mind works."

Bethany glanced at the phone and hated herself for what she was thinking. She didn't want to hear anything else. "Tell me one."

He looked up and stroked his chin. "One?" After a pause, he shook his head as if he wouldn't tell her, but then his eyebrows shot up. "Okay. But only the least of them. The others would freak you out too much." He seemed to be enjoying this.

"I'm listening."

"When I come home on mid-deployment leave, I drug you and take your birth control out so you 'mysteriously' get pregnant." He used his fingers for invisible quotation marks.

A bolt of lightning shot through her. Drugged? Being violated while unconscious. She couldn't even process the idea. She wanted to slam the laptop shut, pack the kids, and run away. She wouldn't let him do that to her.

"I've got access to all sorts of drugs and medication over here. It would be easy to bring some back and slip something into your drink or food."

Bethany's hands shook. She couldn't speak. Couldn't protest. Couldn't move. Couldn't even rip her eyes away from his gloating face.

Carlos snapped his fingers. "Boom. You're pregnant." He laughed and nodded. "I'm really looking forward to hearing your answer. See how much I love you? I'm letting you decide. Based on that, you *force* me to do what I need to do to get what I want."

He put a cigarette between his smiling lips and talked around it while it waved at her. "I need to get to work, baby girl. I love you so much. I'm excited to find out what we get to do next. Strategic." He tapped a finger to his temple. "I'm always thinking, planning, calculating my next move." He pulled the cigarette from his mouth and blew her a kiss before his image froze. The chat window went black.

Her mind relived the conversation. That was nothing like what she'd rehearsed. She would not let him get her pregnant. She was suddenly panicked to know when mid-deployment leave would be. She had to know how much time she was working with. She had to convince him to get counseling. Or tell him not to come home.

He'd kill her. She was dead. There was no win for her. Either the state would take her kids, Carlos would take her kids, or Carlos would kill her.

No matter what she chose, her kids would grow up without their mother. The kids lose. She loses. He was crazy and now he was driving her crazy.

CHAPTER TWENTY-FIVE

BETHANY **Wednesday, June 15**

Bethany had only been reading to Gloria and Maria a few minutes when Kenny had opened the counselor's office door and waved her in. "He wants to talk with us together. We'll leave the door open for the girls."

She nodded and braced herself, sitting on the couch where she could see her girls playing in the waiting area. But she wasn't prepared for what Dr. Davis told her. He believed Kenny would benefit from medication for his depression. Kenny had been struggling with depression for months. The cutting was one sign of it, but it was getting worse. Suicidal thoughts had begun to invade Kenny's thoughts. Dr. Davis suggested a mild dose of anti-depressant while Kenny continued counseling.

Dr. Davis broke a long silence by clearing his throat. "I think it's the best option."

"I don't know. I'm not a big fan of drugs. Even prescriptions."

Kenny scooted closer to her. His voice sounded far away. Strained but decisive. "I want to try it. It's exhausting fighting this all the time, Mom. If it helps, I think I should try it. If you knew what I was feeling ..." His voice trailed off, and his eyes dropped to his clasped hands.

Dr. Davis nodded. "It'll be a very low dose to start with."

Her son. Medication? Depression? Her mom had struggled with depression years ago. But Bethany had been caught up with her own life. She hardly remembered anything about it. If medication would help Kenny, how could she say no? She turned to Kenny. "I wish you would have told me sooner."

"I couldn't talk to you with Carlos around all the time. Besides, I figured his jerkiness was just getting me down. Now, it's so good with him gone. I thought it would get better." He shrugged.

Bethany patted his knee and turned to Dr. Davis, hoping she was doing the right thing for her son. "Can we pick it up today?"

Dr. Davis nodded and pulled a small pad of paper from his desk. He wrote out the prescription and handed it to her. "Take it to your pharmacy. You should be able to get it on your way home."

Bethany's eyes fell to the words on the prescription. The name and numbers meant nothing to her. Was she really helping her son? Everything seemed to get worse.

They stood to leave. "Thanks for coming in. I'll see you both on Monday."

Bethany nodded. She was eager to get home, behind a closed door, and share with her mom. Find out what Stacie knew about depression and the medication Kenny was about to take. She couldn't bear for anything bad to happen to Kenny. She'd never be able to live with herself.

STACIE

Stacie smiled when she saw that Bethany was calling. "What's up, beautiful lady?"

"Did you have depression?"

What was this about? That was so long ago. "Uh, yeah, I did after your dad went to prison. Might've started while he was still home. But that was a long time ago. Why are you asking?"

"Just got home from counseling. Doc wants to put Kenny on meds for depression. Did you take meds for it?"

Stacie frowned and her heart grew heavy. Depression was a tough burden to bear. She remembered how alone she'd felt. "I did. They helped. Are you gonna let Kenny take meds?"

Bethany sighed into the phone. "Picked them up on the way home. I'm scared. Are they addictive? How long did you take them? He won't have to take them forever, right?"

"I don't know how long he'll need to take them, sweetie. I'm not an expert. You'll need to trust your doctor on this one. Keep taking him to counseling. Keep talking with him. No matter how much he seems to push you away or reject you, don't stop showering him with your love. He needs to *see* you love him through this because there will be many times he may not be able to *feel* it."

"I'm so scared, Mom."

"I know you are. Hang in there. You'll get through this."

CHAPTER TWENTY-SIX

Bethany's mind was filled with Kenny all day. Would the medication work? Was he done cutting himself forever? She felt helpless.

She got Gloria and Maria settled in with a movie and headed for the kitchen to make dinner. Kenny glanced up from his medication bottle when she walked in. He opened it and swirled the pills with his finger.

Bethany went to the sink to wash her hands. "Hey." When he didn't respond, she asked, "Have you noticed that Maria doesn't run and hide anymore?"

"Yeah. Um. Mom."

Bethany dried her hands on a towel. She opened the fridge. "When was the last time you caught her banging her head against the wall or hiding in her closet?"

"Been a while. Mom." His voice sounded strange.

She shut the fridge and set a package of cheese on the counter. Kenny flung the bottle as if it had burned him. Pills spilled across the counter and onto the floor. The bottle rolled off the other side and bounced, sending more pills flying.

"Why'd you do that?" She grabbed the bottle and slid pills from the counter into it. She dropped to the floor.

Kenny watched her gather pills on her hands and knees.

"What's going on?" She glanced up. "Kenny?"

His face was pale and he shook his head. "I need you to hide those from me. Just give me what I need each day."

"Why? What's the matter?"

"I didn't used to want to die. I do more today than ever." Tears spilled down Kenny's cheeks.

Bethany wrapped her arms around her son. He dipped his head to her shoulder. When was the last time she'd held her boy while he cried? "Yeah, sure. I'll put them up and call Dr. Davis. We'll get through this." She didn't want to let him go. "Hang in there with me, okay?"

He nodded. Bethany hugged him until he pulled away. She searched his face. "Stay close to me tonight, okay? I'm going to call Dr. Davis now." He was probably gone for the day, but she needed answers.

The recording at his office gave a number to leave after-hours messages. Bethany called and left a message about what had happened. Dr. Davis called shortly after dinner was over. Kenny had barely picked at his meal.

"Bethany, if Kenny is having suicidal thoughts, take him to the emergency room."

"What? He's fine. He just asked me to put his pills up. I did that. Can we just come in tomorrow morning?"

"He's not fine. May I please speak with him?"

"Sure." Bethany gave the phone to Kenny and ran upstairs to grab PJs for her girls.

Kenny handed her the phone when she came back.

Dr. Davis was still on the line. "Can you bring him to my office at 7:30? I'll check in with him before my first patient."

"Okay."

"I think he's okay tonight, but keep him close."

Kenny didn't talk much as his sisters got ready for bed. They wanted him to kiss them goodnight after Bethany had tucked them in. He did it with a smile and tears in his eyes. They seemed to want extra hugs from him. Or maybe they just sensed that he needed extra hugs from them. "I love you, Kenny." Gloria squeezed him extra tight.

Bethany closed their bedroom door and looked at Kenny. "What would you say to us camping out in the family room tonight?"

One side of his mouth lifted. His eyes said, *thank you.* He helped set up their campsite, and they settled into their beds, only a few inches from each other. She was afraid to sleep. Should she hide all the knives too? As far as she knew, he hadn't cut himself recently, but still. "You're not going to hurt yourself tonight, are you?"

"Mom. I still have some self-control. Besides, you got me an appointment first thing in the morning. I want to see what he says. I just don't want to feel like a cry baby. This was supposed to be a good time for us. I don't want to ruin it for everyone."

"It'll get better. Just stick with me. I need you."

"I know. I'm here, Mom. I need you too."

Felicia

Felicia was ticked. She couldn't believe her mom had agreed to it. Danny had come home from work all excited that his best friend was getting married. They wanted to go out for a drink tomorrow night to celebrate. And her mom had actually agreed. What was she thinking? Now, here Felicia sat, the only one in the house not excited about Friday night. Maybe she should call Grammy and see if she could spend the weekend over there. She didn't want to sit home alone tomorrow and wait to see how drunk they were when they got back.

Felicia sat up on her bed when someone tapped her bedroom door. Her mom poked her head in. "Hey. Mind if we talk?"

Felicia shrugged.

Her mom shut the door and joined Felicia on the bed. "You're mad."

"Course I'm mad. You're going drinking with Danny tomorrow. I thought you wanted him to stop drinking?" *Such a stupid idea.* Why couldn't her mom see that?

"We're just going to hang out with friends and have *one* drink to celebrate. Danny promised. *Just one.* I'm the designated driver. I won't even drink. Well, water. But that's it." Her mom tried a playful nudge, but Felicia wasn't having it. She rolled her eyes instead.

"What am I gonna do while ya'll are out *celebrating*?"

"What do you wanna do?"

"Well, I don't want to be stuck here waiting for the fight to roll in the door."

Her mom sighed. "There's not going to be a fight. If you don't want to be here, fine. Go to Jasmine's house."

"What about Grammy or Uncle Nate?"

Her mom cleared her throat and fiddled with her sleeve. "You don't want to spend the night at Jasmine's?"

Felicia did until her mom suggested it. "Why can't I go to Grammy's?"

"Didn't say you *couldn't.* Just thought maybe you'd prefer Jasmine's this time."

Wait a minute. "You don't want Grammy to know Danny's drinking again. Huh?"

"Danny's not drinking again." Too defensive. Even Felicia knew that trick. Her mom waved her hand. "Go to Grammy's if that's what you want."

"Great. I will." *And just wait till Grammy hears why.*

"Fine. Get ready. We're going to dinner."

Her mom left. Felicia flopped back on the bed. Nothing ever really changed. Grown-ups said things would change, but all they did was trick kids into thinking there were changes. Eventually, everything just came back around again and again and again.

CHAPTER TWENTY-SEVEN

Once again, Bethany sat on the couch in Dr. Davis' office with Kenny next to her and watched her girls play through the doorway to the waiting area. How much more could she handle? "I don't want him to live anywhere else." She grabbed a tissue and used it to try and save her makeup.

Dr. Davis nodded with kindness etched into every line on his face. "But you do want him to live."

"Of course!" *What a dumb thing to say.*

Kenny's pain-filled eyes were on his mom. "I think I'm strong enough. I have self-control."

"It's not about being strong." Dr. Davis shook his head and frowned. "Depression is serious. A residential treatment facility is a safe place to work out the best treatment."

Just the thought of Kenny living anywhere else filled Bethany with pain. "How long would he be there?"

Dr. Davis shrugged. "Could be weeks. But most likely, at least a couple of months. Some medications take about six weeks to get fully into the system. But first, they need to find one that makes the symptoms better, without side effects."

The year without Carlos wasn't supposed to be like this.

Kenny took her hand. "How often can Mom visit?"

Dr. Davis handed a brochure to Bethany. "It looks like multiple times a week with this one. It's the best in the area. It's very expensive, but they take your insurance, so

TRICARE completely covers it. They'll take good care of you."

Bethany's sniffs broke the long stretch of silence. Her heart was crushed. She wasn't sure she'd survive this. Kenny was her baby. Her son. He'd been with her through so much.

Kenny leaned on her arm. "Will you visit me?"

Bethany wrapped her arms around him. "Of course."

"Bring my sisters?"

"Yeah. They'll miss you."

They held each other and let the tears fall. Bethany silently cried out to God for strength. She had none left.

STACIE

Stacie sipped a cup of tea after a long day at the shop with Felicia. Now, Felicia was in the guest room, playing a game or talking with her friend on the phone. Maybe both at the same time. Phones could do so much these days.

Stacie took her tea to the recliner with a book. She'd just started a new chapter when her phone buzzed. Bethany.

"Hey, beautiful. Whatcha up to?"

Bethany sighed on the other end. "I'm going to try to update you without crying."

Stacie replaced the bookmark and braced herself. "What's going on, honey?"

"Want me to start with Carlos or Kenny?"

Oh, no. Stacie closed her eyes. "Let's start with Carlos."

"He's crazy. He wants a son. Says if I don't agree, he'll drug me and take out my birth control and get me pregnant when he comes back for mid-deployment leave."

"When's that?" *What kind of husband threatens to drug his wife?*

"No idea. Maybe five or six months. But I don't want to be drugged. And I certainly don't want to bring another kid into this messed up marriage. Have to figure out what to do. He says if I don't agree, he'll take Kenny and me off his insurance—which leads me to Kenny."

Stacie pushed the footrest on the recliner down and leaned forward. "Uh-huh?"

Bethany's voice became thick and tender. "I can't talk about this without crying." During the pause, the hairs at the base of Stacie's skull stood up.

She stood and paced the distance between her living room and kitchen. "I'm still here. Take your time, sweetie." *Hurry up. I'm dying here.*

"I had to drop him off at a mental hospital today. Left him there." Stacie froze. "Counselor called it a 'residential treatment facility.' I guess that's the nice thing to call it nowadays."

"What happened?"

"He's got depression. Started on some meds, but they didn't help enough. Or it takes time to kick in or something like that. He wanted to kill himself, Mom! Can you believe that? My *baby*. I miss him so much. I feel like I'm on the verge of tears all the time. We get to see him day after tomorrow."

"Oh, sweetheart, I'm so sorry." Stacie's mind drifted to her own bout of depression. She had a good idea of what Kenny was going through. She swiped tears from her face. "I'm so glad you were strong enough to get him the help he needs. You did good, sweetie. I know it's hard, but you did the right thing."

"I miss him. I don't know how much longer I can stand this. I shut his bedroom door. I can't even look at the closed door without crying. I can hardly wait to see him. I'm nervous, though. I don't know what to do or think. Oh, and that reminds me. This place he's at is crazy-expensive. It looks so nice. But if Carlos takes Kenny off TRICARE, there's no way he'll be able to stay there. I can't afford that place. I'm freaking out over here. My son needs that, but I miss him, and I don't even know if he'll get to stay because my husband is crazy."

Stacie was at her computer looking up airline tickets to Fayetteville Regional Airport before Bethany had finished her last sentence. Her baby needed her, and she wasn't hesitating this time. "I'm coming. Looking at tickets now. I'll get there as soon as I can."

Bethany sniffed and blew her nose. Stacie thought she heard a choked, "Okay, Momma," but she wasn't sure. Stacie couldn't get there fast enough.

She'd just booked her flight for Sunday when her phone rang. Oh, good. Just the person she wanted to talk to. "Hey, Rich. I'm so glad you called."

"Yeah? I meant to call you earlier this week but got pretty busy at work. I'm sure you've already eaten by now, but I'd love to pick you up for dinner if you haven't."

Stacie closed her laptop and went to the kitchen to warm her tea back up. "I ate. And I have Felicia tonight."

He sounded disappointed. "Oh. I suppose you can't get away for dessert?"

Tempting. She could use his listening ear. But she couldn't leave Felicia on the very night she'd asked not to be left alone. "I'm sorry, Rich. I really wish I could. I want to talk with you anyway. Maybe tomorrow?"

"We can talk on the phone if it's pressing."

"It can wait. Better in person."

"Okay." He cleared his throat. "I can do tomorrow. Dinner or dessert or both?" His voice was strained and she realized what this must sound like so soon after he'd asked to court her. The recent memory made her smile.

Stacie looked around to make sure she wasn't overheard. "It's not about us. We're still good. I'll fill you in over dinner tomorrow. Can't really talk right now."

"Ah. Okay then. Pick you up at six?"

"I'll be ready."

CHAPTER TWENTY-EIGHT

BETHANY   **Saturday, June 18**

Bethany's heart ached for her kids. She mourned the family life she thought she'd have by now. To keep from curling up and crying the evening away, she sat on the floor in Gloria and Maria's room and watched them play. All she had the energy to do was lean against the wall and pretend everything was all right. Her girls seemed to enjoy having her in there with them. They brought her things to hold or asked her to watch something they did. Watching them was medicine to her soul.

Gloria switched out her building blocks for a doll. She walked the doll around in the playhouse. Suddenly, she turned and ran to Bethany, jumping on her lap with a laugh. Maria wasn't going to be left out. She ran and pushed against Gloria, trying to get a spot.

Bethany uncrossed her ankles and grabbed a girl in each arm. "I've got two legs and two girls. One leg for each." She breathed in the scent of their hair as she drew them close. "My precious girls." Each dark head received a kiss.

They snuggled in close. Maria looked up into Bethany's face. "Where's Kenny?"

Just the mention of Kenny brought back the familiar prick in her heart. It had been hard to talk with Carlos the night before. He kept bringing up having a son while her heart broke over the son she already had. She couldn't tell him anything about what was going on. It was a lucky thing

Carlos never cared to talk to Kenny or even ask about him. At least she didn't have to lie.

"When will Kenny come home?" Gloria picked up the topic. They'd been asking since she'd dropped him off. They didn't like driving away without him. They didn't understand and she didn't know how to explain it.

Bethany forced a smile. "Wanna visit him tomorrow?"

Both girls bounced painfully on her legs and squealed their agreement. Bethany laughed and hugged them to get the bouncing to stop.

Gloria changed the topic. "When will Daddy come home?"

"It'll be awhile. Maybe around Christmas, he'll come visit. But then he has to go back again until next summer."

Maria clapped. "Yay."

Did Maria cheer over him being gone so long or that he'd be coming back?

Gloria swung her doll, watching the doll's hair flip from side to side. "When I grow up and get a daddy, I will *not* yell at my kids."

Bethany chuckled. "Well, that's good."

"The daddy will yell. But not me."

Bethany pulled her head back. No. She didn't want that for her little girl. She scooted out from under them and moved to face them. "You do *not* have to marry a daddy who yells."

Gloria's mouth dropped open. She tipped her head to one side and drew her eyebrows together. "I don't? But I want a daddy."

"No. There are lots of daddies who don't yell at their families."

Gloria looked skeptical. "There are?"

Bethany nodded. "Yes." How had she never thought of the example they were setting for their girls?

Gloria fidgeted with her doll and adjusted the clothes for a moment.

"Princess." Bethany lifted Gloria's chin with her finger. "Don't marry a daddy who yells."

"But how will I know? Will you help me?"

"Yes. We'll figure it out." That seemed to satisfy her. "Let's get a snack." They raced each other to the kitchen.

One day, Gloria would wonder how her mother could help her find a good husband when she couldn't even manage to do it herself. But that wasn't today. For now, Bethany could still be trusted. And by the time Gloria was old enough to question that, Bethany determined, she'd have fixed this mess she'd gotten them all into.

STACIE

Everything seemed to be normal at Holly's when Stacie dropped Felicia off. Danny wasn't rude, and Holly seemed well enough. Stacie hurried back to her place to get ready for dinner with Rich. Someone had a feather and kept tickling the inside of her stomach.

What should she wear? She couldn't think of a time he'd ever commented on her clothing, so she had no idea what he even liked on her. Maybe that was a blessing. Did she really want to go down another road of basing every choice on pleasing someone else? She would wear something she felt comfortable in.

She settled on jeans and a floral print shirt with bell bottom type sleeves. It was cute, and she thought the style of shirt was still in. At least, she hoped it was. As she examined herself in the mirror, she noticed a few loose curls popping out at strange angles from her shoulder-length hair. She wet the worst of them and attempted to aim them in more appealing directions just before the doorbell rang. That would have to do.

Rich looked handsome. Every hair was in place, and he wore a gorgeous smile that sent warm waves through her belly.

They caught up over dinner. Stacie told him about her upcoming trip to North Carolina and what was going on there. She somehow managed to do it without tears actually spilling out, which she was thankful for. She shared about Felicia's fear of Danny and Holly going out the night before.

Rich filled her in about the latest at work and one of his new employees. And then, he surprised her. "One of the gals in the office just turned in her two-week notice. If Holly needs a job and if she's interested in a career change, I'd be happy to give her a shot. The other gal in there is real nice. I reckon she'd be happy to train her."

Stacie's eyes stung. "I don't know what to say. That is the sweetest thing ever."

Rich shrugged while the corners of his mouth turned up. "Sometimes, I don't know how to help. But then this came up, and I thought— Well, it just seems like a good fit."

She shook her head. "Rich." She was afraid to say more. No tears tonight. She swallowed and placed her hand on the table, palm up. His large, warm hand was in hers almost immediately. *Wow. Maybe it was too soon.* What holding his hand did to her insides. She squeezed his hand before pulling hers away and hiding it under the table with her other hand. Not yet. "It is a good fit. Thank you, Rich. That's very thoughtful."

He nodded. "Well, little lady, I should get you home so you can rest before yer trip tomorrow." He got the waitress' attention and motioned for the check. "I'm gonna miss you. The selfish part of me hopes you won't be gone long. But I want you to stay as long as ya need to."

Bethany

Bethany's stomach hurt, and she had a headache that had been intensifying since dinner. This was the day Carlos expected an answer. Even though she was sitting in front of her laptop, waiting for the invitation to chat, it still made her jump when it popped up. She accepted and doubled over to hold her achy stomach while it connected.

"Where's that beautiful face?" At least he sounded like he was in a good mood.

Bethany sat up and plastered on a smile. She pressed the record button on her phone. It had become her new habit. Record every conversation with him. Somehow, it helped keep her sanity.

"There she is." Carlos smiled. "I could hardly wait to get online and talk with you today. You put the girls to bed already?"

She nodded.

"Good. Don't want to be interrupted. You know what I want to hear first, right?"

She didn't want to tell him anything. "What?"

"Will you give me a son, or will you force me to do something I'd rather not do?"

"I don't want to decide now."

He slammed his hand on his desk, causing his image to shake. "Why is this so hard? You're crazy about me. You're the only woman I want raising my kids. It's a win/win."

"It's not like we can start trying while you're over there."

"You're really going to make me take you and Kenny off my insurance?" Carlos ran his fingers over his cropped hair and rubbed the back of his head.

"I'm not making you do anything."

"If you refuse to provide me with a son, you force me to do things you won't like."

Bethany leaned back and examined the ceiling.

The tone changed in his voice. Tender. Pleading. "The girls are going to miss you. Why would you deny them their mother?"

Bethany jerked her eyes back to the computer screen.

Carlos nodded. "You expect me to continue letting you raise our girls when you *refuse* to give me a son?"

"I'm not saying you can't have a son. Look at us. We don't even have a healthy marriage."

He shrugged. "We love each other."

"We need counseling. We need a healthy marriage before we consider bringing another child into it."

He shook his head and squinted, leaning forward until his face filled the screen. "You think we have a terrible marriage."

"I think we have an unhealthy one."

"That's what I said. You think our marriage is horrible. You think I'm a bad husband and father."

Bethany shook her head and pulled her bottom lip between her teeth. She looked at the keyboard for a moment while she tried to figure out what to say next. "Look. Gloria came to me and said that when she grows up, she will not yell at her kids, but her husband will."

She thought he'd be upset, but he shrugged and shook his head. "What'd you say?"

"I told her she didn't have to marry someone who yells."

Carlos raised his voice. "What?" She was sure he'd come through the screen and choke her if he could. "Why would you say that?"

Why was he mad at her? "Because she didn't even know there are men out there who don't yell at their families."

"I can't believe you would tell her something like that."

Bethany could hardly believe where the conversation was going. "You actually want her to marry someone who yells at her and her kids?"

"No. But I also don't want you to make her not want to marry someone like her daddy."

This made no sense. She scrunched up her face and shook her head, trying to understand.

He leaned back and crossed his arms over his chest. "How would you like it if I told her that she doesn't have to look like Mommy when she grows up? She can get a nose job."

Bethany's mouth fell open. "How is that even the same thing?"

"It's the same because you're making something about *me* sound *bad*."

"If she wants to change her nose one day, that's up to her. It's not going to hurt her either way. I don't care."

Carlos shook his head.

Bethany was on a role. He needed to get it. "What I *do* care about is that she's healthy and in a healthy relationship. *Yelling* is not part of a healthy relationship." She was thankful he couldn't reach through the screen.

"Look. I talk loud enough for everyone to hear me. You're acting like all I ever do is yell." A vein in his forehead bulged as his face filled with color.

Bethany was not about to back down. "No. You do other things, too. Push. Shove. Choke." She stared at the screen, hanging on his response. She'd never called him out on all of that before, and she had no idea how he'd handle it.

He leaned close to the camera and talked so loudly that she hurried to punch the volume button down a few times. "Yeah. I do those things, and they *work*. They are all effective forms of punishment and communication.

Instantly, Bethany deflated. Her shoulders slouched, and she slumped against her chair. All this time, she'd thought he just lost his temper or had poor self-control. No. He did those things on *purpose*. And he actually thought they were okay. If he thought it was all okay, and even good, what chance was there for change?

She wanted to cry. "I don't want to be afraid of you. I don't want the kids afraid of you. You need counseling."

Carlos scoffed. "I don't want some stranger in our business. Telling me what to do. Telling me that what I'm doing is wrong. I'm a great guy, and my methods work."

"This is not working." She waved her hands and pictured Kenny living in that facility. "I can't bring any more children into this marriage unless it miraculously gets better."

Carlos rested his chin on his folded hands and scowled for a moment. Then, as if he'd thought of a solution, he picked his head up with a smile. "You're saying, if I agree to go to counseling, you'll give me a son?"

Bethany chose her words very carefully. "I'm saying, if we go to counseling, and if our marriage becomes healthy, I would consider having another child." She knew, without that, she'd never be able to agree to his request.

He leaned back and nodded while his laced fingers cradled the back of his head. The expression on his face was thoughtful and calm. "I'll consider what you said. This topic isn't done, but I need a smoke. I just have one more thing to tell you tonight."

Bethany closed her eyes and took a deep breath. He was letting the topic die for now. It felt like a small victory. She opened her eyes, ready to wrap up the conversation.

Carlos smiled. "Good news. I found out I might get to come home early." He laughed.

Bethany was sure all the color had drained from her face as the delicate fabric of her life suddenly unraveled in an instant. Her mind flew to Kenny. Her girls. Their safety. The counselor reporting them to CPS. The son Carlos was demanding. She was supposed to get *a year*.

His smile crinkled the corners of his eyes as his face filled the screen. "Isn't that great?"

"How early?" Was mid-deployment actually the end of deployment?

"Not sure yet. Could be within the next couple of months. Maybe sooner."

Couple of *months*? *Sooner*? *How was this even possible*? She'd never heard of this before. Her heart raced while she worked to keep her face calm.

"Why don't you look happy? We could be trying for that son sooner than expected. By this time next year, you might be changing his diapers." He fist-pumped twice.

Bethany swallowed and cleared her throat. It was odd how her face absolutely refused to be forced into a smile. She felt it twitch, but that was the best she could do.

"They're making a short list. We'll find out who's on it next week, I think."

She had to say something without revealing her true thoughts. "Wow. Unexpected." She swallowed the bile that rose in her throat.

"Right? Okay. I have to go now. Love you." He puckered and blew her a kiss.

"Love you too." Her stomach cramped.

"Love you *more*."

The video chat blacked out. Bethany let out a breath as a shiver raced through her body. She gasped and covered her mouth. Tears sprung to her eyes. Dropping to the floor, she curled up and brought her arms over her face. Fingers tangled in the hair at the back of her head. The sobs started small.

Did God hate her? She was supposed to have a whole year to persuade Carlos to get counseling. A year to help her kids. To figure out what to do about this mess she called her life.

It wasn't fair! The other wives got a year off. Why not her? She cried selfish tears as she mentally interrogated God. How could He let this happen? He couldn't let this happen.

CHAPTER TWENTY-NINE

BETHANY Sunday, June 19

Bethany pulled into a parking space near the entrance of the brick building where Kenny lived. Temporarily. There were park benches sprinkled beneath large trees. It looked inviting, and Bethany was glad for that.

After she signed in, they showed her to a large game room where a ping pong table, board games, tables, bookcases, and chairs were. There was plenty to keep them busy, and Kenny loved ping pong. He showed up a few minutes later with hugs for them all.

"It's not too bad here. Other than missing you guys. Lots of rules but feels safe. Look, we can't even have shoe laces." He pointed to his shoes with a laugh. "We hardly ever get to come in here." Kenny grabbed a ping pong paddle and handed one to Bethany.

He served. Bethany missed. Gloria ran and snatched the ball. "I wanna play." She clung to the ball while picking out a paddle.

Bethany pointed to the spot next to her. "You can be on my team."

Maria wandered to a bookcase and picked out a book. She held it to her nose and sucked in the book scent.

Gloria dropped the ball and swung at it several times without hitting it. She finally just threw it over the net to Kenny. He laughed and served. The ball bounced past Gloria. She shrieked and ran after it, laughing.

They played for several minutes before Kenny set the paddle down. "Wanna sit down?"

Bethany nodded. "Sure. Gloria, you can keep playing, or there are games and books over there for you to look at."

Once they were on the couch and both girls seemed preoccupied, Bethany asked how he was doing.

"I'm good. Only been here a few days, but they treat us good. Things to do. Counseling every day. Groups where we all get to talk about stuff. Pretty cool. Makes me think I don't actually have it that bad—dudes in here with a lot worse issues. Feeling kinda lucky, I guess. And then there's you."

"What about me?"

"Well, I've only been here a couple days, and you're already here visiting me. Some guys have been here almost a year and don't get visits. They're jealous."

Bethany put an arm around him and set her head on his shoulder. "We miss you so much."

FELICIA

Felicia sat in Grammy's car, holding a milkshake from their brunch. She watched sweat roll down the sides of the cup and sighed. She knew she should get out and let Grammy go to the airport. If only her stomach didn't hurt and her eyes would stay dry.

Grammy drew her attention with a pat on Felicia's leg. "You're awful quiet. You okay?"

Felicia shrugged. "Thinking."

"About?"

"You leaving."

"We had a good time today, didn't we?"

Felicia nodded while her chin quivered. "When ya comin' back?"

"What's going on, sweetie?"

"Don't want you to go." Felicia shifted in her seat.

"Why not?"

Good question. Why didn't she want Grammy to go? Grammy was flying all the way to North Carolina without a return date. What if she loved it? What if Grammy had more fun with Aunt Bethy and her kids and decided to stay there? What if Grammy loved her other grandkids more? What if Grammy realized how much work Felicia and her mom were and decided to move to North Carolina? There was no holding back the tears now. "What if you don't come back?"

Grammy gasped. "You're scared I won't come back?"

Felicia studied her straw and nodded. Tears dripped off her chin. She'd been trying to think of ways to get Grammy to stay since Grammy had shared the news.

"Why wouldn't I come back?"

Felicia shrugged. Did it sound weird? But it was true. "What if you like your other grandkids better? There's more of them. And they're not all messed up like Mom and me."

Grammy wrapped her arms around Felicia and pulled her into an awkward car hug. Felicia held her grandma and wished she never had to let go.

"Haven't I ever told you the way a heart works?"

Felicia thought for a moment but didn't know what Grammy was talking about. She shook her head. Curiosity slowing the flow of tears.

"Hm. Guess I haven't shared it since your momma was a little girl. Seems like yesterday. You see. When I was pregnant with Uncle Nate, your mom was scared I'd love the new baby more than her. She already had to share me with her big sister, Aunt Bethy, and she declared I'd run out of love once that baby came along."

Felicia imagined her mother as a child with similar feelings. "What'd you tell her?"

Grammy smiled, lifted her hand, and made an O with her fingers and thumb. "This is about how my heart looked when Aunt Bethany was born. And it was full. All this space," she pointed to the empty O, "was completely filled with love for Aunt Bethy. Then, I got pregnant with your momma."

She smiled and opened her fingers to a C. "Funny thing happened." She brought the fingers of her other hand up to overlapped the fingers of her new C. Her thumb overlapped the thumb on her other hand, making the O bigger. "My heart overflowed with love for your momma and stretched the boundaries a little bigger. I didn't love Aunt Bethy less when your mom came along. My heart just—" she shrugged. "—grew."

Felicia smiled. "Then what?"

Grammy's eyes got big and her eyebrows rose in mock surprise. "Oh, you would scarcely believe it if I told you." They giggled. "My heart stayed about this size for a while. But then Uncle Nate was coming, and I could feel the growing pains start up again."

"It hurts?"

Grammy squinted, wrinkled her nose, and nodded. "Just a little." She sighed. "When new love is born, the heart has to grow to make room for it. But the love is so strong you hardly notice the growing pains." She paused and tipped her face up as if she were looking for something. "Love doesn't always feel good, you know. When you love someone, your heart is open and vulnerable. It can hurt just as deeply as the love flows." She met Felicia's eyes. Felicia imagined she could feel growing pains right then, as her love for Grammy pumped through her heart.

"Then, Uncle Nate was born." Grammy smiled and slid her fingers till the tips just touched, making the O grow. "And what do you suppose happened when I laid eyes on his gooey little face for the first time?"

Felicia giggled. "Ew. Your heart grew."

Grammy nodded. "Exactly. It grew. And you know what?"

Felicia shook her head, hanging on every word.

"When Kenny was born." Grammy's fingers separated an inch. "It grew even more. And when *you* were born. What do you think happened?"

Felicia beamed. "It shrunk!"

Grammy's jaw dropped open, and they laughed together. "Not a chance, silly girl. It grew even more!" She made the circle bigger. "And then, along came Gloria." The circle grew. "And Maria." By this time, she used her arms to help make the circle. "Much more of this, and I'll be fairly bursting with love!" She swung her arms over Felicia's head and snagged her into a bear hug.

Felicia laughed and squeezed. "I love you, Grammy."

"I love you too, Felicia. You are a special girl, and I will never love you less. I can't possibly love Aunt Bethy's family more than yours. You're all my family. All with equal space in my *massive* heart." She chuckled.

Felicia laughed. Grammy was so funny. She didn't know how she'd make it while Grammy was away, but she was already looking forward to her coming back.

STACIE

It was late evening when Stacie stepped off the plane with a wide range of feelings. Her heart beat faster as she thought of seeing Bethany and the kids again. But she missed Felicia, Holly, and Nate already. Nate had offered to join her. He had plenty of leave saved up. Stacie had asked him to stay just in case Holly or Felicia needed someone there. He seemed happy to do it and said he'd call to check up on them every day. Felicia would love to hear from him daily.

She followed signs to baggage and soon found a small crowd gathered with expectant looks on their faces. Warm flutters filled her chest when she spotted Bethany holding Gloria's hand with Maria on her other hip. She waved until she saw the smile of recognition on Bethany's face. Finally, they were able to hug. Stacie could have held them forever. There was nothing like holding her babies in her arms. Didn't matter how big they got.

Stacie reacquainted herself with her beautiful grand-daughters while waiting for her luggage. They'd grown so much. Bethany looked good. Tired but good. They managed to get the luggage to the giant truck Bethany drove and were soon on their way.

"Hungry?"

Stacie had been too excited to notice before. Now that Bethany mentioned it, Stacie's stomach rumbled. She nodded.

"Where would you like to eat?"

"Oh, I don't know my way around here. You pick. I'm happy just to go back to your place if you've got food at the house."

"Home it is." Bethany grinned. "I'm glad you're here, Mom. I've missed you."

BETHANY

Bethany rubbed tired eyes and glanced at the time in the corner of her laptop screen. After she'd had dinner with her mom and daughters, Bethany had put her girls to bed. She wanted nothing more than to sit down, face to face, and chat with her mom. But then, Carlos had called insisting that she get online with him. She wanted to cry.

As soon as they got online, she let him know she was tired and didn't want to talk long, which seemed to set him off. He went into a long lecture about how she should jump to talk with him since she *should* be missing him.

When he was finally done, he smiled and leaned back. "Now, would you like to hear good news first or bad news?"

Oh please. Bethany didn't have energy for bad news. "Tell me the good." She wanted to tell him to keep the bad to himself.

He laughed. "Good news is I might have a better chance of coming home early.

"Why's that?"

"That's the bad news."

Carlos scoffed and looked down while rolling a cigarette in his fingers. When he looked at the camera, his eyes drooped, and his lips turned down. "I don't even want to tell you, but you might hear something. I want you to have the right information."

"Hear what?"

"Some chick doesn't like me here. Trying to start trouble by making stuff up about me."

"Like what?" There would be a speck of truth somewhere in his story. The tricky part was figuring out which speck it was.

"She misunderstood something I said. Ran off and reported me to the commander."

"What was it?"

Carlos shook his head and looked hurt. "Who knows. I heard a rumor that I was sexually harassing some of the female soldiers."

The bottom fell out of her stomach. "Were you?"

His head jerked back as if she'd just slapped him. "Why would you even ask that?"

"Sometimes you flirt. And you've done it before."

"Why does everyone think horrible things about me? I can't believe you'd bring up the past. You're the only woman I want."

"What happened?"

"I didn't do anything wrong. Maybe when I told a joke. That she laughed at, by the way." He shrugged. "Or when she was trying to get by me while I stood in the doorway. As if I was trying to block her. Oh, but I'm a guy and she's a girl, so that's sexual harassment." He waved mocking hands in the air and rolled his eyes. "Commander went around and talked with other soldiers here." Carlos put the unlit cigarette between his lips. "Seems the consensus is that I'm inappropriate, and they aren't comfortable working with me." He scoffed.

"So, now what?"

"They moved me. I can't even do the job I trained for. They stuck me in with the officers." He laughed. "I can do their job better than they can. I really need a smoke. I don't understand why people don't like me. No one understands me. You may be the only person in the world who gets me."

Bethany nodded. She got him, alright. He was fishing for sex in the wrong pond, and someone got offended. "I don't know what to say."

"Don't have to say anything." He smiled and wiggled his eyebrows. "There's one good thing out of all this. I'm not doing my job anyway, so I'll probably be on that list to come home early." He laughed and blew her a kiss. "Can't wait to start making my son. Soon, baby girl. Probably know in a few days."

CHAPTER THIRTY

BETHANY   **Monday, June 20**

Bethany woke from a nightmare. Something had made a loud bang. She was sure of it. The inside of her eyelids felt like sandpaper every time she blinked against the bright morning. She sat up, picturing honey-soaked slices of bread on the counter. Then, she remembered her mom was there.

When she opened her bedroom door, her nostrils were greeted with the smell of bacon and something sweet. Mom's apple cinnamon banana bread? Bethany's mouth watered. It had taken her years to stop craving her mom's secret recipe. Now, here it was baking in her own oven. Had to be. She charged down the stairs.

Mom took one look at Bethany as she rushed into the kitchen and laughed. Gloria and Maria looked from their grandma to their mom with smiles. Bethany stopped and smiled. "Why you laughing, Mom?"

Her mom shook her head and held out her arms. "I'm not sure if it's the way your hair is sticking out everywhere or the way you rushed in here. Maybe both. What's your hurry, anyway? You start a fire upstairs? Should we be rushing out the door?" She chuckled and wrapped her arms around Bethany.

Gloria giggled.

Maria frowned. "Fire?"

Her mom turned to Maria and scooped her up. "No fire, sweetie. Grammy was being funny." She kissed Maria's little nose and handed her a piece of bacon before placing her on a bar stool.

By the time the bread was pulled from the oven, Bethany had scrambled eggs to contribute to breakfast. All she really wanted was the bread, but she forced herself to eat eggs and bacon for protein. And to set a good example for her girls.

Finally, she placed a large chunk of the sweet bread in her mouth and closed her eyes. She smiled as the perfect mix of flavors tickled her taste buds. Memories poured in while she chewed. Gathering around the oven as a kid with her brother and sister while Mom pulled out a steaming loaf. One cold winter, they'd all pulled up dining chairs and Mom had sliced the bread right there on the oven door as the warmth swirled around them. "Wow, Mom. Amazing. Ready to hand over that recipe yet?"

"Not yet. I did write it down at home so you'd have it in case anything happens to me."

"Oh, that's a nice thought." Bethany rolled her eyes.

They ate as much as they wanted, which didn't leave much to put away for later, and got ready for playtime in the park.

STACIE

Stacie had fun watching her daughter and granddaughters devour the bread she'd baked that morning. She'd gotten up early and snuck off to the store to get a few key ingredients for her secret recipe. She must have smiled the entire time she'd put it together as she imagined Bethany's delight. She hadn't been disappointed.

While the girls played, Bethany finally brought the topic of Carlos up. "So, Carlos told me last night that he's got a good chance of coming home early."

Stacie shifted her gaze from her granddaughters to Bethany's serious face. "How early is early?"

Bethany shrugged. "He doesn't know yet. Said his chances improved because someone there doesn't like him, and he got moved. Isn't doing his job anyway, so thinks they'll put him on a list. Never heard of them doing this before. Who gets to come home early? Maybe if they're injured or pregnant. Family emergency. I don't know."

Stacie shook her head. "Doesn't make any sense. Is there anyone you can call? Who's in charge?" She pointed at a bench facing the playground and sat down.

Bethany sat beside Stacie with a sigh. "When a unit deploys, they leave a rear-detachment command team. I have a list of phone numbers."

"Okay. That's a start. Who's in charge of deciding who's on that return list?" She wanted to add *if there's even a list*. If Bethany were ending the relationship, this conversation would be easier. But if Stacie was negative about her son-in-law, and they stayed together, it could wind up damaging her relationship with Bethany. Not worth the risk.

"Guess it would be the rear-d first sergeant."

"Great. Call him when we get home."

Bethany's eyes widened as they met Stacie's. "Just like that? What would I even say? 'Hello, my husband threatened to kill me and the kids, and I was just wondering if you could keep him off the list?' Yeah, Mom. That should go over just swell." She shook her head and dropped her eyes.

It wouldn't be an easy call to make. Stacie remembered how hard it was to make a change. Getting out of the grip of an abuser was nearly impossible without support. "Not exactly like that. Just tell him that you heard there was a list of soldiers coming home early and that Carlos thinks he might be on that list. You're just wondering if they can keep his name off the list. You can use Kenny as an excuse if you need one. Carlos doesn't know, right? Tell the first sergeant you want to keep it that way. For Kenny's sake."

Bethany nodded. "I'll look for the number when we get home."

Stacie nodded. She rubbed Bethany's back. "I'm sorry you have to go through this. I'm here. Keep talking to me."

"I will. I'm glad you're here too."

Stacie wished Bethany would have talked with her sooner. Her mind drifted to Rich. She'd call him later. Even supporters needed support.

BETHANY

Bethany shut the door to her bedroom that afternoon. Her mom was going to keep Gloria and Maria occupied while she called the rear-detachment first sergeant, Wesley Heneghan. She plopped into the chair at the small desk and found the folder she'd received at the pre-deployment briefing with the Family Readiness Group, FRG. She hadn't thought she'd need the phone numbers, but she also hadn't anticipated all that had happened recently.

Her heart picked up pace as she dialed.

"First Sergeant Heneghan. How may I help you, sir or ma'am?"

Bethany cleared her throat and tried to sound normal. "Hi, First Sgt. My name is Bethany. My husband is deployed with your unit."

"Call me Wes. What's your husband's name?"

"Carlos Garcia."

"How can I help you, Mrs. Garcia?"

"He told me they're making a list and sending some soldiers home early. I was wondering if there's a way to keep him off that list."

There was a pause before he replied. "You," he cleared his throat, "*don't* want your husband home early?"

She probably sounded nuts. "That's right. Do you know if he's on the list?"

"A list? I can check. But ma'am, why don't you want him to come home early?"

Bethany's cheeks flushed while her mind raced over all the reasons before landing on the safest. "My son, Carlos' step-son, was recently admitted into a residential mental health facility. Carlos doesn't know. He wouldn't understand. I want my son out before Carlos comes home. Thought we'd have more time."

"You have access to email?"

"Yes."

"Email me all the reasons you don't want Sgt. Garcia to come home early. I'll meet with the rear-d commander and get back with you."

"Okay."

"Get that to me by thirteen hundre—err. One o'clock if you can."

Bethany nodded. "Okay." She took down his email address and hung up. She didn't want to tell him any other reasons. But if she had to convince him and the commander through email, she'd better be very clear about her concerns regarding the relationship between Kenny and Carlos.

She opened the laptop and got started.

CHAPTER THIRTY-ONE

FELICIA   **Tuesday, June 21**

It was three in the morning when something brought Felicia out of sleep. Her heart dropped at the familiar sound of Danny yelling at her mom. She punched her pillow and wanted to scream at him, but her mom was already doing a fine job of that. How could either of them understand anything the other said while they yelled at each other? Maybe they were *both* nuts. Her mom must be since she'd stayed with the loser for this long.

Felicia raged in silence while mixed emotions stormed inside. Did her mom even love her? If she did, she wouldn't have brought them back to Danny again. Felicia felt like the only adult in the house. The only one with half a brain.

There was a loud bang followed by her mom screaming for Danny to get out of her kitchen. A few seconds later, glass shattered. That was it!

Felicia threw back her covers and jumped from bed. She yanked her bedroom door so hard it swung out of her hand, blasted right over the lame doorstop, and crashed into the wall. Then, silence. Crap. Any bravery she thought she'd possessed vanished with the footsteps stomping her way. Her heart in her throat, she slammed her door shut and leaned her back against it, bracing herself with her feet extended, knees bent, and elbows against the door.

Her mom's tone changed from anger to fear. "Danny. Stop!"

The doorknob turned. The door bumped against Felicia's back. But Danny must not have been expecting her to block it because it easily shut again with a little pressure. The next time Danny pushed with more force so Felicia shoved back harder. Her heart thumped against her ribcage. Her fingers tingled in her fists.

She wasn't sure what she thought would happen if she tried to keep him out, but she was too scared to let him in now. The door shoved against her a third time. She pushed back with all she had. Danny growled on the other side while her mom pleaded for him to stop. Energy coursed through Felicia's limbs as she braced herself for the next push.

Danny must have realized Felicia wasn't going to just let him in. This time, he didn't hold back. The door forced Felicia into the wall behind it. With her sandwiched between the door and the wall, Danny smashed the door into Felicia's back several times. Each time it hit, she was flattened against the wall.

Finally, he smashed it into her and held it there, pinning her to the wall. Her heart raced as she tried to slide out, but the doorknob gouged into her back.

She couldn't have dodged Danny's fist in that position, even if she'd seen it in time. White knuckles flew around the door just before pain burst from her cheekbone to her entire head. Black splotches blocked her vision as the door freed her from her prison. She fell to her knees and blinked. Never before had she experienced an instant headache. She embraced her throbbing head with both hands.

Somewhere in the distance, her mom screamed at Danny. Felicia had no idea what her mom said, and she only hoped Danny wasn't in her room because there was no way she could defend herself while she was so off-balance, head throbbing, seeing splotches.

From her hands and knees, Felicia pushed her door closed. Softly. She crawled to her bed and used her shaky hands to pull herself up. He'd actually punched her. She couldn't believe the jerk. She didn't know her head could hurt this much.

She collapsed on the bed and willed the spinning to stop while she tried to think. The first thing she knew to her core was that she was *not* going to stick around. She was leaving. Her mom could come if she wanted, but there was no way Felicia was staying in the same house as Danny for one more day.

She reached for her phone on the nightstand. She needed Grammy.

"Felicia?"

Felicia tried to explain what had just happened, but it felt like a thick fog was rolling into her mind and messing everything up.

"Is your mom okay?"

"Don't know. Shut my door. Come get me, Grammy."

"I can't, sweetie. Remember? I'm in North Carolina. Here's what we're going to do. You call Uncle Nate. He'll come get you. I'll call the police. Stay in your room and be quiet. No matter what you hear, *stay in your room*. If he comes in before the cops get there, pretend you're sleeping or something. Now, I have to get off the phone to call the police. They should get there before Uncle Nate. Do you hear me, Felicia?"

The room was so hot it made Felicia's stomach hurt. She didn't think it would be hard to pretend to sleep as long as she didn't have to throw up. Sleep was the only thing that sounded good anyway. "Yeah." She closed her eyes.

"Felicia." Grammy's tone got Felicia's attention. "What are you going to do as *soon* as I hang up?"

"Sleep."

"No, Felicia. *Listen to me. Call Uncle Nate.* What will you do as soon as we hang up?"

Felicia forced her eyes open. "Call Uncle Nate."

"Good. Do that *right now*." Grammy was gone.

Felicia sighed while tears slipped onto her pillow. All she wanted to do was go to sleep. Why was Grammy being so mean? Danny was mean. Now Grammy was mean too. Why didn't anyone love her? The ceiling wouldn't stop moving, so she closed her eyes before she couldn't hold the puke back anymore. Call Uncle Nate. She had to call him. Grammy said.

She rolled to her side and tried to focus on her phone. It was so heavy, just like her eyelids.

STACIE

The 911 call took a long time as Stacie filled in the dispatcher with the names of all involved, the address, and everything Felicia had told her. Her stomach was full of knots as she relayed the way Felicia had sounded on the phone. "You've got to get an ambulance out there right away. She didn't sound right."

"Are there any weapons in the house?"

"I don't think so. Danny doesn't hunt or do anything but drink."

The dispatcher's calm was both frustrating and reassuring. An ambulance was on the way but would not be able to do anything until the police officers arrived. They were on their way.

Stacie wrung her hands and called Nate.

"Mom?"

"Felicia call you?"

A pause. Nate sounded confused. "Nooo ... Ya mean lately or tonight?"

Stacie couldn't keep the impatience from her voice. "In the last half hour. You haven't heard from her?" The air seemed thin. Stacie pressed an open palm to her pounding heart. Panic was about to take over.

Nate sounded breathless and on the move. "What's going on, Mom?" She heard keys jingle over the phone line.

"Get over there, Nate." Stacie closed her eyes and listened to Nate's front door slam and then his truck door. An engine came to life and revved a couple of times.

"I'm driving. Tell me what I'm gonna find when I get there."

Stacie didn't even want to imagine. "Maybe the cops and an ambulance."

"What happened?"

Stacie spent the next few minutes shaking and crying as she updated her son. She could hear a growing edge to his voice as he followed along and asked clarifying questions. She was glad the cops would get there before he would. She didn't want to know what he'd do to Danny if he got there first.

●●●

Stacie had been on and off the phone since Felicia's first call several hours ago. Now, she was exhausted. She knew Bethany needed her, but she was too emotionally drained to be much support. At least she could spend time with her grandbabies and keep them out of trouble now that there was nothing more for her to do.

Felicia was in the hospital with a concussion. They expected to discharge her soon. Holly had been taken to the police station, along with Danny, for more questioning. Sounded like Danny was locked up. Nate had given Holly a ride to the hospital. They were both with Felicia. Nate said he'd book Holly and Felicia a flight to get them over to Stacie as soon as possible. All she could do now was wait and pray.

Gloria and Maria's voices faded as she dozed on the couch. The phone in her hand vibrated and brought everything back in focus. Nate.

"You wouldn't believe how expensive it is to fly out on such short notice. But—" He chuckled. "I sweet-talked the manager and got me a discount. On account of my service and the situation. They'll be there tomorrow." He sounded proud of himself.

"Wow. So fast?"

"Sure thing. Thought it was best for everyone to get 'em out there right away."

She could hear the smile in his voice. It was contagious. "Nice work, sweetheart. I ever tell you how smart you are?"

"Wouldn't mind them staying here, but they both looked so excited about heading your way. Money goin' to a good cause."

Stacie's heart swelled with love and pride for her son. "You're an amazing man. Thank you. I don't think you realize how much this means to all of us."

"Felicia was discharged. They told her to take it easy for a few days. I'm taking them by their place to pick up some things for their trip. Then I'm kidnapping them for the night."

They wrapped up the travel details. Stacie hung up with her tired mind singing praises that it was all working out. It had been too many years since she'd hung out with both her daughters at the same time. Maybe one day Bethany would heal enough to visit Texas again. A mother's heart could hope.

BETHANY

Bethany made peanut butter and jelly sandwiches for her girls on auto-pilot. She hadn't heard back yet from anyone after sending the email. As if that wasn't enough to consume her concentration, she couldn't stop thinking of her sister and niece. What had Holly been thinking by going back? Holly and Felicia could stay for as long as they needed. Her mom occupied the spare room, but there was a futon in the den.

Holly should press charges and keep Danny locked up and away from them for as long as possible. But who was Bethany to say what Holly should do? Here she sat, planning on stretching the truth about why she didn't want Carlos home yet. *Bah.*

• • •

Bethany's phone rang that afternoon. The sight of Sgt. Heneghan's number made her heart race. Mom gave Bethany's hand a little squeeze as she rushed out of the room. "You've got this, sweetie."

She answered on her way up the stairs.

"Ma'am. Sgt. Heneghan here. Besides the issues with your son, is there any other reason you want your husband to remain deployed?"

Not sure how to answer, Bethany paused. She tried to catch her breath as she sank to the floor in her room.

"It's a very unusual request. Most spouses are eager for their deployed soldier to return home. The earlier, the better. What else is going on?"

The question was so direct and unexpected. Bethany's eyes pricked at the truth. She blinked. "He yells a lot. It's just so peaceful with him gone."

"Okay. Besides your son and the yelling, what else?"

Bethany bit her lip and shook her head. She couldn't do this. Carlos would be so angry. How could she go behind his back like this? "I don't want to interfere with his career. It's important to him."

"This isn't about his career, Ma'am. This is about you and your kids."

"I know. But if he found out—" She couldn't finish the thought out loud.

"I'm meeting with Lieutenant Ortiz and I need to have my facts straight. If you don't want your husband coming home early, you need to give me a compelling reason why."

Bethany leaned against her bed. "It's not going to hurt his career?"

"I can't promise anything, Ma'am."

"Are you going to tell him what I say?"

"No, Ma'am."

Bethany nodded. If this was the only way to buy her more time and keep Carlos deployed, maybe she should share. Maybe they could help. "He thinks pushing and choking are appropriate ..." It sounded too ridiculous to finish saying.

"Okay, Ma'am. You don't have to tell me anymore. I'll see what we can do. You might get a call from Lt. Ortiz. Are you okay with talking to him from here on out?"

Bethany's hands shook. Now she'd done it. She had to talk with the commander. "Do you know if Carlos is on that list?"

"I can't say much about that. You'll have to wait until Lt. Ortiz calls. He can answer all your questions. Might not be till tomorrow."

Her heart raced as she hung up. She wanted a peaceful home to raise her children in. She wanted the Carlos she thought she'd married. Maybe they could help.

CHAPTER THIRTY-TWO

BETHANY **Wednesday, June 22**

The next morning, Bethany slid two cups of juice across the counter to Gloria and Maria. They sat on bar stools and finished the breakfast their grandma had cooked. Bethany and her mom had been chatting in the kitchen.

Gloria licked her lips. "Mm."

Bethany smiled.

Her mom stepped close. "Doesn't seem very long ago when you were little like that. Just as eager for a cup of juice." She rubbed Bethany's back.

The familiar scratch of work-worn hands across cotton, occasionally snagging the material, made her mom's reminiscent image more real to Bethany. "I love you, Mom."

The phone rang and they looked at each other. Seemed Lt. Ortiz didn't waste any time. Bethany plucked the phone from the counter and wrinkled her nose. Her mom nodded toward her granddaughters. "I've got this. You go tell him whatever you need to convince him to get Carlos off that list."

Bethany nodded and ran out.

"Mrs. Garcia? This is Lt. Ortiz. You can call me Victor. I read your email and spoke with First Sgt. Heneghan about your request. Do you have a minute to talk?"

Bethany closed her bedroom door and perched on the corner of the bed. "Yes. Can you keep Carlos off the list?"

He cleared his throat. "It's not quite like that. I did make some calls to find out about this list you mentioned. I spoke directly with the commander who's deployed with your husband."

"Does Carlos know any of this?"

"No. And I can't tell you why, but they cannot keep your husband deployed with them. He will return home soon."

Color drained from Bethany's face. The temperature dropped. Deep in her chest, she shook, making her voice sound wobbly. "How soon?"

"We don't know yet. Could be a couple of weeks or a month at most."

Weeks? A month at *most?* The shaking extended to her limbs. Knots grew in Bethany's stomach. But Carlos was supposed to be gone a *year*. Not *months!* How could this happen? What was *wrong* with these people?

"Ma'am?"

Bethany hugged herself and tried to stop the shaking. It didn't help. Her teeth chattered, so she clenched them.

"I need you to tell me about the things that have happened at home. What's your husband been doing?"

Bethany drew her knees in and wrapped her arms around them. She tried to clear the clouds in her mind. Her tight jaw made speaking hard. "I don't know what to do."

"We can't help you if you won't tell us what he's been doing."

What's Carlos been doing? "He yells a lot. Gets mad about everything. He chokes. After he left, I took my son to counseling and found out he's been choking Kenny. Not just me."

Bethany rocked side to side and squeezed her knees as her guilty confession tumbled out. "I should have known. Should have paid more attention to Kenny. He started cutting himself. Then wanted to—" Her voice broke off. "But now, he's in a hospital while he learns to cope and get adjusted to meds." She couldn't believe this was happening to her. This was actually her life. How had it gotten so out of control? Control was a sick and twisted illusion.

"What else?" Victor's voice held an edge. He must know it was all her fault. She was a failure as a mother and a wife.

There was so much to tell. Carlos' spin on things danced with her memories giving the events fuzzy edges in her mind. Maybe she was crazy. Someone needed help. Maybe it was her. Maybe it was Carlos. "He wants a son. Said if I won't agree, he'll drug me and get me pregnant or kick me and Kenny off his insurance."

Victor's sigh stopped her disclosure. His tone demanded her attention. "Okay. Just so you know. He *can't* take dependents off his insurance."

Bethany's eyes popped open. A flutter rushed through her chest. "He can't?" Kenny would get the medical care he needed. Carlos couldn't do anything about that.

"No."

She took a deep breath and sighed it out. There was hope. Words came easier now that one weight had been lifted. "I didn't know. I've been so scared. Things have been getting worse. He shoves, pushes, and he said he'd kill us if we called the police. I think he needs help." Her teeth chattered so hard she was afraid he'd hear them. Her jaw and neck ached the longer she tried to stop from shaking.

"Ma'am. If even half of what you're telling me is true, you need to report this to Family Advocacy on post."

Report it? "What happens then?" A faint memory seeped to the surface of her mind. Family Advocacy flyers on the inside of the women's bathroom stalls at the Commissary, the military grocery store. Somehow, she'd never thought they applied to her. Never considered calling them. What could they do anyway? What if he found out? "I don't want him coming after me."

"They can help keep you and your children safe. That's what they're there for."

"Will Carlos lose his job?"

"That's not something you need to worry about. You need to think of your kids and yourself. Let us worry about Sgt. Garcia."

"But if I ruin his career—Will this affect his career?"

"You don't need to worry about that. What happens to Sgt. Garcia will *not* be your fault. Your first concern needs to be you and your kids. Do you have a pen and paper?"

Bethany hurried to the desk. "Yes." He believed her. Maybe it wasn't crazy to be scared of Carlos. Her heart fluttered as she wrote down the number he gave her.

"Ask for Jennifer. She's very nice. She'll answer your questions. Please, call her today. I'm going to call back in a couple of days to check on you."

Bethany nodded in a daze.

"Are you going to call her?"

"Yes." How could she report her own husband? A man she had vowed to love, respect, and honor all the days of her life? Even if she survived such a thing, how would her marriage? Her family? Making Carlos angry was not the way to get the healthy marriage and family she'd always wanted.

Downstairs, Bethany shared the conversation with her mom. As she talked, her hopes of getting Carlos off the list evaporated like a morning fog. There probably wasn't even a list.

He *was* the list.

At least now she had choices. She could stay where she'd been all along, watching her life and children fall apart. Or make that call to Jennifer at Family Advocacy. Besides, if she didn't get help, CPS would take her kids anyway. Doing nothing was no longer an option.

Her mom unwrapped a granola bar and slipped it into Bethany's hand. "Eat that. You need fuel." Eating. Great idea. "I'll make lunch while you call Jennifer. Don't worry about us. Take as long as you need." Bethany chewed as she hauled her heavy legs back up the stairs.

Her choices had shifted the pieces of her life in unexpected directions. She wasn't sure she liked it.

She'd taken Kenny into counseling, and now he was in a hospital.

She'd stood up against Carlos' request for another child, and he'd threatened to take Kenny off insurance, drug her, and take her girls from her.

She'd called the rear-detachment command, and now she had the name and phone number to someone at Family Advocacy. Should she call?

It was just a phone call. One tiny step toward keeping her kids safe.

FELICIA

Felicia's heart pounded along with her head. They'd just landed in North Carolina, and she was nearly bursting in anticipation. She wasn't sure if she was more excited to see Grammy or Kenny. When she'd woken up in the hospital yesterday, she'd ached to feel Grammy's rough hands push the hair from her forehead to make room for a kiss.

But what was Kenny like now? She'd always looked up to Kenny. He was four years older, and that made him seem big. Last time she saw him, she'd just turned nine, and he'd stepped into his teens. Now, she was about to join him. Her thirteenth birthday was only a week away. Well, technically, eight days. But who was counting?

The headache she'd had since Danny's punch in the face had faded until their plane took off. It seemed to creep back in while they were in the air. Now, every hurried step made it hurt a little more. "Mom."

Her mom looked over her shoulder. "Baggage claim is this way."

"Mom." A wave of nausea hit Felicia. She swallowed— no way she wanted to throw up in front of everyone at the airport.

"Come on." Mom glanced back at Felicia and then hurried to her side. She dropped her bag. One arm went around Felicia's waist while the other pushed the hair from her clammy face. "Oh my gosh. Are you okay?"

Felicia shook her head. If only she could ignore the nauseating dizziness. People shot curious glances her way as they rushed to their next destination. Someone's shoulder clipped her on the way by, forcing her to take a step to keep her balance.

"Hey! Watch it!" Her mom stepped toward the culprit, shook her head, and sighed. "Wanna slow down?"

Felicia wanted to throw her chin up and plow through to baggage claim. Aunt Bethy and Grammy were meeting them there. She hoped Kenny would be there too. But she didn't want to show up feeling like this. "Can we sit down for just a minute?"

Her mom's eyebrows twitched for a second before she gave a quick nod and scanned the area. "Over there." She picked her bag up and took the handle of Felicia's bag in the same hand. She never let go of Felicia's waist with the other arm.

Felicia was thankful for her mom's support as they crossed the path of hurried travelers. Once on the bench, her mom pulled her phone out. "Gonna send Aunt Bethy a text and let her know it'll be a few minutes. No worries." She met Felicia's eyes with a smile. Maybe she'd get to see her mom smile more again. Happened at Grammy's. Could happen at Aunt Bethy's too.

She was feeling slightly better by the time they strolled into the baggage claim area. Most of their flight companions had already left with their bags, so it was easy to spot

Grammy and Aunt Bethy. But no Kenny. Bummer. Gloria and Maria were there. Where was Kenny? Bathroom?

Hugs were passed around and they claimed their suitcases. Grammy squeezed her extra tight. Her head would have exploded for sure if Grammy hadn't let go when she did. "So glad you're okay, sweetie. Was worried." Felicia nodded.

The women talked over the top of each other, clearly happy to be together—but still no Kenny. Aunt Bethy picked Maria up. "Ready to go?" Gloria grabbed Grammy's hand and they all turned toward the exit.

Felicia's heart dropped. She trailed behind the rest of them. Why hadn't Kenny come? Didn't he want to see her? Too grown up to come meet her at the airport. "Where's Kenny?" Maybe he wouldn't want anything to do with her the entire time. Tears sprung to her eyes. She'd been so excited. Did he know what had happened to her? Seems he would have at least come to make sure she was okay.

But no. He hadn't given her a single thought. What a jerk. Just like all the other guys Felicia knew. Except Uncle Nate. He was still cool. Unless he forgot about her while she was gone. Lightning struck her chest. She couldn't lose Uncle Nate too. Why'd they have to come here? Maybe she could stow away on one of the returning planes. As they drove away, she watched a plane disappear in the clouds and wished she was on it. Going home to Uncle Nate, the only guy on the planet who cared about her.

BETHANY

That evening, Bethany sat in front of the laptop at the desk in her room. Her mind was downstairs with her mom and sister. But she didn't want Carlos to know they were there visiting. He had an insulting opinion of each of them. She wasn't in the mood to hear anything negative about these women she loved so much. She stared at the chat window. Carlos had stepped away for a few seconds.

The invitation to start a video chat popped up. Bethany hovered her mouse over the accept button and took a shaky breath. Did Carlos know she'd talked with the commander? She'd find out as soon as she saw his face. She clicked accept and prepared the most realistic smile she could muster. How would she keep it from him? She'd made an appointment to talk with Jennifer on Friday at 11am.

Carlos filled the laptop screen with a warm smile. "Hey, beautiful. I was thinking of what you said. About counseling. I spoke with the deployment psychologist here."

Bethany raised her eyebrows. "You did?" He actually did it! She never expected him to start counseling on his own. And before he even came back. "How'd that go?"

Carlos laughed. "He had me take a test and asked a lot of questions. He thinks I have narcissistic personality disorder. Something like that." He shrugged.

"Oh?" Bethany grabbed the mouse and used it to drag the chat window to the corner of the screen. She opened a search engine and typed it in while he answered.

"It means I've got good self-esteem." He smacked his desk and laughed. "Figures. If your self-esteem is high enough, they call it a disorder." He snickered and shook his head.

"Looking it up." She squinted as she scrolled and clicked a link that listed the signs.

"Yeah. Look it up. I'm confident and strong, and they actually have a name for it. It's great!"

Bethany tuned him out a bit as she scanned the page. Maybe he hadn't looked it up yet because it didn't sound flattering to her. She wouldn't have been able to describe him any better. It was like they knew him. "It does sound a lot like you."

She didn't dare read any of it out loud. Arrogant. Self-centered. Demanding. Manipulative. Think they're superior. Require constant attention and flattery. Lack empathy. Her mouth dropped open as she continued to scan. Memories flew through her mind to confirm each description. "He might be right. If so, then what?" *Was there a medication for this?*

Carlos shrugged one shoulder. "It's not official. Just us talking. I'd have to see someone when I get back."

Bethany nodded.

"Which, hopefully, will be soon. I can't wait to have a son with you." He licked his lips.

She wanted to change the subject. "Wanna talk with the girls?" She was surprised that he never asked to speak with them. If she were deployed, she'd be talking with them every chance she got.

But Carlos shook his head. "You know what I want. Come on. It's been too long."

"I can't. They need a bath before bed tonight."

Carlos squinted and leaned close to the camera. "You've been denying me all sorts of things since I left. Don't you love me?"

Gloria and Maria burst through the door with a squeal and laugh. Gloria ran up to the laptop. "Daddy!" She clapped her hands.

Maria skidded to a stop when she saw Carlos on the screen. She spun and ran out.

Carlos stretched his lips into a strained smile. "Hi, baby girl."

"I'm playing tigers with Maria."

"That's nice. I need to talk with your Mommy. Go to your room and play. Okay?"

Gloria's face dropped, but she nodded.

Bethany kissed her cheek. She was relieved Gloria hadn't mentioned their company. "It's okay, sweetheart. I'm almost done."

Gloria sulked out the door and disappeared down the hall.

"I've got to bathe two little girls. It's almost their bedtime."

"I'm doing what you wanted. I talked with a counselor. Don't you miss me?"

Gloria ran in but stayed near the door. "Maria won't come out of the closet."

Bethany nodded. "Yes, Carlos. But I have to go. The girls need me." She didn't give him a chance to object. "Love you. Bye." She closed the laptop.

He was probably freaking out right now. She couldn't remember ever hanging up on him before. No doubt he was about to blow up her phone and email, but on this one day, she wasn't going to worry about him. Her sister and niece had just arrived. Her mom was there. She was going to enjoy herself. Carlos could wait.

CHAPTER THIRTY-THREE

FELICIA   **Thursday, June 23**

Felicia slept in late the next morning. The travel and excitement from the day before must have worn her out more than she thought. When she found out about Kenny being in a hospital, she was happy to know it hadn't been his choice to miss her arrival. She wanted to see him. Depression sounded terrible. Maybe seeing her would cheer him up.

They used to be close when Aunt Bethy and Kenny lived in Texas. She was a little fuzzy on the details. She was only six when they'd left. Felicia remembered living close to them. Kenny would watch out for her on the bus ride to school and back. They'd played together a lot.

Apparently, Uncle Carlos had come to Fort Hood for a training and met Aunt Bethy. She used to work on post, but Felicia had no idea what her job had been. They fell in love and kept talking after Uncle Carlos went back home. He convinced her to leave everything, except Kenny of course, and marry him. She did. And she never came back to Texas again. Felicia had cried herself to sleep and refused to ride the bus many times that year. Somehow, it had gotten easier, but she still missed Kenny. He was like a big brother to her.

Tomorrow evening they were going to see him. Blood surged through Felicia's veins at the thought. She hopped out of bed and quickly exchanged her PJs for a pair of shorts and a tank top. The house was quiet and unfamiliar so she tried not to make any noise as she crept downstairs. Her mom's voice drifted from the family room. Felicia tiptoed closer, hugging the wall as she went.

"… my fault. I could tell he'd been drinking—"

"Don't own that. He made his choices that day." Grammy sounded so serious.

"Yeah, but I should'a just stayed out of his way. Pretended to sleep or something. I was just so *mad*. The later it got, the more sure I was that he was out drinking again. By the time he walked in—" Her mom sighed.

"I know what you mean. Carlos doesn't drink very often, but just before he deployed, he stayed out late drinking. I pretended to be sleeping when he came in. As if anyone could sleep through all that racket." Sarcasm seeped into Aunt Bethy's voice.

"It worked?" Grammy sounded different than usual. Serious. Sad. Her voice was deeper.

"No. He wanted to talk." Aunt Bethy cleared her throat.

The long pause made Felicia want to look around the corner and see what they were doing. Did they know she was listening?

But her mom broke the silence. "What happened?"

Felicia shifted her weight to the foot closest to the family room. She wanted to know what happened too.

Grammy spoke next. "It's okay, sweetie. Let's talk about these things. It hurts, but we have to go through the hurt to find the healing." How'd Grammy know all this stuff?

Someone sniffed. Probably Aunt Bethy, since her voice sounded wet and gooey. "He said he loved me. Touched my throat and said it was small under his strong hand. Said he could crush it if he wanted to. Then he started to squeeze."

Felicia just about fell around the corner. Uncle Carlos? She slid down the wall and sat with her back to it and her ear as close to the edge of the family room as she dared get it.

"He asked me if I love him enough to *die* for him. The pressure didn't really hurt, but it was getting hard to breathe.

I was so scared." Someone blew their nose. "I just tried to stay calm. I didn't want to die."

"No. Of course not." Grammy had tears in her voice.

"What a loser." Felicia recognized bitter anger in her mom's voice.

"He asked if I would *let* him kill me, and then he'd raise the kids on his own." Aunt Bethy's voice had gotten so thick and broken that Felicia had to strain to make out all the words.

Felicia's thoughts took her out of the conversation. Her heart raced. *Why would he do that?*

Uncle Carlos. Another jerk. She knew it! The cement was hardening on her opinion that all guys were jerks. Felicia's feet tingled. She shifted to let the blood flow.

If Uncle Nate or Kenny got married someday or lived with someone, would they become jerks too? Did it happen to all guys? She was never getting married.

There was a cute guy at school, Ethan. Her heartbeat picked up a little when he talked to her, but he would probably end up being a jerk too.

Felicia tuned back in on her mom's soft voice. "Had no idea, sis.

"And I don't want to ruin his career, so I don't know what to do."

Grammy spoke. "You're doing it. Seems impossible, but it'll get better."

Aunt Bethy sighed. "It didn't seem that bad until. Hm. Wow. I've been thinking it's only recent but Gloria's *five* already. First time he really scared me was when she was a baby. He's thrown furniture around. Broke one of our dining chairs and then made up some story about how it broke when we moved. Think he told it so many times, he started to believe it himself. Always making up stories, changing facts, twisting the truth. Can't believe it's been five years. And here

I am, still thinking that it'll get better. But it's only gotten worse."

"I know how that is." *Grammy understood?* "I was always trying harder and taking the blame for your dad's temper." *Wait. What?* Her mom's dad was a jerk too? "Most the time, his temper flared up whenever I caught him cheating. It took a while, but I finally realized that the times he accused me of cheating or flirting were the times he was doing that very thing. It was his own guilty conscience that brought on his accusations."

"Oh. Sounds like Felicia's dad." Felicia's eyes about popped out of her face. Her mom never talked about her dad. Every nerve was on alert. She held her breath to hear what her mom would say next.

"The last time was so bad that he almost had me convinced—"

"Felicia!" Gloria's happy voice called from just over halfway up the stairs where she could see Felicia's hiding spot from between the fancy wooden rails.

Oh crap! Felicia held a finger to her lips to shush Gloria and avoid getting caught. She was so frustrated with her miniature cousin that Gloria didn't even look cute anymore. Not even with her hair sticking out at all angles and her mouth stretched into a delighted smile. "You playing hide and seek?"

Felicia rolled her eyes. She hurried to the bottom of the stairs. Maria appeared at the top and started down after Gloria. Felicia's only hope of salvaging this was to pretend she'd just come down. She faked happy. "Good morning! You were right behind me. Just got up."

Her mom stepped out of the family room and squinted at her. Felicia threw on a huge smile. "I'm starved! What's for breakfast?"

"You hear us talking?"

Oh great. She hated lying to her mom. "I heard voices ..." Maybe if she played dumb.

Grammy didn't even hesitate when she came out of the family room. She strolled right over and wrapped an arm around Felicia's shoulders, looked her straight in the eyes, and asked, "How much did you hear?"

Felicia fidgeted. Grammy's arm never felt heavier. "I … um … a little." She swallowed.

Everyone was gathered between the base of the stairs and the family room doorway. Aunt Bethy scooped Maria up and shushed Gloria.

"It's probably time, anyway." Grammy took her eyes off Felicia and bounced them between her daughters. Her voice took on a spunky tone. "I say we all get full of something amazingly delicious. After we eat, we'll put on a movie for Gloria and Maria to enjoy while us *four women* gather around the kitchen table and talk."

A brief pause while her mom studied Felicia's hot face. Aunt Bethy nodded. "Sounds like a plan. I think I've got just the thing." She took Gloria and Maria to the kitchen with her. Grammy followed.

Felicia's head dropped. She should paint her toenails. Aunt Bethy probably had some cool colors. Maybe they could go to the store.

Her mom's bare feet appeared directly in front of Felicia's. Felicia followed the feet all the way up until she met her mom's gaze. Instead of rebuke, she found tenderness in her mom's pale, grayish-blue eyes. Felicia's eyes stung, and then her mom's arms were around her in a fierce hug. Felicia leaned into her as tears spilled down her cheeks. "I'm sorry, Mom. Just wanted to hear. And then you said something about my dad. Why'd Gloria have to come down right *then*?"

"It's okay. We'll talk about it after we all eat."

Felicia nodded against her mom's shoulder. She was about to learn their secrets. Hear about her dad. She wouldn't have to hide around the corner to know what was going on. They were going to let her into their circle.

CHAPTER THIRTY-FOUR

Bethany was down on one knee as she squeezed Gloria and Maria tight against her. She'd tried not to think about this Family Advocacy appointment, but there was no ignoring it anymore. She didn't want to do this. But as she held her girls, she told herself she was doing this for them too. If she had to choose between what was best for Carlos and what was best for her kids, she'd have to choose her kids. They were innocent. Carlos was a grown man.

When Bethany let go of her girls and kissed each smiling face, Felicia appeared. For a moment, she just eyed Bethany. "Ya getting ready to go?"

Bethany nodded and stood.

Felicia squatted with a smile for Gloria and Maria. "Wanna play with me?"

"Yay!" Gloria jumped, grabbing Felicia's hand. "Let's go!" She dragged a sheepish Felicia to the stairs. Maria followed. The girls would have fun. Felicia was sweet with them.

Bethany watched them until they reached the top and disappeared around the corner. She shook her head and blew a quick puff of air from tight lips as she trudged to the small closet near the front door. If only her mom were back from the store with Holly.

Her heartbeat picked up speed as she examined the neat row of shoes on the closet floor. She tried to think about which shoes to grab, but all she could see was Carlos sneering at her through their bathroom mirror. If she did this, there was no going back. She could never undo it. Up to this point, it was just words. Nothing in writing. No report made. Nothing official.

With a shaking hand, she reached for a pair of white sneakers. Every time she moved, she felt frozen as she tried to remember what she should do next.

She sank to the floor and pulled a shoe close while a tear rolled down her cheek. Laughter floated down the stairs. She was alone. Tears flowed. Some traced a line over her jaw and down her neck. Carlos was her husband. She'd vowed to love him in sickness and in health. He was just sick. He needed help. He needed her support, not her betrayal.

But no. She'd tried to talk with him about it. He said it was okay to choke them. He thought being narcissistic was funny and cool. If he didn't see anything wrong, he'd never change. She had to pull herself together. She sat up, wheezing, as she talked herself through the motions. "Get your shoes on. Don't think of anything else. Put your shoe on. Tie your shoe." Her hands shook. She growled at the stubborn laces. She managed to get them tied and dropped back against the bottom steps. The entryway chandelier hung over her head. It needed cleaning.

She sniffed and wiped her moist eyes with the heels of her shaky hands. She took a moment to calm her breathing—deep, slow breath in. Smell the flowers. Push all the breath out. Blow out the candles. Smell the flowers. Blow out the candles. Again. Again. Her heartbeat slowed a bit. She shuddered as she stood and scooped up her keys.

In the truck, she rested her head against the headrest and forced herself to think of the best way to get to the Family Advocacy office. She'd never been there before but had the building number and street. She could find it. She'd better get going, or she'd miss her appointment. Would that be so bad?

Her mom's white rental car pulled into the driveway next to her. Stacie said something to Holly and jumped out of the car and into the passenger seat of Bethany's truck. "Sorry it took us so long. You ready to go?"

Bethany nodded.

"Want me to come with you?"

Bethany nodded again.

"I'm ready. Let's go. You got this."

Bethany gave Holly a little wave and backed out of the driveway. She had this.

STACIE

Bethany's eyes were pink, and she didn't seem to care that her face was completely void of makeup. Not even her customary mascara darkened her blonde lashes. They hadn't talked about whether or not Stacie should go with Bethany, but one look at her daughter when Stacie had pulled in, and there was no way she was sending Bethany off on her own.

The drive was quiet. Stacie didn't mind. It gave her time to think. This had to be hard on Bethany. Stacie couldn't imagine. She hadn't reported her husband. She wished she had.

"How are you feeling, sweetheart?"

Bethany's knuckles were white on the steering wheel. "Fine." She loosened her grip and let one hand drop to her lap. "Scared."

Stacie nodded. "Why are you scared?"

"What am I going to do? He's going to be so mad when he finds out."

"It's going to be okay."

Bethany's lips pressed together as she pulled into the parking lot.

• • •

Four and a half hours later, Stacie looked up as some-one walked by. She'd hung back when Jennifer had called Bethany in. If she'd known it would take this long, she'd have brought a book and food. Her phone was almost dead after talking with Rich so long. It was worth it.

A door down the hall opened. Stacie scooted to the edge of her seat. When she saw Bethany's trim form appear in the hallway, Stacie jumped to her feet. She was so hungry that she could hardly think of asking Bethany how it went. Instead, her mind raced through the fast-food restaurants she'd seen on the way in.

Bethany looked better than she had earlier, even if some-what dazed. Stacie smiled and opened the door for her. "You hungry?"

Bethany nodded. "Think so."

"You were back there a long time."

They climbed in the truck. "Was I?"

Stacie laughed. "Um. Yeah. Over four hours."

Bethany's eyes rounded. "Seriously? I'm sorry. Had no idea. You waited that whole time?"

"It's okay. Must have been a lot to say."

Bethany nodded and pulled onto the road. "So many questions. So many things I thought were normal."

"Please stop at the next restaurant. I've got to eat."

"Sure, Mom. I'm sorry."

• • •

Once they had eaten and were back on the road, Stacie's mind was full of questions about the appointment. "You said there were things you thought were normal. Wanna talk about that?"

"Well. So many. Like walking on eggshells. When I talked about that, Jennifer said that wasn't healthy. Healthy relationships don't have one person constantly afraid of upsetting the other person. I thought that was normal. It was that way with Dad." Bethany shrugged one shoulder. "With Kenny's dad. Now with Carlos." Bethany took her eyes off the road long enough to shoot Stacie a questioning look.

"No. It shouldn't be that way."

"I can't imagine it any other way." Stacie waited for Bethany to share more. A few miles later, Bethany continued. "His temper. I just figured all men get mad easy. I mean. Dad didn't do a lot of yelling. Neither did Kenny's dad. But they got mad in their own ways. Carlos yells a lot. A whole lot."

Stacie nodded.

"Oh my gosh. Whenever Antonio comes over, he stirs his coffee with a spoon and then leaves it on the counter. If I don't catch it before Carlos comes in the kitchen, he explodes. Starts yelling at his dad that he's sloppy and disgusting. Asks his mom how she puts up with his messes all the time. She joins right in and they make fun of Antonio together. Sometimes, he tries to defend himself. Other times, he just shrugs it off. Guess he's used to it. But I've never gotten used to Carlos exploding over the tiniest thing. I don't want to. It's no fun."

"No, that wouldn't be."

"He blows up if someone makes a sandwich or toast and leaves a crumb on the counter. Literally. A crumb. One time I came in while he was yelling over the nasty counter, and there was *one crumb*, Mom. It's nuts."

"I had no idea you were living like that." Stacie shook her head. Bethany's chatter was bringing back unpleasant memories from her own marriage. There was a lot of truth to girls choosing men like their fathers.

If mothers asked themselves if they wanted their daughters to marry a man like their husband, they might be inspired to do something to change their situation. "So, what's next?"

"I need to move before he gets back. File for protective order."

Stacie's brows flew up. "They're making you move?"

Bethany shook her head. "No. But after sharing everything and learning about my choices and the risks—" She shook her head. "It's just not safe to be here when he gets back. I don't want anything to happen, and he's not stable."

Made sense. Stacie nodded. She was impressed that Bethany looked and sounded so much stronger than she had when she'd went in. Jennifer knew what she was doing. She had empowered Bethany.

"Jennifer said there are funds for this. She's putting in for us to get Army Emergency Relief. They'll pay for our flights to another state. Relocate. Just don't know where to go yet."

"Could always come back to Texas."

Bethany shook her head. "Can't go back there, Mom. Too many memories."

"Maybe it's time to face the past and find healing."

They rode in silence for the next couple miles. Finally, Bethany croaked a response. "Aren't I doing enough right now as it is?"

Stacie sighed and nodded. "Maybe you are. I just miss you. Can't I be a little selfish and hope for you to come back?"

Bethany cracked a smile and rolled her eyes. "Sure, Mom."

"Besides, it'll be easier if you're close to people who love and care about you. You'll need that support during this time."

Bethany nodded. "That would be good."

FELICIA

Felicia scooped macaroni and cheese from a small pot on the stove into hot pink, plastic bowls. She didn't know how to make much, but boxed mac and cheese was one of her specialties. She slid the steaming bowls across the counter to her cousins. Maria flung her chubby arms in the air. "Yay."

No one had appreciated her cooking more than Gloria and Maria. Felicia giggled. Was this what having little sisters was like? She felt a twinge of jealousy for Kenny.

Gloria copied her sister, waving her hands in the air and laughing. "I love macaroni!"

She hadn't heard Aunt Bethy come in, but when Felicia looked up from her hungry cousins, her aunt was watching with a smile. "And I love my girls!"

Gloria and Maria turned and gasped. "Mommy's home!"

Aunt Bethy leaned between them and smooched each of their faces. "Mmm. My sweet princesses. I see Felicia made you dinner.

Felicia smiled. She hadn't really thought about it being dinner time. She was hungry and figured they'd want something more than crackers and cookies too. "Want some?" There wasn't much left, and Felicia's mouth watered, but she could make more if Aunt Bethy wanted it.

"No, thanks. Me and your grandma grabbed something on the way home. I had no idea it would take so long."

Felicia was curious about her aunt. So brave. Aunt Bethy had went to talk with someone about what Carlos was doing. Like, who does that? She'd never seen her mom do that. What happened next? She wanted to ask but thought it might be better just to hang close and overhear once Grammy and her mom were around. "Where's Grammy?"

"Using the restroom and taking a little break. I feel bad. She was in the waiting area the whole time." Aunt Bethy shook her head. "Wouldn't have left her out there without the keys or anything if I'd known it would take so long."

"What was it like?" She plopped a scoop of mac and cheese on a small plate and sat at the end of the kitchen table to see Aunt Bethy's face while she answered. She was feeling very grown-up since her mom, Grammy, and Aunt Bethy had let her in on so many secrets about the men in their lives.

Bethany glanced at Gloria and Maria and then pulled a chair close to Felicia. She set an arm on the table and propped her head up with that hand. Something in the way Aunt Bethy's blue eyes looked made Felicia set her fork down and wait.

Aunt Bethy didn't speak right away. It was as if she were searching for the words deep in Felicia's eyes. "I'll tell you why it wasn't easy."

Felicia leaned closer and breathed shallowly so she wouldn't miss a single, gently spoken word from her Aunt Bethany's lips. "At first it was hard because I was scared Carlos would find out. I almost expected him to come in at any moment. But it got easier the more I talked. She asked me questions I never expected. I shared more than I even knew I had to share. There were the obvious things. And then—" Aunt Bethy licked her lips. "Well, I was surprised at how much I thought of as normal. Not nice or fun, but still normal. Talking about it was sort of like getting an infected appendix removed. Didn't you have that done last year?"

Felicia nodded. The pain had been so bad she'd wanted surgery. It hurt afterward, too, but a different kind of hurt that wasn't nearly as bad.

"Well, this infection has been building up for years. And the symptoms were getting obvious. The appendix was ready to burst. When I walked in today, it was time for surgery. No more home remedies and hoping for a change. Took a while to clean it out."

Aunt Bethy sighed. "I walked in, terrified of what Carlos would do when he finds out. The more I shared, the more clearly I was able to see things. I think I'm finally ready to stop *waiting* for something to change. I might be ready to *make* it change. Now that I got all that infection out, I need to seal up the wound and not let it back in. But the thing you need to know, sweetie, is that *Uncle Carlos* was *not* the infection. The things he *did* were wrong. But *I* put up with it. *I* didn't tell anyone. *I* didn't leave. And he didn't stop."

Her mom and Grammy walked in and paused to listen a moment before taking seats at the table. Aunt Bethy continued. "We all lose our tempers and act selfishly sometimes. The dangerous poison comes in consuming the abuse without vomiting it back out. I didn't get away from the poison. I drank it. I let my children drink it. My kids watched me drink it. *That* part is on *me*."

Grammy shook her head. "You can't blame yourself for what he did."

Aunt Bethy looked peaceful as she smiled at Grammy. Something had shifted and it captured Felicia's fascination. "Oh, I'm not blaming myself. We each made our choices. What he did is on him. He has to live with whatever happens now. Maybe he'll become better one day. Maybe he never will. Either way, that part is up to him. The part *I* have to live with is that I didn't really do anything about it. Sure, I tried to calm him down when he got angry, keep him happy, get between him and the kids whenever I saw a need for it."

Aunt Bethy shook her head. "But here's the thing I realized as I talked with Jennifer today. Some of the things I did probably made it more likely to happen again. Stick with me for a minute. Carlos gets angry and scary. What did I do? Well, many times, I ran to him and kissed him or hugged him to get him to calm down or forget what was upsetting him."

She scoffed. "Those are all *rewards*. I may as well have been telling him that in order to get my most devoted and loving attention, he needed to be a jerk or blow up. If we disagreed on anything and he wanted his way, all he had to do was become threatening or scare me, and I'd back off."

Grammy started to say something but Aunt Bethy held up her hand. "I know. He probably learned these things *years* before he met me. He'd already mastered them. I can see how he does it with his parents too. But the thing is, I should have set clear boundaries. If I *wanted* to be with him, I should have made it clear from the start that those things would not work on me. He would have either left and found a woman who was easier to control and manipulate, or he would have changed before it became a norm in *our* relationship. Either way, we wouldn't have gotten to this point. So, here we are. Now what? Now, I'm forced to do something extreme. Something I've never wanted."

Aunt Bethy's voice grew thick and tears filled her eyes. "I have to leave." The end of her nose turned pink. A tear fell off her lashes to the table. "I have to talk with Victor again." *Who was Victor?* "I have to tell him how it went today and what I need to do." She sighed and slouched in her chair.

Felicia had forgotten all about Gloria and Maria until Grammy popped up. "Hold that thought. The girls are done eating. Gonna throw a movie in for them."

The rest of them sat in silence. Aunt Bethy kept her eyes closed. Felicia's mom stared at something only she could see. Felicia worked to wrap her mind around the things Aunt Bethy had shared. She wasn't used to hearing someone share blame. Her mom usually blamed Danny at first and then later said it was all her own fault. Danny never took any blame. That's the way she'd gotten used to thinking about things too. It was all one person's fault.

Grammy came back in and sat down. "Okay. They're occupied for a little while."

"Thanks, Mom." Aunt Bethy opened her eyes. "I want him to go into one of these abuse intervention programs. I think that would be best. I don't want another divorce. If he agrees to go, there's a chance he can change. But we have to separate. I have to leave before he gets back. Jennifer said the Army will pay for us to leave."

"Really? I never heard of that." Her mom's eyebrows were raised.

Felicia thought it was really cool. Why hadn't her mom gone and talked to someone about Danny before? There had to be someone in Texas who could help the way Aunt Bethy was getting help. Just had to be.

"Yup. She said Carlos is dangerous. If I'm going to leave, I need to do it without telling him where I'm going. They're worried Carlos will send someone to stop me. They'll pay for our plane tickets out of here and won't tell him where we went."

Felicia's heart picked up. *Wait. Now it sounded scary. Uncle Carlos was that dangerous?* Aunt Bethy just made it sound like he was mean.

Grammy patted Aunt Bethy's shoulder. "When do you leave?"

"I think I can have us all ready in a couple of weeks. But I have to figure out what to do about Kenny. I'll talk to his counselor at the facility and see what they think."

Kenny. They were planning on spending as much time with him as possible. Felicia could hardly wait.

STACIE

Stacie was glad when Felicia wandered off. Holly had appeared to listen intently to Bethany as she shared, but at every pause, Holly's eyes glassed over, and she looked deep in thought. "That's some pretty intense reflection you've been doing, Bethany." Stacie turned to Holly. "What do you think about all this?"

Holly leaned forward and placed folded hands on the table. "I'm thinking about Danny and me and what Bethany said about boundaries. I don't really get it. So—" She pushed her hair back and tucked it behind her ears with a sigh. "I think I need to get our stuff from Danny's. Maybe he'll really change someday. But not with us there. I don't know how I'm going to do this on my own. I don't have a job. My credit is shot. I already looked into getting an apartment, but I need a job. I can't keep staying with you and Nate. When I'm staying with someone, I start to get antsy to have my own place again. I don't want to be a burden. I want my own room. My own bed. My own space. How am I going to do this?"

Stacie wasn't sure what to say. Holly hadn't mentioned those things before but it made sense. Her mind raced through different options. Maybe Holly was ready for that job Rich had told Stacie about. Taking calls and booking appointments. Office-type work with growing responsibilities that she could gradually learn.

Bethany surprised them both when she cleared her throat and offered an idea. "I can't believe I'm saying this. Maybe I should move back to Texas." She looked like she was going to chew a hole threw her bottom lip when she paused.

Holly tucked her chin in with a frown. "Why now?"

Bethany shrugged. "Maybe it would be good for me. Painful. But …" Her voice trailed off before coming back with decisiveness. "We could use my credit to get into a place together. Get this guy mess straightened out together. Mom. Would you hire me until I can find a real job?"

Stacie opened her mouth to respond but couldn't hold back the laugh that shoved its way in front of her words. She would never have been able to imagine today's turn of events. It sounded like she was going to get both her girls back. All her kids living within driving distance from her for the first time in years. Her girls looked at her with amused curiosity. "You haven't seen my shop. It's rarely busy enough to need hired help. But since you asked." She nodded. "Yes. You have a job as soon as you want it."

"That's all it took, Mom? And here I've been worried about where to find work all this time." She rolled her eyes and winked at Bethany.

Bethany giggled. "Okay. Mom says, yes. What about you, Holly? Wanna be my roommate? Just like the old days."

Stacie's heart was so full. She wanted to get up and start dancing. Her girls were going to be okay. Soon, she wasn't going to have to worry about them every day. They could help each other. Stacie would be free to focus on her growing relationship with Rich. Maybe, between him and Nate, her girls would see how a man was supposed to treat a woman. Their family would finally heal and be what she'd always dreamed. It was happening.

Holly's smile lit her face. She was so beautiful. Finely cut features. She'd better hurry and figure out how to set boundaries because the men would come knocking just like they always had. Holly nodded. "Roommate. I think I could get used to that. Do I get to decorate?"

Bethany's laugh filled the room. "You haven't forgotten about the apartment?"

Holly shook her head too hard.

"But that was so long ago. Haven't you forgiven me yet?" They were both laughing now.

"Never. You could have at least told me what you had planned. But no, I had to come home to *that*! I'll never forget. It's settled then. We get a place together, and I get to decorate. You can decorate your room. But after you see the rest of the house, you'll be begging me to at least do Gloria and Maria's room."

Bethany giggled. "You might be right about that."

Stacie was eager to make all of this planning a reality. It was time to talk to Rich about that job for Holly. She wanted the offer to come from him.

Holly jumped up. "I'm going to call Nate and see if he can get our tickets bumped up. I don't know how much longer Danny will be in jail. I want to get over there and get our stuff moved before he's out."

"Can't you wait till we all go together? Just a couple weeks."

"Momma. He might be back home by then. No. Best to get it done right away."

Stacie nodded. Holly had a point. Getting packed up and out of there without worrying about another run-in with Danny was smart.

CHAPTER THIRTY-FIVE

BETHANY   **Saturday, June 25**

Kenny sat next to Bethany in the game room. He'd been thrilled to see Felicia. Bethany couldn't wait, so she cut the greetings short and told Kenny she needed to talk with him for a moment. Stacie and Maria stood at one end of the ping pong table with Felicia and Gloria at the other end. All had their paddles up and ready except Maria. She looked like she was trying to swat at a fly over and over and delighted in every swat. Holly sat nearby and watched.

After Bethany shared a short version of her experience at Family Advocacy, Kenny's mouth formed a small circle with one side of his lips curved upward. She loved this expression. It was the one he used when he was pleasantly surprised. "Wow, Mom. You actually did it." He laughed, grabbed her arm, and gave it a happy shake.

Bethany smiled. He may not like her next bit of news. "We have to move before Carlos gets back. Sounds like it'll be soon. Like within the next month."

"Move?"

"Yeah. The only way to keep safe is to get out of his reach and get a protective order. But he can't know where we went. Where do you think we could go that he'd suspect the least?"

Kenny's smile came back bigger than ever. "We're going back to Texas?"

Bethany nodded.

"Whoo! When we leaving?"

That was the question Bethany had been dreading. She pulled a piece of fuzz off her pants. With a deep breath, she looked into Kenny's eyes. "I spoke with your counselor. He wants me to leave you here. He said you're better, but he wants you to finish the treatment to prevent any potential issues."

Kenny jumped to his feet. "What? Leave me here?"

The ping pong ball flew past Stacie as they all turned toward Kenny. Bethany pulled Kenny's hand until he sat next to her. "I don't want to leave you. But I don't want to take you before you're ready, either."

"I'm ready. I've learned better ways to deal with negative emotions. Don't leave without me, Mom."

The desperation in his voice tugged at Bethany's heart. She nodded, not knowing quite what to do. She wanted them all to go together, but if Kenny started hurting himself again, or fell back into depression, she would have a hard time forgiving herself for taking him. Looking at his hopeless expression got to her. "I'll take you. First thing we'll do is get you set up with a counselor. And you'll cooperate with *everything*."

Kenny nodded. "Of course. I don't ever want to feel that way again. It'll be fine. Besides, I don't want you doing all this without me. I can help move stuff."

Bethany took his hand. "Okay. But I'm not checking you out of here until a couple days before we go. Fair enough?"

"Okay. When do you think that'll be?"

Bethany shrugged one shoulder. "I don't know yet. We're going to share a house with Aunt Holly and Felicia. They're set to fly out on Wednesday. Holly's gonna start house hunting for us."

Kenny smiled, popped up, and strolled to Felicia. "Hey, roomy." He nudged her.

Felicia giggled and nudged him back.

Maria laughed and smacked Kenny's butt with the paddle. He fell to the floor with an exaggerated groan while his sisters squealed and jumped on him.

CHAPTER THIRTY-SIX

BETHANY   **Sunday, June 26**

Church the next morning was fun with everyone there. It was a small distraction from the pang of missing Kenny in a seat next to her. At various points, Bethany wondered what her sister thought of the message. How much church had Felicia experienced?

When it was over, people formed a line and trailed out the sanctuary doors. Bethany scanned for Trudy. "Mom. Can you get my girls from their class? Wanna update Trudy."

"Yup." Her mom turned to Holly. "Come on. Let's grab the little ones."

Trudy was talking with a woman near the back. Pastor Eric's eye was on his wife while he covered the short distance toward his goal. As Bethany approached, Pastor Eric joined Trudy with a smile. Bethany stopped a few steps behind the woman while the conversation wrapped up, and the woman walked away.

Trudy's smile was big and warm. "How you hanging in there?"

"Pretty good." Bethany gave them a condensed version of her Family Advocacy meeting. She shared how dangerous Jennifer believed her situation was.

Pastor Eric's forehead creased as he listened.

Trudy shook her head. "Wow. What are you going to do now?"

"Been thinking a lot about that. I can't stay here. It's not safe. I'm taking the kids out of state. Don—"

"You're leaving?" Trudy's eyebrows shot up. "Thought you wanted marriage counseling or something to help your relationship with Carlos? You're just going to leave him?"

Bethany squirmed under their disproving gaze. "I—uh— It's just that. I'm scared. He threatened to kill me, Trudy. I did exactly what he didn't want me to do. I'm scared. I need to keep my kids safe. I need to be safe."

Pastor Eric shook his head. "God hates divorce."

"I'm not filing for divorce. He needs help, but I need to keep me and the kids safe while he gets that help." Bethany shook her head. "I can't stay."

Trudy placed a hand on Bethany's arm and dropped her voice. "Pray about it, Bethany. Compare what you're planning with the Bible. Wives are to submit to their husbands. Divorce is wrong. I understand you're scared, and you want to keep your kids safe. But are you sure Carlos is a threat? We've never seen you or the kids with bruises, black eyes, or broken bones. I get it that sometimes he doesn't seem very nice, but you're a Christian woman, and you need to think very seriously about your role as a submissive wife. Not only to your husband but to God. Your submissiveness could lead to Carlos' salvation."

Bethany wanted to crawl behind some chairs and cover her shame-filled head. Did God mean for her to stay? She needed answers.

• • •

Bethany plopped down at the desk in her room before she'd had a chance to eat lunch after church. Carlos had blown up her phone on the way home. Wanted to know why she wasn't at home waiting to talk with him. As if she had nothing else going on other than to wait on him. A twinge of guilt plucked at her chest when she remembered that he had no idea she had family visiting or where Kenny was.

While the rest of the family enjoyed lunch downstairs, Bethany waited for the video chat to connect. Trudy's words ricocheted like a hundred tiny BBs in her skull. She pressed her palm to the side of her forehead and rested an elbow on the desk.

The screen blinked and there was Carlos. Clearly unhappy. "Where've you been? I've been trying to reach you all day."

Bethany sat up. "Church. Got on as soon as I got home. Haven't even eaten yet."

"About time. I have good news. I've been excited to share with you, but maybe I should just let it be a surprise. Not sure I'm in the mood to tell you now."

"I'm sorry. I'm here. What's the news?"

"Do you love me?"

"You know, I do."

"I'm not so sure today." He scoffed.

"You gonna tell me your good news?"

He paused before a smile broke out on his face. "I'm on the list! I don't have to stay a whole year." He laughed. "Might be leaving in a few weeks! Shorter than my last TDY." He smacked the desk making his image bounce.

"You're coming home in a few *weeks*?" She couldn't keep the horror from her face or voice. *Pull it together. Smile. Do something. Look happy.* She forced her mouth closed and felt the corners of her lips twitch.

Carlos just stared at a spot below his camera. Probably her image. Emotions raced across his features, but none stayed long enough for Bethany to read until his expression settled on rage. A vein grew in his forehead as color flooded his face. "You're not happy." It was just loud enough to hear through the speakers.

The initial shock over, Bethany managed to pull her face into something that had to be more pleasant and shook her head. "It's not that. I'm surprised. What's the date?"

"You should be excited. I don't have a date yet. Don't you want me home?"

If she was going to leave, this was the perfect opportunity to let him know what she was worried about. One last chance to see if he knew that what he'd done was wrong. If maybe he could change.

She took a deep breath. "I'm scared for you to come home early. It's been so peaceful here. Maria doesn't hide and bang her head on the wall anymore."

Carlos shook his head and narrowed his eyes.

"No yelling. More laughing. It feels good. No more fear when you walk in the door."

He looked frozen. Bethany paused to see if the chat had stopped. No. He blinked.

She needed a reaction to gauge how much more she should say.

He grunted. "You'd rather I didn't come home at all. Killed in battle."

"I didn't say that. I'm saying, I'm scared of things being the way they were." She waited, but he just stared. The longer they sat there, the stickier her palms got. Her shoulders and neck ached, but she found it impossible to move. She waited.

His voice was low. "Let me talk with Gloria."

Bethany pulled her head back and frowned. What was he up to? "You haven't asked to talk with any of the kids before. Why now?"

His eyebrows rose and he leaned forward. "Just get her. I need to talk with her. *Now*."

Automatically, she jumped to her feet and stepped away from the desk. Her rapid heartbeat thumped in her eardrums as she took a second to examine her husband's face while he thought she was running to do his bidding. His expression had relaxed as he chewed one of his fingernails. He didn't look at all intimidating. Yet, she was intimidated.

Gloria was happy to hear that her daddy wanted to talk with her. She ran ahead of Bethany and climbed into the chair in front of the laptop with a giggle. "Hi, Daddy."

Bethany lifted her daughter and sat in the chair with Gloria on her lap.

Carlos gave her a big smile and gushed. "Hi, baby girl!"

"I got a new shirt. See?" Gloria smoothed the front of her shirt and pushed her chest out.

"I have some questions."

Gloria dropped her hands to her lap and nodded.

"Do you love your daddy?"

She nodded with a smile. "Yes. I love you, Daddy."

"Do you miss daddy?"

"Uh-huh." She nodded.

"Last one. Do you want daddy to come home as soon as he can?"

Gloria bobbed her head once and pressed her hands together. "Yes."

"Daddy loves you and wants to come home. I'm trying to get back as soon as possible. Maybe you and Mommy can plan a big party for me."

She gasped. "A party! Yay!"

"You can go play now."

Gloria frowned. "Do you want to hear my ABCs?"

"Not now, baby girl. Let me talk with your mommy again. Go play. Love you. Bye." He waved the back of his hand at the camera as if shooing her away.

Gloria spun to face Bethany with moist eyes.

Bethany stood, picking Gloria up with her. "I'll be right back." She reached over and clicked the mute button before carrying Gloria toward the door. Bethany knelt on the floor and turned Gloria to face her. "What's wrong?"

Gloria sniffed. "I wanted to talk with Daddy but he doesn't want to talk with me."

Bethany hugged her and talked against the top of her head. "He just has a lot on his mind, sweet pea. I'm sorry. Wanna help me make cookies later?"

Gloria nodded and grabbed a handful of Bethany's long hair. She used it to dry the tears on her face. Bethany pretended to be offended, which always made Gloria laugh. Silly girl.

Bethany laughed. "Give that back."

Gloria giggled and buried her face in Bethany's hair while squeezing Bethany's neck.

Bethany grunted with a grin. "You're so strong!" She poked Gloria's side. A squeal tore from Gloria's throat as she jumped back with a laugh.

Bethany stood and opened her bedroom door. "I'll be out soon."

Gloria ran down the hall. "Maria! We're making cookies."

Bethany shook her head, closed the door, and then took her seat at the desk, wondering how fast she could wrap up the chat. As soon as Carlos saw her, he looked like someone had stolen his last cigarette. "At least Gloria misses me. She loves me and she wants me to come home."

Bethany sighed. "We all love you."

"Then why aren't you happy that I'm coming home so much sooner? I want you to be happy."

"I want to be happy too. I can't help it that I'm scared. Things have to be different. No more eggshells."

"You're too sensitive. Things are fine. We all love each other. That's all we need."

She shook her head.

"Whatever. I need a smoke. I'll call you back later. You better be home and answer."

The chat screen went black. Bethany rolled her eyes. *Yeah. Whatever.*

She'd be home. But she was turning off her phone. She didn't want to deal with any more of this today. She was going to make cookies and relax with her family. Tomorrow, she planned to get up before the others and spend some time asking God to show her what to do. She pulled her Bible from the lower shelf of her nightstand and set it next to the alarm clock. There had to be some answers in there.

CHAPTER THIRTY-SEVEN

STACIE **Monday, June 27**

Stacie tucked her legs up at one end of the couch and faced Holly doing the same at the other end. They settled in for a chat while each cradled a fresh cup of coffee. Bethany had asked them to keep an eye on Gloria and Maria and disappeared into her bedroom right after breakfast. Felicia had taken the girls outside to jump on the trampoline.

Stacie enjoyed this time with her daughters without having to worry about their men or work. "What'd you think of church yesterday?"

Holly nodded and tilted her head to one side. "Was good. But it did make me start to wonder? What if *my* life matters?"

"Course it matters."

Holly shook her head. "No, I mean. Why am I here? Am I missing out on something bigger that I'm supposed to be doing?" She blew over her coffee before taking a sip. "Mom. You know that support group you dragged me to?"

Stacie chuckled. *Wouldn't have put it that way.* "Sure. What about it?"

"Well. Obviously, I need to go. But there have to be ways me and Felicia can help others going through what we went through. I wanna make a difference. Everything I've been through can't be for nothing."

Wow. Holly had clearly been doing some soul searching. Maybe this was her turning point. Stacie was more grateful to Nate than she'd ever been. And he was missing out on what his tickets had really purchased.

"You know it's not always going to be easy." Stacie leaned forward. "There may be times you miss Danny. And at some point, another guy will come along. Don't jump in too soon. You have to start saying no and setting boundaries. Living with your sister will make it a little easier, but it's not the cure." Stacie placed a hand over her chest. "It's got to come from deep within." She took a sip of coffee.

Holly dropped her gaze and traced the outline of a hole in the thigh of her jeans. "I know. But since Bethany has been through a lot too, we'll be able to help each other stay strong. I'll get this figured out, Mom. Don't worry. Maybe soon you won't have to worry about any of us. What would you do with yourself?"

Stacie's mind flew to Rich. She missed him. Rich was very different from her first husband. And she was different. Had learned a lot. It had taken her almost twenty years to feel ready for another relationship. Rich was worth the wait.

Holly sipped from her cup and shifted. "One thing really bothers me about yesterday, though. I'm not sure I'm ready to jump into *church*."

"What bothers you?"

"I don't get Bethany's friend. The pastor's wife." Holly rolled her eyes.

Stacie lifted her eyebrows and tipped her head, waiting for Holly to continue.

"What the heck is wrong with her? Bethany is *scared*. She's trying to keep her kids safe. Herself safe. Carlos is a jerk. Worse than a jerk. Mom. Can't you tell it's Carlos every time he calls just by the look on Bethany's face? Before she even answers."

Stacie nodded. You'd have to be blind not to notice.

Holly's voice dropped. "I know that feeling, and it makes me sick to see my big sis go through it." She shook her head and glared past Stacie. "What would possess anyone to discourage a woman from leaving a man she's scared of? Like, Bethany was totally ready to go." She slapped her leg. "Then, she talks to the pastor and his wife, and suddenly, she's second-guessing herself all over again."

Holly's voice rose and she spit the words as if they tasted bad on the way out. "*Submit to abuse?* If that's what religion is about, I don't want *anything* to do with it." Bitterness tinged her sarcastic laugh. "Just cuz she made the mistake of *marrying* him doesn't mean she should be sentenced to a lifetime of fear. What the heck is wrong with those people?" She shook her head. "Nope. I don't need anyone like that in my life."

Stacie wanted to defend her faith and leaders of her faith, but she couldn't defend Trudy and Eric's position on this topic. She drank deeply from her cup as she thought about how to respond. Marriage was a covenant, but who talked like that anymore? Contracts were different, but close enough for this conversation. "Marriage is not a life sentence. It's more like a contract."

"Tell that to the pastor's wife."

"Okay, Holly. Forget about Trudy for a second. Think about me. Think about Zalika. Your brother. Do you see the same in us?"

Holly hesitated before shaking her head.

"Is it possible that it's not necessarily a religious viewpoint but more of a personal one?"

Holly shrugged one shoulder. "I guess. But they acted like it's based on the Bible. That makes it religious."

"I see what you're saying. I'm not going to pretend I have all the answers. I'm not a Bible scholar or anything like that. But I do have a relationship with my Heavenly Father, and I read my Bible regularly. I believe I have a pretty good understanding of His character. Do you want to know what *I* think on this topic?"

Holly nodded. "Sure."

"Okay. So, the Bible does have passages that call a wife to submit to her husband."

Holly was already shaking her head and opening her mouth as if she wanted to interrupt.

Stacie held up a hand. "Let me finish."

Holly clamped her mouth shut, tucked her chin, and watched Stacie through narrow slits.

"In one of those places, right before it says for wives to submit to their husbands in Ephesians, it tells *all* believers to submit to *each other*. You see, wives are not the only people who are told to submit." Stacie shook her head as she reflected. "Even Jesus confidently submitted on numerous occasions. It's not a sign of weakness."

"Okay, but it calls wives out specifically. Husbands can just walk all over their wives?"

Stacie scoffed with wide eyes. "Oh, husbands don't get off that easy." She laughed. "In fact, there's actually a verse that tells husbands not to be *harsh* with their wives. Abuse is pretty harsh, don't you think?"

Holly's eyebrows drew together.

Stacie shook her head and raised her eyebrows. "Not only that, but it says that husbands are to love their wives as their own bodies. It explains that no one hated his own body but nourishes and cherishes it. That's the way a husband is supposed to treat his wife."

"Huh." Holly's expression softened, and she rested the side of her head against the back of the sofa while studying Stacie's face.

"Yeah. Even in the Old Testament, God calls husbands out on the way they were treating their wives. He says they've dealt treacherously with their wives." Stacie raised a challenging eyebrow. "Sound like the Bible condones the mistreatment of wives?"

Holly shook her head. "But why doesn't Bethany's friend see what you just told me? Shouldn't people who call themselves Christians all believe the same things?"

"It's a touchy issue. Marriage is a covenant, sort of like a contract. It's not meant to be broken. The vows are basically like promises of what each will do to uphold their end of the deal. When a husband is abusive, he's clearly broken his promise to love and cherish."

Stacie examined Holly's face to make sure she was still following and then nodded. "Yes. The Bible says God hates divorce, but it doesn't call divorce a sin. Cruelty and abuse are sins. And get this, in James, it says that whoever knows the right thing to do and fails to do it, for him it is sin. So, my thinking is this. On their wedding day, a couple knows it's right to treat each other the way they've just promised. And when abuse is introduced into marriage, by either the man or the woman, the abuser is not doing what they've already agreed is the right thing to do. That's sin. God doesn't want us divorcing *and* he wants us to treat each other right. So, what happens if one partner cheats or becomes abusive? Some believe that with the vows broken, if the behavior continues, the other is freed from the covenant. Others don't agree."

"Still seems like they should all agree if they're getting their beliefs from the same book."

Stacie shrugged. "Remember that journalism class you took in high school?"

"Sure."

"Sometimes, you and your classmates had to report on the same issues or events."

Holly nodded.

"Do you remember what you used to say after hearing the others?"

"Yeah. Sometimes it was cool to see different perspectives, and other times, it was annoying."

Holly slapped her leg. "Like that one time. The Beauty Queen Killer had just been found. The entire class had to cover the story. This guy was driving all over the country, killing pretty girls, and he was finally off the streets. It was a relief when they got the sicko. But some people reported it as tragic that he was killed before he could stand trial. As if it mattered that he didn't get punished for what he'd done to all those girls. The point was he was done. He didn't need a trial or prison. He couldn't kill again."

"So. Same facts. Different points of view. Different emphasis. Probably based on each of your pasts. Your experiences. Your upbringings. Maybe even what was going on in each of your lives at the time. If you talked with some of those same people today, some might change the way they report it."

"Maybe. So?"

"But it still doesn't change the facts. Points of view don't change facts. May change the way we see the truth, but won't change the truth."

Holly wrinkled one side of her nose and smirked. "Just because two people read the same thing in the Bible doesn't mean they'll get the same thing out of it at the same time."

"Exactly."

"Well, what's the point then? I mean, if people just interpret it any way they want." Holly lifted her shoulders in the start of a shrug but froze. Her eyes stared at a spot somewhere above Stacie's head. "Wait. That's why Bethany is upstairs right now, isn't it?"

Stacie smiled. "You got it. She's searching for answers *and* asking for guidance. She knows wives are to submit. She knows God hates divorce. She also knows God loves her and doesn't want her mistreated. And she knows better than any of us what Carlos has done and what he's capable of. Now, what choice should she make based on all of these facts? She's not taking this lightly. It's a big decision. She's going to have to live with it no matter what she chooses. She needs to be sure."

BETHANY

Bethany had been on her knees, begging God to tell her what to do. Her mind bounced between her options as she thumbed through her Bible. She wanted to avoid all passages about marriage. She found herself in Ezekiel. Weird place to stop, but chapter thirty-four caught her eye. Something about God taking care of his flock as a good shepherd. Her heartbeat quickened when she reached verse twenty-two, "So, I will rescue my flock, and they will no longer be abused. I will judge between one animal of the flock and another." By the time she finished the rest of the chapter, tears flowed freely. Some of the words bounced around in her head and washed her with a new sort of hope. "… They will live in safety, and no one will frighten them."

The words pierced Bethany's heart. They could be rescued. It would not be a superhero rescue. No one in a cape or suit of armor would come flying in and swoop them off to a safe tower somewhere obscure and unknown. Neither would she suddenly become a Kung Fu master and bring her tormentor to his fateful end. No. She had to take wise steps. She saw the open door but it wouldn't stay that way long.

Snares of doubt wilted and fell at her feet as she rose from the floor and went to the bathroom. She knew what she had to do. She washed her face and was amazed at the determination in her eyes. She would take her children and flee to Texas. There, they would be safe and secure. Carlos may come for her. But if she stayed here, she was dead anyway.

CHAPTER THIRTY-EIGHT

Everyone was in a great mood the next morning as they talked and laughed over a late breakfast. The air sparked with anticipation. No one would let Felicia lift a finger because they had decided to celebrate her thirteenth birthday today, two days early, since she and Holly were flying back to Texas tomorrow.

After lunch, they planned to take the celebration to Kenny. Bethany decided to make the most of her nice, big kitchen before saying goodbye to the home she'd shared with Carlos. No telling when she'd have so much space again. Breakfast looked like a banquet. They all ate until they were stuffed.

Afterward, the women cleaned up together while Gloria and Maria sat at the table, drawing and coloring birthday cards for Felicia.

Felicia sat on the counter and pretended to boss the others around. "You missed a spot." She pointed and smirked at her mom.

Holly laughed. "Why, you little turkey." She lunged at Felicia and grabbed her sides, causing Felicia to jump off the counter in peals of laughter.

"Hey. No fair. You can't tickle me. I'm thirteen now."

"Not until Thursday!" Holly laughed and swiped her dishrag over the counter. "There's no spot, silly. I'm a pro at wiping down counters."

Bethany let out a laugh. "Good. You can be the designated counter cleaner in our new place then. I can never seem to keep them clean enough."

"I'll keep the counters clean if you do my laundry."

Bethany shook her head. "Not the way you go through clothes. Do you still try everything on five times before leaving your room? Leave it all on the floor for later?"

"Nope. Outgrew that, I don't know, maybe fifteen years ago! Brat." Holly chuckled as she rolled her eyes at Felicia. "Big sisters. Sheesh!"

The doorbell rang, and everyone looked at Bethany. Stacie raised her eyebrows. "Expecting someone?"

Bethany shook her head. Her fingers tingled as the last conversation with Carlos shot through her brain. What if he was back and wanted to surprise her? What if he was waiting outside the door now? She pretended to be brave as she went to answer.

Patricia, a single, older woman from church, stood on the porch wearing a confident smile with her hands behind her back. She always looked so proper. Today was no different. Pressed slacks and a flowery button up shirt with a pearl necklace. Eyebrows perfectly drawn over each eye. Everything in place. Not even her lipstick dared to bleed into the wrinkles forming around her mouth. For some reason, her bold self-reliance had always intimidated Bethany. Patricia seemed to be able to see right through Bethany's cheerful front. Almost as if she knew all of Bethany's secrets, which made Bethany very uneasy and apt to avoid Patricia whenever possible. What was she doing here? She forced a polite smile. "What a surprise!"

Patricia searched Bethany's face and lost just a fraction of the lift to her perfect smile. "May I come in?"

Oh great. "Sure." Bethany opened the door wider and stepped aside.

As soon as Patricia was inside, she pulled a small gift bag from behind her back and held it out to Bethany. Pale blue tissue paper stuck out from the top. The entryway filled with her family as everyone gathered around and wanted to see who their unexpected guest was.

Bethany blushed as she accepted the gift. *What was Patricia up to?* "Did you meet my family at church?" Her wave encompassed the curious group.

Patricia shook her head. "I saw them, but you seemed a little distracted after service."

Got that right. She introduced Patricia to her family. Her mind was only halfway on the introductions as she tried to figure out what could possibly possess Patricia to show up with a gift. How'd she even know where Bethany lived?

Patricia greeted them by name as she was introduced. Her warmth seemed to put everyone at ease. But after the introductions, an awkward silence filled the air. Bethany lifted a hand toward the rest of the house. "Would you like to sit down?"

Patricia nodded and followed Bethany to the living room. She settled at one end of the love seat and patted the space next to her. "Join me?"

Bethany shot a glance at her mom as she sat down.

Stacie smiled and waved her hands toward the doorway. "Let's finish up in the kitchen and give Bethany a moment with her guest."

Patricia lifted the bag from Bethany's stiff fingers and placed it on the floor at their feet. Her soft hands wrapped around one of Bethany's cold ones. "You know I'm on the prayer team and read your prayer request cards, right?"

Bethany hadn't known. She filled those things out and dropped them in the offering tray when it came by, but she'd never thought about who was reading them or praying for the things she wrote down. For some reason, Bethany thought if anyone read them, it was just Pastor Eric and Trudy. It was a good thing she'd usually been vague. Her shirt was hot and scratchy but she worked at seeming nonchalant. "Oh. That's nice. Thank you for your prayers." She tried to smile.

"I was gathering my things after service when you came in behind me to talk with Trudy. I overheard a portion of the conversation. I did *not* intend to eavesdrop, and I want you to know that I hurried out of earshot as soon as I realized how sensitive it was."

Bethany was sure her face was red. She nodded. "It's fine." It wasn't. "I'm sure everyone will know soon enough. It's a small church." She could imagine what people would say since she didn't plan on making an announcement or anything. She only hoped the talk wouldn't start until after she was gone. Maybe she wouldn't go back. Only a couple weeks until she was leaving the state anyway.

Patricia nodded. "I started praying about what I heard on Sunday, along with what I already know from your prayer slips. A verse came to mind that I felt led to share with you. I was going to wait and tell you next time I saw you at church. But then, I was in the bookstore yesterday—" she picked the bag up and placed it between Bethany's hands "—and came across something which had that precise verse printed on the cover. I knew it was for you. I bought it and was compelled to bring it over today." She poked the bag. "Open it."

For some reason, Bethany's hands trembled as she pulled the tissue paper out and looked inside. A hardcover, spiral-bound book rested on a bed of white tissue paper.

"It's a journal. If you're not journaling yet, you should be. This will help you sort things out and remember what's important."

Bethany pulled it out. On the cover was a picture of a valley between two, out-of-focus hills. In focus, on the lower half of the cover, was a green field alive with about a dozen of her favorite flowers. Purple irises. In the cloudy blue sky, above the valley, was fancy print that read, "The Lord will guide you continually … You shall be like a watered garden, And like a spring of water, whose waters do not fail." As she examined it, her vision blurred until she could no longer read the words. She didn't know what to say, so she just stared at it in her lap until a silent teardrop fell on it. She blinked and wiped it off.

Words stuck in her tight throat, but Patricia didn't seem to mind. She scooted close to Bethany and wrapped an arm around her, drawing her close. "It's going to be okay. I don't normally say this but," she leaned back and waited for Bethany to make eye contact, "don't listen to Trudy or Pastor Eric on this one." She stood with a heavy sigh. "They mean well. But they just don't understand."

Bethany sniffed as she basked in the tender reassurance from a woman she would never have expected to understand. This unexpected visit was confirmation that she was making the right choice. Despite what Pastor Eric and Trudy thought.

CHAPTER THIRTY-NINE

FELICIA   **Wednesday, June 29**

Felicia folded her clothes and stuffed them in a bag the next morning while Grammy watched from the bed. That afternoon, she'd be flying back to Texas with her mom. It was going to be so cool to live with Aunt Bethy and Kenny. Felicia's mind bounced between all that she'd learned on this trip, along with the exciting changes her mom was making for their lives. "I'm never getting married."

"Like your mom?"

Felicia's head snapped up, and her wide eyes looked at Grammy as if she'd just suggested Felicia would rob a bank. "No!" She shook her head. "Why would I want a boyfriend to screw it all up?" She looked around the room for more to pack. "No husband. No boyfriend. No man." Her eyes met Grammy's. "Except, of course, Uncle Nate and Kenny. They're different."

Grammy nodded. "I can understand why you'd say that. You haven't had very good examples, have you?"

Felicia shook her head with her nose wrinkled. "But it might be hard. Seems like everyone at school either has a boyfriend or is trying to get one. What if I don't want one? I mean. I sort of do. Looks fun. But only at first." She shook her head. "Not worth it." But something in her heart tugged even as she said the words. Did she believe it? But what if she wanted kids?

Grammy patted the bed. "Well, you know there's nothing wrong with being single, right?"

Felicia sat facing Grammy with one leg tucked in front of her and the other dangling. "Seriously?" That's not what she saw on TV. What about finding *the one*?

"Did you know Paul wrote in the Bible that it's better to be single?"

What? And here, Felicia thought it was her idea. Her expression must have given away her thoughts because Grammy nodded with a smirk.

"Oh, yes. Actually, Jesus sort of said the same thing years earlier." Grammy shrugged. "But then, he basically said not everyone could handle the single life, which is what Paul taught later. You're right. It's not easy. But *if* a person can accept it without giving in to temptation …" Grammy lifted one shoulder and tipped her head toward it. "It's better for some people. My point is, sweetheart, that you do not need to go looking for a relationship, boyfriend, or even worry about getting married one day. Instead, think about what to do with your life and take steps to follow that path. If one day you realize there's a man you'd like to spend the rest of your life with, then you can always reconsider. But, please, learn from your mom and Aunt Bethy. Take your time and choose carefully. There are a lot of wolves in sheep's clothing."

• • •

Felicia rested her head against the airplane seat and closed her eyes. Everything out her tiny window had become too small to keep her interest. She replayed some of the fun from her birthday celebration. Kenny was so cool. She couldn't wait to hang out with him again. It'd be like having a big brother. He'd made a big deal out of her becoming a teenager. Even though, technically, she wasn't thirteen until tomorrow. Still.

She turned her head toward the window to hide the smile that lit her face. A teenager. Soon, she'd be able to get a job. Boys would be more interested in her now that she was so much older. Thirteen. She could see it now. A cute guy asks how old she is and she could say, "Thirteen."

But then what? What good would it do to have him like her if she was too afraid to have a relationship? What Grammy had said made sense in a weird way. But how would she ever stay single when everyone she knew was crazy about hooking up? She'd look like a weirdo. Or worse. It would look like no one wanted her.

She wanted to be wanted.

Sometimes a boy would flirt. It felt good. It was exciting. She didn't want that to stop. Sometimes she even wanted to try the things she saw others do. She'd been looking forward to becoming a teenager.

Now. Well, now she was all mixed up inside. She didn't want to go through anything like what her mom or Aunt Bethy kept going through.

Men were jerks.

But were boys?

Maybe she could find one before he became a man. Before he turned into a jerk like the rest. But Grammy said she could stay single. Like, she never had to be with anyone. Ever. Was that what she really wanted?

Grammy was single. Felicia had never seen her with a man. Well, Rich lately, but not in a romantic way. Grammy seemed happy. She smiled a lot. She laughed. She was fun to be around. But she was old. It was easy for her. There wasn't anyone to be with anyway.

Her mind shifted to Ethan. He was so cute. And funny. And nice most of the time. He didn't pull mean pranks like some of the other popular boys. Only Jasmine knew he'd been Felicia's crush for the past two years. If Felicia decided to do like Grammy, would she miss something amazing with Ethan?

BETHANY

Bethany and her mom strapped Gloria and Maria into their car seats in the airport parking lot. They'd walked with Holly and Felicia as far as they could go and hugged them goodbye just outside of security.

Now, all strapped in, Bethany kissed Maria's chubby cheek before shutting the back door and hopping into the driver's seat.

"Mommy." Gloria had been quiet since they'd started the long walk back to the truck.

"Yes?"

"When will Felicia come over?"

"Why? You miss her already?" Bethany put the truck in reverse and smiled at Gloria as she turned around to check before backing out.

Gloria nodded. "She's nice."

"What if we lived closer to her? Close enough to see her every day? Would you like that?"

Gloria's face lit up and she nodded.

"Hm. Maybe we can do something about that." Bethany shot a smile at her mom as she pointed the truck toward the exit.

Her mom smiled. "Sounds like a good idea to me."

Bethany nodded. "Now, who's hungry? I say we get pizza for dinner. At Chuck E Cheese!"

Maria and Gloria gasped and squealed. It was a silly idea. She shouldn't spend the money, but she had to do something to take her mind off her racing thoughts. Holly and Felicia were going house hunting. Soon, Bethany and her kids would join them.

This was all outside of her comfort zone, but the thought that nagged at her the most was that she couldn't tell Carlos herself. She hated lies. When the dust settled and Carlos, hopefully, got help and changed, would their marriage survive her betrayal? If she could just tell him *why*. Explain before she left …

FELICIA

She must have fallen asleep because the next thing she knew, her mom patted her hand. "Sweetie. Put your seat up. We're descending. Almost home." She smiled.

Felicia rubbed the side of her neck. "Already?"

"I know. I dozed off too. Not for long, though. My mind is racing. Let's grab dinner and then head to Grammy's for the night. First thing in the morning, we'll go find our new home. I know it might not be the most fun way to spend your birthday, but …" her mom giggled.

Mom was almost bouncing in her seat. A thrill shot through Felicia. This was real. "I don't mind. Good birthday present. We gonna get our stuff out of the old house too?"

Her mom shrugged. "I'll check with some friends and see if Danny's still in jail or what. Figure out the best time to sneak in. We won't be able to take a lot. Just some clothes, pictures … Important stuff. You okay with starting fresh with everything else?"

Felicia nodded. "Uh. Yeah, Mom. Duh."

"Good. Grammy said to check out a place one of her friends has for rent first."

Felicia tried to imagine their new home, but it was hard.

"I feel a little sorry for Kenny, though." Mom snickered.

"Why would you feel sorry for Kenny?"

"He'll be the only boy in a house full of girls. Five of us to deal with." Rich laughter rolled from her mom. Felicia pictured Kenny surrounded by girls and dropped her head to her mom's shoulder as she joined in the laugh.

A skinny girl in front of them shifted in her seat and shot them a curious look. For some reason, that just made Felicia laugh more. Mom's arms came around Felicia and held her as they brought their laughter under control. Only a spontaneous giggle escaped here and there. As Felicia melted into her mother's embrace, she felt like a little girl again. Maybe she wasn't in such a hurry to grow up. Nothing felt as good as being tucked safely in her mom's arms.

BETHANY

Hours later, Bethany was beginning to drag. Her girls seemed to be having a blast. Bethany was too distracted for the fun to really soak in and refresh her. Wearing a smile and pushing out laughs had drained her. She was ready to go home and put her feet up.

"Okay, girls, last game!"

"Awe." Gloria pushed her bottom lip out.

"Potty." Maria did the potty dance.

Stacie smiled. "I'll take her."

"No. I'll go. Just don't let Gloria play any more games. I'll meet you outside." She dug the keys from her purse and handed them to her mom.

Bethany scooped Maria up and hurried to the bathroom. As the bathroom door shut, her eardrums were bathed in silence. Well, maybe not total silence, but compared to the other side of that door, it was amazing.

They squeezed into a well-used stall where a lingering odor still hung in the air. Bethany held her breath as long as she could as she lined the toilet seat for Maria. She hated putting her babies on nasty public toilets. Maria was so tiny and wanted to hold onto the sides of the toilet seat to keep from falling into the bowl. Gross. Instead, Bethany carefully placed Maria on the seat and told her to hold onto Mommy's arms. It wasn't the most comfortable position, bending over so Maria could cling to her while trying to keep her purse from touching anything inside of the germ-infested stall.

As she held Maria and waited for the sound of her pee to hit the water, her back already complaining, her phone rang from her back pocket. Her daughter stiffened and squeezed Bethany's arms. "It's okay, sweetie. Just relax and go." When Maria was finally done, Bethany lifted her from the toilet seat and handed her a wad of toilet paper.

Bethany opened the stall door. The phone rang again. Must be Carlos. "Go wash." She pointed to the sink as she swiped the screen to answer. "Hey, honey!"

"Where are you?"

Bethany tucked her phone between her shoulder and ear. "In the bathroom with Maria at Chuck E. Cheese." She lifted Maria and stuck a leg out to help hold her high enough to reach the water and the soap dispenser.

"Fun. Wish I was there with you."

"Yeah. Me too. Done now, though. About to leave." Maria wiggled as she tried to get soap out of the dispenser.

"Good. Start a video chat with me when you get home."

Bethany leaned over Maria, wrapped one arm around her, and reached for the soap with the other hand. Nothing. "Okay. See you soon." Trying to keep the phone pinched between her ear and shoulder, she reached for the next dispenser over. The phone slipped and bounced off Maria's shoulder. It cracked on the edge of the sink before coming to rest under the faucet of running water.

"Owie!" Maria fussed and squirmed.

Bethany snatched the phone out of the sink. "Oh, sorry, sweetie." The top corner of the black screen was chipped with cracks stretching across the rest. Bethany pulled her leg back and slid Maria to the floor. "Let's go." She grabbed an extra paper towel for her phone and dabbed at it before stuffing it into her pocket and pushing the bathroom door open. Just what she needed.

• • •

At home, Bethany sat at the desk in her room, video chatting with Carlos. He'd been sweet from the start. He smiled and leaned close to the camera. "You're so beautiful, baby."

His clear eyes seemed to overflow with affection, and she felt a blush creep into her cheeks. "Thanks."

"I didn't know I'd miss you as much as I have."

Bethany's mind raced over all the sneaky things she'd been doing since he left and felt the color in her face deepen. A lump formed in her throat.

"I know you've missed me too. You don't have to say it. I can see it in your eyes." His lips turned up in a tranquil smile. "Always so sweet. Loving. It's why I fell in love with you so fast." He chuckled. "No. I didn't stand a chance against those innocent eyes. Delicate face. Can't wait to get home to you."

Bethany swallowed hard. She was evil—pure evil. No one would ever love her as much as Carlos did. But he could get so mean and scary. Yeah, but he loved her. She didn't doubt that. *Wasn't love enough?* It was in the movies. But this wasn't a movie. This was her life. She blinked, and a tear escaped, rolling down her cheek.

"Aw, baby girl. Don't cry. We'll be together soon. See. I knew you wanted me to come home early. You need me. A love like ours just shouldn't be apart like this." He propped his chin on his folded hands and gazed into the camera.

More tears spilled. She did love him—this version. Love wasn't the issue. This was the man she'd married. Would he ever come back to stay? She wanted to tell him everything. Explain why. She never wanted to hurt him. But Victor had been adamant. Don't tell Carlos anything. Victor was sure Carlos would send someone to stop her from leaving if he knew. Victor said he'd tell Carlos once his plane landed. Before coming home to an empty house.

Carlos leaned back with a smile. "Are you going to have the girls make a big 'Welcome Home' banner to hang outside for when I get home? Knowing you, it's going to be amazing."

The image he described was so far from what he was in store for, Bethany's stomach turned. She had to tell him. She couldn't let him think he was coming home to a happy family, eager to see him. She opened her mouth, but he didn't seem to notice.

"Make sure Kenny's with you." One dark eyebrow arched high and seemed to pull a small sneer from his lip on that side. It was gone as fast as it had shown up. "I know that kid might not agree, but I've only ever tried to prepare him for the real world. It's tough out here. One day he'll appreciate all I've done."

Bethany nodded. Her confession died before it left her lips. "Okay, honey."

He smiled. "Better have the girls start coloring on that banner soon. It's a big project."

"Yes, it is a big project."

He leaned to one side, reaching for something. When he straightened, he held a pack of cigarettes and pulled one from the carton. "I can't wait to see how it turns out. Going to smoke. Love you." He blew her a kiss before the chat screen went black.

Bethany slouched in her chair. This sucked.

CHAPTER FORTY

Thursday, June 30

Stacie couldn't help the joy that bubbled up every time she thought about her girls living together, safe, and close by.

Bethany brought Gloria and Maria downstairs and sniffed the air. "I smell coffee."

Stacie jumped up to pour her daughter a cup. Bethany looked awful. Well, she did say she had to talk with Carlos last night. Must have been up late.

After handing Bethany a steamy mug, Stacie grabbed two plastic cereal bowls for her hungry granddaughters. "Up late?"

"Yeah. Not too late with Carlos but had a tough time sleeping after that."

"Your sister's heading out a little later to look at a house a friend of mine has. Pretty cool, huh?"

Stacie watched Bethany's retreating back as she left the kitchen.

After Stacie got the little ones settled with breakfast, she found Bethany on the couch and sat next to her. "Talk to me."

"Carlos was so sweet last night. He loves me. He's going to be so hurt when he finds out. He's so excited to come home. I'm a horrible wife for not even telling him."

"No, you're a wise mother, protecting her kids and herself."

"Doesn't feel that way right now." Bethany sighed and curled up with her head on the armrest.

Doubts were inevitable but must not be given room to grow. Stacie patted her daughter's leg. "Run up and get dressed. If you still want to bring Kenny, I think we should get him out today."

They were ready within the hour and headed toward Kenny.

Stacie dialed Rich. Bethany shot her a sideways look.

He answered on the first ring. "I'll be home sooner than expected. Don't have much time to talk but my Bethy is moving back to Texas with her kids."

"That's great! I can't wait to meet her."

Stacie smiled. "And Holly's already back in Texas. Out looking for a new place they can rent together. Told her to look at Lizzy's place first."

"Good idea. Reckon she'll be needing that job right quick."

"It's time, but I want you to tell her." Stacie hung up with a smile.

Bethany pulled into the parking lot. "Let's bust Kenny outta this place."

Gloria mimicked Bethany and her sister joined in, making it sound more like a chant. "Bus Kenny out. Bus Kenny out. Bus Kenny out."

• • •

It wound up being much easier than either of them expected to get Kenny discharged. Of course, the staff weren't happy to see him go before his treatment was complete. But once they were filled in on the situation, they quickly put things in order and got the discharge paperwork together.

Kenny strolled out with a grin on his handsome face. "Man. Feels so good to be free."

Bethany glanced at him through the rearview mirror and smiled. She'd started looking better as soon as she'd signed the paperwork and had her arm locked with Kenny's on the way to the truck. They were on the road, and the mood was noticeably lighter. Bethany smiled. "Feels good to have you back. Missed you so much."

"Missed you too. And my sisters." His poke in each of their sides was rewarded with squeals and giggles. "Missed home. My room. Hey, Mom, I even missed your cooking!"

Stacie reached back and swatted at Kenny's long legs. "Be nice. We've got a lot of work to do."

Bethany nodded. "First stop is Family Advocacy. Need to update Jennifer. Then we've got to get some boxes from the store and pack them up with a few things we can't live without. My mixer, food processor...."

"We'll pack those and mail them to my house before we fly out."

Bethany nodded. "We're not taking any furniture. Just personal items."

Kenny rubbed his hands together. "I'm ready. Can't wait to see Uncle Nate again. What's he think of all this?"

Stacie smiled. "He's excited ya'll will be living close enough to see all the time. He's missed you."

Kenny nodded. "I'm excited too."

• • •

Stacie knew something was off as soon as Bethany came out of Jennifer's office. She was pale and distracted. She forced a smile for her girls when they greeted her but immediately handed them snacks from her purse. "Eat as much as you want."

Stacie pulled Bethany's elbow and led her outside. She shot Kenny a look on her way out. "Keep an eye on them?"

He nodded.

"What's wrong?"

Bethany's eyes filled with tears. "My phone's broke."

"What?"

Bethany nodded. "Yeah. I dropped it in the sink with water yesterday and broke it."

"Okay. Want to get a new one before we go home?"

"He's coming. Victor's been trying to call since yesterday, but I didn't know."

Stacie's heart thumped against her eardrums. "Why's he been calling?"

"Carlos is flying out tomorrow. He's coming."

Stacie grabbed Bethany's arms and gave them a little shake. "Carlos is coming tomorrow? Are you sure?"

Bethany nodded, tears streaming down her cheeks. "Jennifer said Victor called and wants to know why we're still here." She shook her head. "We have to go. We have to go." Bethany's hands waved, and she looked like a cornered rabbit, ready to run but not sure which direction.

Stacie nodded as she gulped in shallow breaths trying to get more oxygen to her fuzzy brain. "What time will he be home? We should go tonight."

Bethany shook her head. "No, Mom. He's leaving tomorrow. Supposed to stop overnight. Home sometime Saturday. Unless he doesn't spend the night, then, late tomorrow, but probably Saturday. At least, that's what Victor told Jennifer."

Stacie shook her head and closed her eyes. "Still ..." She had to think.

"Jennifer wants me to come back in the morning. She's going to take me down to the Emergency Relief office. She's doing the paperwork."

"For what? What does that mean?"

"They'll pay for our plane tickets. Me and the kids. Wherever we want to go."

"Texas."

Bethany nodded. "Yeah. What will I tell the girls?"

Stacie wrapped her arms around her daughter. She couldn't tell if the shaking was coming from Bethany's body or her own. "I don't know, sweetheart. I don't know."

FELICIA

This was a birthday Felicia would remember forever. Her mom treated her like a grownup while they looked at a couple houses for rent in Cedar Park. The first house was Felicia's favorite. It had four bedrooms, and there was a bonus room that Felicia would be totally cool with. Mom seemed a little worried about the price, but Grammy had sent them to this one first because she knew the owner.

They had a third house on their list, but then her mom got a text from Grammy saying there was a change of plans. Carlos was coming back sooner than expected. They were on their way to Texas tomorrow. *Tomorrow!* Felicia clapped her hands when she heard the news. "Let's just get the first one, Mom. It was perfect."

"You might be right. Sort of crunched for time now. We'd split the seams at Grammy's."

"You should call and tell her that's the one we want."

"How'd you get so smart? I'm seeing peeks of the woman you're turning into. It's fun."

Felicia sat a little straighter and smiled. "I am thirteen now."

Her mom chuckled. "In that case, how about *you* call Grammy?"

Felicia grabbed her phone with a grin.

"Think about where you want to go for your birthday dinner."

Felicia nodded as Grammy answered.

• • •

Whatever Grammy did worked, because before they were finished eating, they got a call saying they could pick up the keys to their new place. The deposit had been waived. Whatever that meant. Aunt Bethy could sign her part on Monday morning.

Felicia pushed her half-eaten meal away with a squeal. She bounced in her seat and begged her mom to go pick up the keys. "*Please*. I'm done." She probably lost all her grownup points, but she couldn't hold still. They could move in today. They had a home. A safe place to live. "Let's go, Mom."

Her mom laughed. "You'll be hungry later. Finish eating."

Felicia rolled her eyes. "I'm fine. I want to go. I have to see my new room again. Can I decorate it any way I want?"

"Yes. But probably not all at once. I still have to get a job."

BETHANY

There was so much to do before they left in the morning. First stop was the cell phone company. While she was there, she asked for a new number. This was one time she was glad it was all in her name. She removed him as an approved contact before they left. She might not have thought to do that if she hadn't broken her phone.

Two hours later, they stopped to get lunch on their way to the store for boxes. She didn't want her girls to be confused about why they were packing, so the first thing she did when they got home was ask her girls to come sit on the couch. She knelt on the floor in front of them to see both of their faces and read their reactions. It was hard to get started, but she took a deep breath and smiled.

"Do you remember when Daddy was home?"

They nodded. Maria pushed the back of her head into the couch and bounced it softly.

"Has it felt different since he left?"

Two dark heads bobbed. Gloria offered, "Maria doesn't bump her head in the closet anymore."

"No. She doesn't. Why do you think that is?"

"She's not scared. Daddy yells a lot."

Bethany nodded and placed a hand on the knee of each daughter. "Well, Daddy's coming home sooner than he was going to."

Maria's head bounced against the couch a little harder, faster.

"I want Daddy to stop yelling so much. He *can*, but he needs practice. I think it would be easier for him to practice if we were not here when he gets home."

Both girls froze and examined her face.

Bethany tried to look calm. "We're going to move close to Grandma's house for a while." No reaction. Maybe they didn't understand what she was saying. She sighed and picked Maria up, sitting in her place and pulled Gloria close. "I need you girls to pack your favorite toys because you might not see the rest of them for a long time. Tomorrow, we will get on an airplane and fly all the way to Texas, where Grandma lives, and we'll have a house there with Aunt Holly and Felicia."

Gloria looked at her. "Kenny?"

Bethany chuckled. "Yes. Kenny's coming too."

Maria nodded. "Okay."

"You're okay with that, Maria?"

She nodded.

"How about you, Gloria?"

Gloria looked sad as she nodded. "Okay, but I will miss Daddy."

"I know you will, sweetheart. I will too. I love your daddy. I just want him to get better so we can all be together again."

The plan was to get all the boxes mailed off before the post office closed. In the morning, she would leave her mom home with the kids and meet Jennifer to get their airline tickets for that evening. Carlos would freak. But Victor would take care of him. He would have a Military-No-Contact-Order ready to give Carlos when he landed.

FELICIA

The house was perfect. Felicia hoped Kenny and Aunt Bethy loved it as much as she did. They'd picked up the keys and spent at least a half-hour walking through every room and talking about what it might be like to live with Aunt Bethy's family. They'd imagined who would occupy each room. Her mom shared decorating ideas that sounded perfect to Felicia.

Now, Felicia was ready for her stuff. She'd convinced her mom to go to their old house and get as much as possible in one trip. One of Mom's friends said she thought Danny was still locked up, but another said she thought she saw him at the bar playing pool the night before. Mom decided to drive by the house and check it out.

Danny's truck wasn't there. The potted plants on the front porch were dried up and looked dead. "Looks like he hasn't been here since we left." Mom backed into the drive-way and popped the trunk. "This place gives me the creeps. Let's just hurry."

On the porch, Mom lifted a stiff vine with a frown. A dead flower broke off and dropped to her feet. She sighed. "Wonder if we should take these with us and try to revive them."

Felicia rolled her eyes. "Sure, Mom. But can you unlock the door? I wanna get my stuff."

"Sorry." Her mom opened the door and peeked inside before crossing the threshold. The blinds were shut. It took a minute for their eyes to adjust. "Just leave the door open. Be easier to load the car, and it stinks in here." Sure did. Old food and stale cigarettes. Maybe something else. Gross. Her mom hurried to the kitchen. "I should take out the trash. Reeks."

Felicia followed her. "Whatever. We don't live here any-more anyway." As Felicia said it, she found herself smiling. They didn't live there. It wasn't home. Giddy vibrations filled her belly. Best. Birthday. Ever.

Mom opened the cupboard under the sink, grabbed a roll of trash bags, pulled three off, and handed them to Felicia. "Put your stuff in these. Try to hurry. I just wanna get out of here."

She rushed to her room. No. To the room that *used* to be hers. Not anymore. Her door was wide open. For a second, she saw Danny smashing her behind that door. Her heart beat a little faster. She shook her head and pressed her lips together. No more. Felicia sailed through the doorway and tossed two trash bags at the bed. They didn't quite make it and fell to the floor instead. She rolled her eyes and shook open the one in her hand.

She started with her clothes, scooping them up and shov-ing them in the bag. She'd missed some of these. Happy Birthday to me! She wasn't sure how to pack her few pieces of jewelry and pretty figurines Grammy had given her. She looked around and then smacked her forehead. Duh. Digging around in her bag of clothes, she found a few soft tee-shirts. She carefully wrapped each item in a shirt before placing them in a second bag.

Felicia didn't want to forget a couple of treasures she'd stowed under the bed. As she crawled under, she giggled. Buried treasure. This was like an adventure. She grabbed a small stack of notebooks and pushed them out.

When she reached for an old stuffed animal, she heard it. No way. But she knew that sound—Danny's truck. Still running in the driveway. Just outside her window. She rushed to get out from under the bed but didn't clear it before trying to get up, slamming the back of her head against the frame. Pain shot through her skull and made her blink a couple times before she slid out a few more inches and jumped to her feet. The engine shut off. One glance out the window showed Danny sitting in his truck, staring at their car in the driveway with a sneer on his ugly face. "Mom! Danny's here!" She tripped over the bag of clothes and sprawled on the other side of it. As she bounced to her feet, Mom rushed in and put a hand out, motioning for Felicia to stop. "Stay in your room."

Felicia was wild and shook her head, trying to get past. "We have to get out of here!"

Her mom grabbed her shoulders and forced her to make eye contact. "It's okay. I won't let anything else happen to you. Stay in your room."

Felicia nodded and let her mom close the bedroom door. For a moment, she just stood there, straining to hear him walk through the front door but unable to hear anything except the pounding of her heart. Pack. She swung around and grabbed the last empty trash bag and started throwing stuff into it. She didn't care what she took or how it was packed. Her mission was to get it all in the trash bags and get out of there.

At first, she heard Danny's voice occasionally. He was drunk. Loud questions and accusations. The walls were thin. He wanted to know who Mom had been sleeping with since she clearly hadn't been at Stacie's this time. Felicia couldn't make out her mom's soft answers.

But then Danny exploded. "Leaving? Ya think ya'll can just come into my house, take my crap, and leave? I'm supposed to be okay with ya cheating on me, stealing from me, and then walking out on me?"

There was a crash. Felicia jumped and looked around. She couldn't stay there—another crash. Felicia ran to the window and opened it. She shoved the screen out of the way and tossed her trash bags into the front yard. She was halfway out the window when something hit her bedroom door. She hesitated.

Her mom screamed, but the sound was cut off and muffled, followed by dull thumping sounds.

Felicia jumped back into her room and ran to open her door. She found Danny in the living room on his knees in front of her mom. Mom's hands and forearms blocked few of the punches Danny threw at her. Felicia froze. Danny pulled his fist back and hit her mom in the stomach. She cried out and moved her arms from her head and grabbed her stomach.

Her face was a mess. Blood smeared. One eye fixed shut. The other eye blinked and looked at Felicia. Her mom moaned. This was all wrong. It wasn't supposed to go like this. He wasn't supposed to be home. They just wanted to leave.

Felicia had to get Danny away from her mom. Then, they could run, jump in the car, and never see his horrid face again. She darted into the kitchen and grabbed the biggest knife she could find. Screw the stuff. He could keep it all. She ran to the other side of her mom to get Danny's attention and screamed as loud as she could. "Stop hitting her!"

Danny took in Felicia holding the knife and laughed as if he'd just heard the punchline to some sick joke. He stood up and swayed. Looked like he tried to bounce the way a boxer does in the ring. It would have been more intimidating if he could've kept his balance. He looked stupid.

Felicia backed up, luring him away from her mom with her heart slamming around in her chest. Her mom moaned from the floor and tried to grab Danny's leg as he stepped over her. *Don't grab him, Mom. Get ready to run.*

Danny shook off her weak grasp and chuckled. "Hey, baby. Check it out. Felicia thinks she's a big girl now. You big enough to take a beating like a woman?"

Felicia took another step back. No. She was ready to get out of there.

"Thirteen and all grown up, huh? What ya plan to do, cutie? Ya wanna kill me?" He chuckled and blew her a kiss. Maybe she did want to kill him.

But how could she ever manage to hurt him? She took a step back. She'd succeeded in distracting him from her mom and wanted to run. But her mom didn't look like she could get away fast enough. Even with Danny all wobbly like this. *Get up, Mom.*

"You're just a little girl, Felicia. Can't even take you seriously. Especially the way you're holding that knife. Probably just gonna stab yourself."

She glanced at the knife. How was she supposed to hold it?

Her mom staggered to all fours and coughed. Blood mixed with saliva dribbled from her lips. *Oh my gosh. No way Mom's running anywhere. Crap. Now what?*

"Leab hu." More coughing. "Stay way."

Danny laughed and threw his voice into a high pitch. "Leab her." His hands waved in the air in mock protest. "Stay away from my baby."

Blood surged through Felicia's veins and made her hands tingle as she tightened her grip on the knife. Her thoughts were like a railway train that had jumped tracks from fleeing with her mom to making Danny pay for what he'd just done to her.

She braced herself, ready to plunge the knife into whatever reached her first. Shoulder. Hand. Arm. Chest. She focused on every twitch and unsteady step he took closer. He would be in her knife's range soon, and her entire body was tense and ready to pounce.

He leaned back as if swaying. This was her chance. She lunged toward him with all her might as his knee rose. Before she could stop her momentum, he'd leaned into his leading foot and planted it into her stomach, pushing so hard, it knocked the air from her lungs and sent her flailing backward. She slammed into the wall and crumpled into a choking, gasping heap on the floor. Tears pricked her eyes as she worked to drag oxygen back into her lungs.

Danny kicked her side. Searing heat engulfed the left side of her ribcage. Felicia pulled her legs in close and wrapped her arms around them. It was hard to see through the blur of tears and pain. She tucked the knife under her leg, flat side against her calf. She didn't want it in Danny's hands. At least now, Danny wasn't focused on her mom. Mom. Where'd she go?

Felicia caught sight of her mom from between Danny's legs. Her mom stumbled away, down the hall, using the walls for balance. Felicia's eyes stung. Her mom had said she wouldn't let Danny hurt Felicia. She'd lied.

Pain burst through her thigh with the next kick. She was a disobedient dog. Kicked into submission. Danny sneered. "How does it feel to be a big, tough teenager? You enjoying this?" The pain in her thigh couldn't compete with her broken heart as her mom lunged out of sight. Into the master bedroom. Gone. "Welcome to womanhood, Felicia." Danny pulled his leg up. His boot stomped just above her ankle creating a loud snap and hot pain. She couldn't hold back the scream that ripped from her throat.

Her hand shot down to protect the area while her good leg kicked against the floor, trying to scoot away from Danny. Her breaths were quick and shallow. She had to get out of here. He was going to kill her.

Felicia was afraid to blink, but the stupid tears made things too blurry. She couldn't let Danny take her by surprise again.

"Danny." Someone far away called to him. It came again. Louder this time but followed by a fit of coughing. "Danny." Her mom. The pronunciation and tone were a little different, but that was definitely her mom's voice. "Danny. Help me."

Danny grinned and looked toward the bedroom. "Knew she'd come around." Felicia's stomach turned. She heaved and puke poured from her mouth, getting on her shirt, arms, and knees. She moaned and cried like the baby she really was. Danny's lip curled as he looked down at her. "Disgusting. Yer no woman."

"Danny." Closer this time. Mom clung to the wall as she inched her way toward them.

Danny nodded his head toward her. "That there's a *real* woman. Can take a beating better'n most men. Time to make up." He grabbed his belt buckle and chuckled before giving Felicia a half-hearted kick to the shoulder and strutting away. "Comin', babe."

Felicia couldn't make out her mom's face in the dim hallway. Danny opened his arms and said something too soft for Felicia to make out.

BOOM! The walls vibrated with an unfamiliar and deafening sound.

Danny cried out and staggered two steps back. "What—?" He looked at his left shoulder—another boom. Danny stumbled, cursed, and then hurled himself at her mom. He grabbed her in a bear hug on his way to the floor, bringing her down under him. She screamed.

Felicia scrambled to get up, but her hand slipped in the puddle of puke. It was all over the front of her shirt when she pushed herself up a second time.

Danny cursed and got to his knees. He leaned over Holly. "Can't believe you shot me! Where's the gun?" He unleashed a string of obscenities as he pushed to his knees and examined his bleeding shoulder.

Felicia tried to run to them, but pain shot up her leg as it gave out. She dropped to her hands and knees, one hand landing on the cool, flat steel of the knife she'd forgotten about.

"What. Were. You. *Thinking?*" Danny punctuated each word with a punch to her mom.

Felicia grabbed the knife and crawled as quickly as she could. Almost there. Her mom lay sideways in the hall. Her face just visible around Danny's crouched form. Blood was everywhere. One of Danny's shoulders was drenched with blood running from his sleeve. Felicia crawled up behind him and pushed to her knees, raising the knife to chest level, she closed the gap. She focused on his back, hunching over her mom, and shoved the knife in as hard as she could and with all her weight behind it.

Danny arched his back and roared. Felicia toppled to his side. He turned, eyes and mouth wide. He dove at her, fist first. Fireworks burst in her head as his fist caught her in the eye.

She would die in this miserable house.

Blood sprayed her face as he coughed over her. He pulled his fist back. Felicia braced herself. His punch was clumsy, but pain still sizzled through her already throbbing ribs. Danny stopped and fell to the floor in a bloody, coughing fit. She scrambled to her mom's side. "Mom." The damp carpet stuck to her palms, trying to slow her down. "Mom."

Her mom's chest rose and fell with wet, wheezing sounds. "Mom." Felicia was afraid to touch her. So much blood. Her mom's face was swollen and misshapen. "I got him, Momma. I got him for you."

Her mom's fingers twitched. Felicia laid down and wrapped her arm around her mom's waist. "It's okay, Momma. I won't let him hurt you anymore. We're going to be okay." Felicia squeezed her eyes shut, but that didn't stop the tears from escaping under her lashes.

Someone touched the arm she'd wrapped around her mom. Her eyes flew open. It was Mom's hand. Her fingers rested on Felicia's arm. "I love you, Momma."

Mom moaned through unmoving lips. Felicia got the message. Her mom loved her too. Felicia had the best mom any teenage girl could ask for. Felicia lifted her head once, but when the hallway spun, she laid it against her mom. She'd stay here for a little while longer.

CHAPTER FORTY-ONE

STACIE   **Friday, July 1**

Stacie was pulled from her dreams by the vibration of her phone on the nightstand. She opened scratchy eyes and looked at the clock while reaching for her phone. 12:12. Strange. She squinted at Nate's smiling face lighting up the screen. She didn't try to mask the confused concern in her voice when she answered.

Nate sounded out of breath and almost rude. "You need to come home—*now*."

"What's going on, Nate?" She popped up and threw the covers to the side.

"I'm on my way to Cedar Park Regional to see Felicia."

"Why's Felicia in the hospital? She okay?"

"Momma, she's." Nate paused. Stacie pulled her feet from the covers and placed them on the floor, one at a time. When Nate spoke again, his voice was thick. "I'm driving. Gonna take me almost an *hour* to get there." There was a loud thump in the background. "God, no!"

"Nate. You have to tell me what's going on." Stacie dropped to her knees on the floor and braced herself.

"Danny's dead."

"Danny's dead?" Chills swept her body. *How'd he die? And what did that have to do with Felicia?* "Why's Felicia in the hospital? Where's Holly? Nate, tell me what's going on."

"Had to call you. Can't. Oh, God, Please."

Stacie's heart thumped against her ribs.

Nate started speaking in a whisper, which gradually rose to a yell. "Please, God. She can't be. My sister, God. My *sister*!" Nate's voice caught on a sob. "Not my *sister, God*!"

"Nate." She didn't want to know. "What are you saying, Nate?" She grabbed the phone with both hands and pressed it hard to her ear. She didn't want to hear the words Nate was struggling to say. "Tell me where Holly is."

Nate whimpered. "No, Momma."

"*Where is she, Nate*?" She wanted to reach through the phone and shake him. "Tell me!"

"Oh, Mom. They said she's." He coughed. "I'm going to see Felicia. She's in the hospital. They took her to Cedar Park. That's where I'm headed. Take me almost an hour to get there. Maybe not the way I'm driving. I'll get to Felicia, Mom. Know more then. They'll take me to see Holly. Took her there too. Said I could see her. I'll see her. Know more then."

"Wait. So, Holly's in the hospital too?"

"No. Yeah. She's there. But they said she's." He cleared his throat. "I'm sorry, Momma. I shoulda been there. They said Danny was dead when they got there. Felicia had her head on Holly. Her arms were wrapped around her momma but Holly was ... already." He cleared his throat. "Gone." His voice was a hoarse whisper by the time he got to the last word. Stacie must not have heard him right, but Nate's words picked up speed. "That's what they *said*. Felicia's hurt bad. Hasn't woke up yet. Danny's dead. They killed Danny. I wasn't there, Momma. I'm so sorry. I wasn't there, but I shoulda been. I'm sorry I let ya down. Let all ya'll down."

Nothing Nate said made any sense to Stacie. It was hard to breathe. Nate's voice was too thick and hard to understand. "Gotta get to the hospital. See my sister. My niece."

But Holly had just found a new home for them. It was all set. Holly and Felicia already got the keys. They were waiting for Bethany and the kids to join them in their new place. Stacie was helping them get set up. A fresh start for all of them. Holly couldn't be *dead*. How had Danny even *found* them?

Stacie shook her head. Nate was wrong. "No. They were in a new place. Danny didn't know where the new house was. He couldn't know. Why was he even out of jail? How did he know where to *find* them?"

"They weren't at the new place. They were at the *old* place. With Danny."

"Holly left Danny. She was done. She just got the keys to the new place. Why would she be at the old house with Danny? She left him!"

"Mom! I don't know why she was there. That's all I know. I just gotta get to the hospital and see. Pray, Momma. Maybe it's a mistake. Pray they bring Holly back. And get to the airport. Felicia needs you. I need ya too."

"This can't be happening." Holly wasn't dead. There was a mistake. But if they were hurt, Stacie had to be there. She should have flown back with Holly. She shouldn't have let them go without her. "I'll get down to the airport and get on the first flight. You gonna pick me up from the airport?"

"I'm not leaving Felicia till I know she's okay. I can't leave her."

Stacie nodded. "I'll call Rich. Be there as soon as I can."

Stacie slid to the floor in a daze. Holly. Felicia. Danny. Holly's smiling face filled her mind. Holly's laugh. Holly's hugs. Holly's tears. Holly's temper. Her baby girl. Her eyes fell to the phone, still in her limp hand. She flung it away from her as if it were the viper that had taken her daughter.

Stacie groaned as she brought both knees to the carpet and folded over on top of them, her forehead against the floor, hands overlapped on the back of her head. Nate's words played in her mind. Felicia held her mother. Did they get a chance to say goodbye? *Why, God?* Sobs rocked her body. Please don't let it be true. She pounded the floor with her fists. No! No! She tucked her arms and clasped her hands to her chest and cried, begging God to wake Holly up. Begged for the life of her daughter and granddaughter. Her daughter's life was just beginning. She was filled with hope. Promising future. New job. New home. A new start.

Her own words of caution haunted her. How many times had she spoken with a woman in one of her support groups, looked them in the eye, and warned them? The most dangerous time in an abusive relationship is when the abused leaves the abuser. Stacie knew this. But Holly had already left. Holly shouldn't have been there.

She should not have been there!

Rage flowed through Stacie's veins. Moans rose from the deepest parts of her core and ripped from her throat as she hammered the floor until she could no longer lift her arms. Loud sobs took over. She tried to cover her mouth to quiet them. She struggled to her hands and knees and pulled the pillow off her bed. She flattened out and scooted under the bed. She was in the deepest pit she'd ever known. She wanted to bury herself. Wanted to hide in the dark and make it all go away.

Under the bed, with the pillow against her face, she cried for her baby. She should have been there. Holly had still needed her. But she'd seemed so strong. So excited. So sure. Stacie should have known better. How many women had she counseled? How many times had she been there for women as they were leaving their abusers? And now, she hadn't even been there for her own daughter. When Holly needed her most, she'd been thousands of miles away. Had Holly cried out for her? While Holly lay there, dying, what had Stacie been doing? Laughing and having a good time with Bethany? What time did all of this happen? When Stacie should have been coming to Holly's rescue, what had she been doing instead?

And Felicia. She was unconscious when they found her. Would Stacie's granddaughter be ripped from her life too? Stacie couldn't bear it. Felicia needed her. Nate's words drummed in her mind. "Felicia needs you. I need you." Stacie had to be strong. She appealed to the only one strong enough to carry her through this. *God, give me your strength because I can't do this on my own.* She slid halfway out from under the bed and retrieved her phone, pulling it back under with her. Her hands shook as she tapped Rich's number. His deep, sleepy voice answered on the second ring.

"Stacie?"

The sound of his voice brought fresh tears to her eyes but not the hopeless ones she'd been crying before. These were the tears cried when falling into the arms of someone stronger and able to take some of the burden. She shared everything she knew. Although her eyes never stopped flowing, strength began coursing through her veins at Rich's words of empathy and understanding. "Darling. I'm so sorry."

His voice was thick. Stacie could picture tears on his face.

And then he prayed. "Heavenly Father. We're stunned and broken-hearted. We don't want it to be true. Please, give Stacie the strength she needs for those who need her. If there is any way Holly could make it through this, please let it be. And for Felicia." His voice broke, and Stacie cried as quietly as she could, clinging to every word. "Preserve her life. Give her the strength to bear whatever losses she must endure." He sniffed and cleared his throat. "Be with Nate. Breathe your peace into him and give him the strength to bear whatever he's about to see and hear. And give me wisdom to know how to help."

Stacie wiped her eyes with the heel of her hand, but it was pointless. The faucet would not be shut off.

"Sweetheart. I'm so sorry for what you're going through. I feel helpless. But here's what I can do. I can go to the hospital. I can update you if anything changes. As soon as you have a flight, let me know what time it lands. I'll be at the airport to pick ya up. But until it's time to get you, I want to be with Nate and make sure he's eating and taking care of himself. He's gonna need his strength for when Felicia wakes up. She'll need him. And she'll need you, too. Make sure you're eating and taking care of yourself. It's not going to be easy. Do it for Felicia."

Stacie pushed her words through a raw throat. "Okay. Thank you." Stacie could hear him getting ready with drawers closing, water running, and rustling noises in the background. Rich didn't have to do any of this. She hoped he understood how much he meant to her right then and how much she appreciated him because she had no words to express any of it. She didn't want to hang up. Didn't want to be alone.

The phone went silent for a moment before his deep voice floated over the line. "You sure you don't mind? I don't want to step on your toes, but I do want to help. I'm sure not going back to sleep tonight."

It felt like the moment of truth. Here was a man who actually respected her opinion, her boundaries, and her family. Instead of taking over, he paused. He asked. He waited for her approval. She respected him more than she'd ever respected any other man for the way he respected her.

"Thank you for making sure. Yes. Please be there for my babies until I can get there. I'll text as soon as I have an arrival time and flight number."

Keys were scooped up in the background and a door shut. Rich was on the way. But he'd waited. He'd actually waited even though it was obvious he was eager to get going. He'd waited for her. But then, it seemed Rich had been waiting for Stacie for a very long time. She'd never felt more loved and respected than she did in that moment.

Bethany

Bethany woke Kenny up just after 3 am. He took one look at his clock and buried his head under his pillow with a groan. She sat on the edge of his bed and gave the corner of his pillow a gentle tug. "Good morning." The usual joy those words held fell like a stone in an empty pool—no happy ripples. Everything had changed last night.

Stacie had woken Bethany up an hour earlier. Her mom's crying made Bethany uncomfortable. As if she should be crying too. Instead, her eyes were dry and scratchy. Holly had just been at her house. They were going to move in together. That was the plan. Holly dying was not part of the plan. Somehow, Bethany still expected to see Holly when she pulled up to their new driveway. Standing in their new doorway, jingling an extra set of keys, and saying she'd saved all the dirty dishes for Bethany and had already started decorating.

Bethany forced the words through her brain. Holly is dead. But no. Just no.

She rubbed Kenny's back. "Change of plans. Grandma needs to get back to Texas right now. I'm taking her to the airport. You can go back to sleep, but leave your door open so you'll hear if your sisters get up."

Kenny mumbled. Bethany squeezed his arm. "That mean you heard me?"

He pulled the pillow down and squinted at her. "Yeah. You leaving *now?*"

"Yeah. Go back to sleep, but take care of your sisters if they get up while I'm gone."

The pillow went back over his head as he rolled away from her.

Bethany wouldn't tell him anything until she had more answers. As it was, Nate had called once he'd arrived at the hospital and seen both Felicia and Holly. Felicia was in ICU.

Something about head trauma, brain swelling, cracked ribs, and a broken leg. The information was all muddled.

Her mom came up behind her and put a hand on Bethany's back. "Ready?"

Bethany nodded. "Wish we were all going together."

"Me too, but I can't wait." Mom's puffy eyes filled with tears. Bethany wished she could cry. Wished she could believe it. Was glad she couldn't. Maybe she didn't feel anything because it wasn't true. A cruel and horrible nightmare that she'd wake up from soon.

Bethany was eager to get to Felicia's bedside. She wanted to be there when her niece woke up. It was a strange feeling. Believing one part of what had happened but not believing the other part. Maybe it would be easier if she knew what had happened.

• • •

Bethany didn't want to leave her mom at the airport. "Want me to hang out with you?"

Stacie shook her head. "I'll be okay. You need to get your plane tickets. You shouldn't be far behind me anyway. Sorry I couldn't wait for you. I need to get to Felicia."

Bethany nodded. "Why'd they go there?"

Mom shook her head as tears spilled down her cheeks. "If Felicia wakes up—No. *When* Felicia wakes up, she'll be able to tell us."

• • •

Jennifer was waiting for Bethany in the parking lot of the emergency relief office. "You okay?"

Bethany nodded. She was absolutely not okay. She'd pulled her son from a safe place. Her sister was dead. Her niece was in the hospital. Her mom had abandoned her. And she was deceiving her husband.

Together, they went inside. "You don't need to say anything."

Bethany nodded. The middle-aged woman at the counter wore her hair cropped short and pressed her lips together, forming a thin, straight line. There was a brief, business-like exchange between Jennifer and the haughty woman. But Bethany's racing mind couldn't absorb the conversation.

The way the woman kept shooting glances at her made Bethany feel inferior and unworthy. Did this woman know Bethany was in the process of betraying the trust and love of her husband?

The woman spoke to her, but Bethany had no idea what she'd said. Jennifer placed a hand on her arm and handed her a pen. She pointed to the signature line at the bottom of the paper. Bethany nodded and signed. Whose signature was that? Jagged edges that Bethany didn't recognize contorted her name on the page. Just like her life.

The woman handed Bethany a check and copy of the paperwork. Did the woman know what compassion was? Had that face ever held a smile? Bethany doubted it. Jennifer smiled and nodded. She seemed pleased with the transaction and led Bethany back out to the parking lot.

"You're all set. If there is anything you need, please call my cell phone. I'll be waiting to hear from you. Let me know when you leave and when you get to where you're going. Everything is going to be okay. I'll check on you in a couple days. Okay?"

Bethany nodded. "Thank you." Jennifer's arms wrapped around Bethany.

"This is one day. You are brave. You are strong. Don't think of other days. Just think of today." Jennifer grabbed Bethany's hands, squeezed, and looked into her eyes. "I'm proud of you. This is *hard,* and that's okay. It's worth it. You're not the first to go through it, and you will not be the last. Today is your day. You live in it. Embrace it. Conquer it.

Don't look too far ahead. Only enough to do the things you need to do in each new day. That's it. Got it?"

Bethany nodded.

"What are you doing today?"

Bethany swallowed. "Flying to Texas."

Jennifer nodded. "Plans are good. You make them, stick with them, and only change them as needed in order to keep you and your kids safe. We'll stay in contact. If I don't hear from you, I'll be calling. Please answer my calls, or I'll worry."

STACIE

Somehow, Rich had sweet-talked his way into getting a ticket past security and was standing at the terminal as Stacie walked off the ramp and into the Austin airport. He looked a little sheepish and shrugged when she saw him. "How did you ...?"

On the way to baggage claim, Rich explained, "I got here way too early and was going stir crazy out there. I finally went to one of the ladies in the first-class line and explained the situation. I may have let her think we were a little more than friends." His ears turned a deep shade of pink. He cleared his throat. "She was very understanding and cleared me to meet you at your gate."

Stacie shook her head as emotions wrestled in her chest. She'd worked hard for over two decades to only rely on God and herself. But now something inside yearned to rely on Rich. To share her burdens with this man. To share her life with him. She blushed. Had she really just thought that? How could these thoughts and feelings dare to enter her mind at a time like this?

Bethany

A strange car sat in her driveway when Bethany pulled in. Her heart hammered against her ribs. Maybe Victor had been wrong. Was Carlos here already? Inside with the kids? Had he seen the suitcases? The truck crept to a stop as her mind raced with how she was going to get the kids out of the house without the sort of issue Holly and Felicia had just went through.

She opened the front door and peeked inside. Kenny flew into her and pulled her outside, quietly shutting the door once they were out. "Carlos' parents are here."

"Carlos?"

Kenny shook his head. "Just his parents. Said Carlos is coming home, and they wanted to be here for it. We gotta get out of here. What do you want me to do?"

Breathing came easier now that she knew it wasn't Carlos. "I'll talk to them."

Kenny took his sisters upstairs while Bethany greeted her in-laws. "I didn't know you were coming."

Antonio nodded. "Carlos will return soon. He asked us to come."

"What is this?" Luciana pointed to a packed suitcase.

A string of lies passed through Bethany's mind, but she was not going to keep Carlos' secret abuse hidden from his parents any longer.

"I need to tell you something that's been very hard for me to talk about or admit." She swallowed. "Carlos is not safe for me and the kids."

Antonio looked confused, but Luciana scoffed loudly. "He's good. You are not safe for Carlos. He do everything. He work, he cook, he clean. What you do?"

Bethany bristled and opened her mouth to defend herself but snapped it shut. No. She would not allow herself to be baited into defending herself and get sidetracked from the real issue. Her tone hardened. "I don't want to make him sound bad, but he needs to get counseling and learn how to be a healthy husband and dad."

Antonio put a hand on Luciana's arm. "What'd he do?"

"He pushes Kenny, yells at everyone, grabs our throats …"

Antonio's eyes grew round. "No."

Bethany nodded. "Yes."

Luciana clicked her tongue. "Lies."

Antonio glanced at the suitcase. "You are leaving before he come home."

She nodded. "Yes. I want him to get help. He'll be angry and maybe sad too. He'll need you."

Luciana moved close to Bethany. "No. You will stay. Talk to him."

Bethany shook her head. "No. I will leave with my kids before he gets home. I tried talking to him. He won't let me leave if I don't go before he gets back."

"No. Is for him to decide. Not you."

There was no way she was about to let Luciana bully her into staying. She was done being intimidated, and her voice dared Luciana to disagree. "He's not safe. No more choking. No more pushing. No more yelling. No more abuse. Carlos has a problem, and he needs help."

The rims of Antonio's eyes were pink and watery. "So sorry, Bethany."

Luciana threw her hands up. "You believe this?"

Antonio took Luciana's arm. "We will go. We could not stop you."

"No." Luciana pulled her arm away and snatched the suitcase dragging it out the door.

Bethany looked at Antonio. He shook his head as they watched Luciana take it to the car and struggle to get it in the backseat.

He sighed. "I keep her outside. Come out when you're ready. I give you suitcase."

Bethany nodded. "Don't ask where we're going."

Antonio nodded and shut the door on his way out.

Bethany started up the stairs to get Kenny but saw that he was already on the stairs, probably listening to the whole thing. She clenched angry teeth. How dare Luciana treat her as if she were the one in the wrong. "Let's get moving. We don't have much time."

Bethany hardly spoke as they worked to get the last of their things crammed into a couple of suitcases. She only barked orders as she moved from room to room, checking to make sure she didn't forget anything important.

Holly was never far from her mind as she worked. She was ready for a fight. She almost wanted Luciana to come back in and try to stop her. Furious energy drove her as if fighting her way through Luciana would undo what she couldn't bear to be true.

STACIE

Stacie texted Nate when she was close to the hospital. Rich dropped her off at the door and told her he'd meet her in Felicia's room after parking. Nate met Stacie in the hall outside Felicia's room with swollen, red eyes and a long hug.

"How is she?" Stacie pressed her face against Nate's and spoke into his ear as she stroked the hair on the back of his head. He was precious, and she was thankful for him. She didn't want to let him go.

He squeezed her in no hurry to step away. The pain in his hoarse voice brought fresh tears to her eyes. "Danny bust her up pretty bad. Cracked ribs, broken leg, lots of bruises all over. Doc says her body should heal just fine. But they said she hadn't fully healed from the last concussion he gave her, so this one's more serious. Was lots of brain swelling. Doc says it's gone down, and they just changed her meds. They want her to wake up. I was hoping you'd get here in time. I gotta say, I sure am lookin forward to seeing her eyes. Hearing her voice. Detective been here askin' questions and trying to piece together what mighta happened. He asked if Holly and Felicia ever talked about getting rida Danny. Said he'd be back after she wakes up. I didn't like what he was implying."

Rich appeared and placed a tender hand on Stacie's arm. "You heard about a detective asking questions?"

Rich's eyebrows dropped as he glanced at Nate. "Yeah. Just doing his job. Don't let it worry ya. Let's go see Felicia."

Nate turned and led the way. As soon as he entered the room, he swung around and almost bumped into Stacie. "I'm gonna find the doc for ya."

Stacie nodded and stepped aside to let Nate pass. Felicia's face was so pale, it made her dark blond hair look brown in contrast. Everything else disappeared from the room. There was only Felicia on her hospital bed. It seemed as if the bed floated up to Stacie until their faces were close. The breath left Stacie's lungs. She stroked Felicia's forehead but stopped at the matted hair. Her hair didn't look darker because Felicia's skin was so pale. Dried blood was caked into it, staining the color a deep brown. Stacie pinched a clump of stiff hair and lifted it, looking for the wound or stiches. Traces of dried, flakey blood clung to Felicia's skin near her hairline, ear, and side of her neck.

Rich's voice broke through from somewhere far away. "Blood didn't come from her head, Sweetie."

Stacie looked at him then ran her eyes over Felicia's body and back up to her face. "But there's so much. Where ...?"

Rich cleared his throat and put a hand on Stacie's shoulder. His voice was so low Stacie barely caught his words. "It's Holly's."

Tears sprung to Stacie's eyes as she lowered the clump of hair as if it were made of fragile glass. Felicia was found with her head resting on Holly. Stacie just hadn't imagined the blood. Would she be able to see her baby girl and tell her goodbye? Could she bare it? She blinked, trying to unblur her vision, but more tears took the place of the ones that fell. "Have you seen Holly?" She had to know what to expect.

"No. Not sure if I wanted to. Or if they'd even let me. Thought I'd wait till you got here and see how you feel about it."

Nate walked in and stood so close his arm pressed into Stacie's shoulder. "Doc'll be here soon."

Stacie picked up Felicia's limp hand and squeezed it. As she rubbed her thumb back and forth over the back of Felicia's hand, she spoke in a mother's soothing tone. "It's alright, Felicia. Grammy's here. You're going to be okay. Nate's here too. We're here and we love you. Just rest, and don't worry about a thing."

Felicia's pinky finger twitched. Stacie nodded as a tear escaped the corner of her eye. "That's right. You know we're going to take good care of you, sweetheart. Do you wanna open those pretty eyes and show us all that you're okay? We've been worried about you."

Felicia moaned and shifted as the doctor appeared next to Stacie.

He nodded and smiled. "Keep talking to her. Let's see if she's ready to wake up."

Nate picked up her other hand and smiled at Stacie with a new light in his eyes. "Hey, Felicia. I had me a sleepover here with you last night, but you weren't very talkative."

Felicia's eyes opened and immediately closed. It looked as if she struggled to get them open, only to have them slam shut a couple more times. Stacie, Nate, Rich, and even the doctor all spoke encouraging words together.

"Come on, girl. You got this."

"You're almost there. We wanna see you."

She took a deep breath and let out a low groan as if she were annoyed that she hadn't been able to sleep in. This time, when her eyes opened, she looked at her cheerleaders and frowned. "Wha—"

The room was filled with joyful noises. Felicia was the only one who didn't look thrilled.

The doctor nodded as he gave her a quick look over. "We'll take it slow, but she should heal just fine." He smiled and left.

Stacie's chest was about to burst. She wasn't losing a granddaughter. "Hey, sweetheart. How you doing?"

Felicia's lip trembled. A tear slid from the corner of her eye. "Momma."

Stacie's eyes filled as she nodded. "Do you remember what happened?"

"Where's Momma?"

Stacie shook her head. She couldn't do this. She could not look Felicia in the eyes and tell her. Stacie hadn't even had a chance to say goodbye. She stroked Felicia's hand and cleared her throat. "I just got here, sweetie. I haven't seen her yet."

Both Rich and Nate watched her. Nate shook his head and mouthed, "No."

Rich smiled at Felicia. "Can I borrow your grandma for a minute? Uncle Nate's here. I'll bring her right back." He looked at Stacie. "If that's okay with you?"

Stacie nodded and went with Rich.

"What do you want to do, dear?"

"I need to see Holly." Tears spilled, and her heart broke, but she had to do this. It was as if Holly were there, waiting to say goodbye. Stacie's heart ached to run to her baby girl and make everything better one last time. Holly would know her mom had come to check on her. Had tried to reach her in time.

Stacie hadn't meant to fail her. She'd tried to keep Holly safe. She should have come back with her. Or convinced her to stay until they could all go together. It was a terrible idea to let Holly and Felicia come back alone. No matter how many times Holly said it was over. No matter how safe she seemed, no matter how much she declared her trust in men was lost forever, still, she trusted them.

She had to be strong for Holly one last time. She needed to tell her that Felicia was okay. That Danny would never hurt them again. Holly needed to know that her daughter would be safe and that her momma had come. It was time to say goodbye to her beautiful daughter.

BETHANY

Once they were all checked in and sitting outside their gate at the airport, Kenny pulled some toys out and handed them to his sisters. They appeared thrilled and immediately began to play together. He looked at Bethany and motioned for her to join him a couple seats away.

"What's up?"

"Thank you, Mom."

"What for?"

"For being so strong. You're the strongest person I know." She shook her head. "Stop, Kenny."

"I'm not stopping, Mom." He grabbed her hand. "Listen to me. I've been watching you. Sure, things haven't been easy for a really long time. Maybe not ever. But I've never seen you closed off and angry the way you've been today." His eyes brimmed with unshed tears. "Don't leave us, Mom, and don't be mad. You're strong. You're brave. You're so important. I can't make it through this without you."

It seemed that her very soul wobbled. "Holly's my baby sister. Felicia's my precious niece." She shook her head even while her eyes began to fill. "It's not fair."

Kenny put an arm around her. "I know, Mom. It's not fair."

Bethany leaned on her son's shoulder. "I was so worried about myself when it was Holly who needed protecting the whole time. I had my mom. I had the Army. I had Jennifer, Victor, everyone protecting *me*. Holly had *no one*, and she needed it more."

He shook his head. "What would have happened if you hadn't done all that stuff over the past few weeks? If you were just worried about Aunt Holly?"

Bethany shook her head.

"I was hurting. I was cutting myself, and I wanted to die. What's Carlos been telling you since he deployed? You don't have to say, but I could tell it must've been pretty bad. So, you focused on me, on Gloria, on Maria, and you. Guess what, Mom? If you hadn't, we'd all still be sitting at the house with Carlos about to get home."

She stared at this son of hers, transforming into a man. He was right.

"Mom, what happened with Holly and Felicia could have happened even if you'd kept us here. It just feels different because you had one eye on Texas while packing up North Carolina. That's all. What you gave Holly was hope. And, you know what? That's what you give me all the time. That's what you give my sisters. That's what you gave Felicia."

Bethany shook her head. He gave her too much credit. She was only doing what she had to do.

"Oh, you think I didn't notice the way Felicia looked at you when ya'll came to visit? Yes, Mom. You inspire people to do brave things because *you* are brave. And you're not done."

They sat there in silence, deep in their own thoughts. Her mind wandered over all that had happened during the past several weeks. There was no denying she'd changed. And the change wasn't a lack of fear because there was still a lot she was scared of. So many unknowns. And knowing Carlos, the fight wasn't over. So, what was it then?

A cheerful voice called over the loudspeaker, announcing that they were beginning to board. As people lined up, Bethany realized this was the first flight in years that she didn't have Carlos by her side. There were no eggshells to walk over as she and Kenny joined her daughters and put their toys away. There was no intimidating face she had to constantly read to determine when it was time to rush to the line.

In fact, she didn't even need to stand in that horribly long line at all if she didn't want to. She looked at how slow the line moved and made her own decision right then and there.

They would take those toys back out. Her daughters could play a little longer. And she could chat with her son about anything at all. They would wait comfortably until the line disappeared. Until they were ready to board the plane. Maybe that's what had changed. The suffocating chains of intimidation that had held them all captive were broken.

Her heart ached for her sister. But it was almost as if Holly were there. A tear escaped as memories of Holly played through her mind. All the way up to the most recent ones with their plans for freedom. She imagined her sister sitting down beside her and giving her a message. Stay gone. No more chances. Now that Bethany had her kids safely out, never go back. Nothing was worth that price. It was just too high. Bethany got the message and nodded. Thank you, Holly. She drank in the sight of her children's relaxed faces. They were daunted no more, and she planned to keep it that way.

Today I Will Live

Today I will live.

I will believe in myself even when others don't.
I will speak positive words even if others won't.

I will trust that still small voice in my head
And let it rise above doubts and fears.
With new confidence I'll climb out of bed.

There's no going back to yesterday.
And I'm not promised tomorrow.
So, in this moment is where I'll stay.

Today I will Love.

I will stand up where I used to cower in fear.
Speak for hope, justice, encouragement.
I'll let my voice be heard loud and clear.

I'll open my eyes and take a look around.
See that it's not all about me in this busy world.
People are hurting. Afraid to make a sound.

Today I will Live.

I will stop holding myself back.
Accept that there will be naysayers.
But their opinions are not fact.

Today I will Love.

Let others see the real me and know.
It's not about being perfect, none of us are.

My vulnerability may help others grow.

Today I will Live.

Sunshine or rain. Snow, sleet, or hail.
Remembering I'm not in this alone.
No more excuses. Today I'll prevail.

—S.R. Luviek

CHAPTER QUESTIONS FOR DISCUSSION, REFLECTION, OR JOURNALING

Chapter 1
1. How could a casual attitude be considered a defense?

2. What does Carlos' obsession with his reflection tell us about his character?

3. Why do you think Bethany masked her true feelings multiple times throughout the first chapter?

4. Why did Bethany wonder if she was losing her mind?

5. Is it Bethany's responsibility to keep Carlos happy? Why or why not?

Chapter 2
1. What reason might Bethany have for not wanting her mom to visit?

2. Do you agree with Stacie's assessment that there is "something far worse for kids than divorce?" Why or why not?

3. Why did Danny stop pursuing Holly once they caught the attention of a neighbor?

4. Describe Bethany's internal struggle over Carlos' plans.

5. Do you think that the way Bethany changed Carlos' mind would be more likely to prevent or inspire Carlos to behave like that again? Explain.

Chapter 3

1. Why might Carlos want to see Bethany get angry with Kenny?

2. Why would Maria hide in the closet and repeatedly bang her head against the wall?

3. What was the purpose of Carlos telling Bethany that if she ever left, she'd never see her girls again?

Chapter 4

1. Why do you think Bethany believed Carlos' threat after she told him about her dream?

2. Did Stacy overreact to Nate's request not to challenge Danny? Why or why not?

3. Do you think Nate's fear of becoming like his dad is legitimate? Why or why not?

4. What reason could Carlos have for bringing Bethany flowers?

Chapter 5

1. Why do you think Stacie didn't ask anyone for help when she didn't know where Holly and Felicia were?

2. What reasons might Carlos have had for giving Bethany the Power of Attorney the way that he did?

3. How do you think Bethany should have handled Carlos' accusations to get a better result?

4. In Bethany's flashback, why would Carlos take the baby and treat Bethany as if she were the dangerous one immediately after choking her?

Chapter 6

1. Was Maria's reaction to the delivery man typical behavior for a three-year-old? Why or why not?

2. What does it say about Kenny, and his relationship with his mom, that he shared his impulse to self-harm with her?

3. Did Carlos intend to scare Bethany when he had the gun? Explain.

4. Was Bethany's fear valid? Why or why not?

5. Do you agree with Bethany's thoughts that God was fair and wouldn't force Carlos to change? That it was actually up to Bethany to make the change? Explain.

Chapter 7

1. Do you think it was wise for Bethany to email her brother, Nate, and her friend/pastor's wife, Trudy? Why or why not?

2. Do you agree with Bethany's doubt, that Carlos hadn't hurt her, and she might sound crazy?

3. Why does abuse rely on isolation and secrecy?

4. Would a domestic violence support group be helpful for Holly? Explain your answer.

5. Do you agree or disagree with Stacie's idea that "guys like that seemed to have a sixth sense about which women would put up with their crap?" Why or why not?

Chapter 8

1. Do you agree with Trudy that Bethany needs to work harder at seeing the good in Carlos? Why or why not?

2. Bethany begins to think she was wrong to send that email and wrong to be afraid of Carlos. Do you agree with her feelings? Why or why not?

3. What things did Zalika do that made Holly feel valued? Explain.

4. What's your understanding of a "domestic violence support group," and do you think they are helpful?

5. Should they explain the term "domestic violence" to Felicia at her age? Explain.

Chapter 9

1. Why did Stacie's phone conversation with Bethany raise concern? Was she right to dismiss the concern? Why or why not?

2. Why do you think Bethany didn't answer her mom's question?

3. Do you think Rich is a safe man for Stacie to develop romantic feelings for? Why or why not?

Chapter 10

1. What reasons might Bethany have for feeling the same nervousness around Luciana as she does around Carlos?

2. Do you agree or disagree with Carlos when he tells Bethany, "Look what you made me do"? Explain

3. Bethany feels like she doesn't have a choice but to pretend to be normal and join the family for dinner.

Does she have another choice? If so, what else could she do? If not, why not?

4. Why do you suppose Maria is afraid of her grandfather, Antonio?

5. What do you think is Antonio's reason for cutting their visit short? Do you think this decision will be helpful or harmful to Bethany and the kids? Explain.

Chapter 11

1. Do you think it would be smart for Stacie to move into a bigger house so that Holly and Felicia could move in with her? Why or why not?

2. Why does Stacie say that "she wanted to tell Holly what to think? But that never worked"?

3. Holly mentions that a couple of women in group still live with their abuser and that they just "set boundaries." What sort of boundaries would need to be set in order for it to be safe to stay in the relationship?

4. Describe what Felicia may be feeling and why. Do you think her feelings are justified? What should she do about them?

Chapter 12

1. Do you think Carlos is truly sorry for the bruises? Explain.

2. Why do you think Carlos made Kenny bowl in the lane with bumpers?

3. What reasons might Bethany feel solely responsible for bringing chaos back into order?

4. Why did Bethany rush to get them out of the bowling alley? Why did Carlos?

5. Kenny wanted to tell the MPs about Carlos while they were there, but Bethany didn't agree. Explain each of their reasons and if you agree with them or not.

Chapter 13

1. Explain why Stacie believes it's dysfunctional when Holly tells her Danny said he'd quit for her, and that if she comes back, she can help him get sober.

2. Why would hope need to die in order for things to get better?

3. Explain how fear or hope could keep someone in an abusive relationship.

4. Why do you think Stacie believes the heart always follows hope?

5. What were some things Stacie could have tried to keep Holly from seeing Danny again?

Chapter 14

1. When Carlos came home drunk, why did Bethany say she loved him even though she felt like running from him instead?

2. What could Bethany have done differently when Carlos questioned her?

Chapter 15

1. What's the worst thing that may have happened if Bethany had let her brother, Nate, fly over and get her and her kids? What's the best thing that could have happened? Should she have said yes to him? Why or why not?

2. What do you think about Felicia, a twelve-year-old, being allowed to choose where she lives?

3. Are there any risks to forcing Maria to hug against her will? If so, what are they?

4. Why do you suppose Gloria ran to hug her dad and asked him to play with her in that moment? Is that a sign of a healthy father/daughter relationship? Why or why not?

5. Why do you think Carlos left? Where do you think he went for so long? Why did he bring gifts back for everyone?

6. What does Bethany mean when she says they are all Carlos' puppets?

Chapter 16

1. Is it okay for a person to request pictures from their spouse that they're not comfortable giving? Why or why not?

2. Why do you think Carlos told Bethany that she always gets between him and the kids?

3. Why did Carlos blame Gloria for not listening to him in the grocery store? What might that sort of thing do to a child over time?

4. How might Carlos' logic over the way they each remember the shopping cart event affect Bethany's mind and emotions?

5. Was there any harm in Bethany's use of alcohol? Explain.

Chapter 17
1. What should Bethany do when Carlos rewrites history, as he did when talking to her about how she got the bruise on her arm?

2. Why do you think Bethany laughed so uncontrollably when Carlos left?

3. What reasons might Holly have for missing the support group meeting?

4. Is it wrong that Bethany doesn't at least pretend to miss Carlos in front of the kids? Why or why not?

Chapter 18
1. Consider Bethany's thought about keeping what happened at home a secret, and that her father had taught her well. What are the implications of this reality for Bethany and others like her?

2. Is it okay to squeeze someone's throat only enough to scare them, as Bethany said of Carlos? Why or why not?

3. What could be the reasons Dr. Davis wants to see Bethany as well as Kenny?

Chapter 19
1. Does Bethany have sound logic behind her plan to keep the counseling from Carlos? Why or why not?

2. What do you think of Bethany's thought that "Christians weren't supposed to get divorced?"

3. Explain what Bethany means by not wanting to trigger the bad times. Would it be realistic to think that if these women could avoid "triggering the bad times" that there wouldn't be "bad times" or abuse?

4. In what ways might Bethany's realization, that she had access to someone who'd already been through similar things, benefit her?

5. Was there anything different that Stacie could have said to Bethany on the phone to help the situation? What would you say if it was your daughter? What would you do?

Chapter 20

1. Describe Felicia's struggle with her thoughts and emotions toward Danny.

2. Should Felicia have tried to explain to her mom how she really felt about Danny? If so, how should she have done it? If not, why not?

3. How might Carlos be feeling by the end of this chapter? How about Bethany or the kids?

Chapter 21

1. Do you think a relationship can successfully transition from longtime friends to romantic partners? What could be the benefits and drawbacks of such a transition?

2. What do you think the playtime with the stuffed dog and monkey indicate about Gloria and Maria?

3. How do you think Bethany should respond to Carlos' request for a son and why?

Chapter 22

1. Why might Felicia get the feeling that Danny doesn't want her around?

2. Why do you think Holly appears to prioritize her boyfriend, Danny, over her daughter?

Chapter 23

1. With the stakes so high and no way to fulfill Carlos' request for several months anyway, would it be better for Bethany to just agree with the request for now? Why or why not?

2. Why do you suppose Kenny is behaving so differently?

Chapter 24

1. If you were Bethany in this chapter, what would you think Carlos was planning to do?

2. Does Bethany have a reason to be scared? Why or why not?

3. In what ways does Carlos' plan sound logical? In what ways does it sound illogical?

4. What are Bethany's options, including those she's not seeing?

Chapter 25

1. Is Bethany making the right choice to put her son on medication? Why or why not?

2. What do you think of Stacie's advice, to keep showing Kenny love and that he won't always be able to feel it?

3. What more could Stacie have said to her daughter at that moment?

Chapter 26

1. What would be your best advice if you could talk with Bethany in this chapter?

2. What would be your best advice if you could talk with Kenny in this chapter?

3. Why do you think Holly would agree to go out and have one drink with Danny to celebrate with a newly engaged friend? Does Felicia have the right to be angry?

Chapter 27
1. Do you think it's wise to put Kenny in a residential treatment facility? Why or why not?

2. If you were Stacie, how do you think you'd handle the news her daughter shared in this chapter?

3. Is there anything more Stacie could have done? Should she have done anything differently? Explain.

Chapter 28
1. Why would Gloria look forward to a day when she could marry a man who yells at her and their kids?

2. What are some ways Bethany can help prepare her daughters to make healthy relationship choices?

3. At this stage in their relationship, is it a good idea for Rich to offer Stacie's daughter a job? Why or why not?

4. What do you think about Carlos' word choices, such as when he states that he's "letting" Bethany raise their girls, that Bethany is "forcing" him to do things, that he "talks loud enough to be heard," and that his methods of punishment are all "effective" and that they "work"?

Chapter 29
1. Why do you suppose Felicia believes her grandmother would prefer her family in NC? What is the core issue Felicia is struggling with in this scene?

2. What do you think of Carlos' story about the female soldier? Should Bethany believe him?

3. What's the worst thing that could happen if he came home early?

4. What advice would you give Bethany if you were in Stacie's position?

Chapter 30
1. What do you think of Stacie's logic about wording things differently depending on whether or not Bethany planned to be with Carlos again?

2. Should Stacie just come right out and say what she thinks about it all? Why or why not?

3. Is Bethany right in using Kenny's condition to try and get Carlos off the list? Explain.

Chapter 31
1. Why do you think Felicia tried to prevent Danny from coming into her room?

2. Why would Stacie have Felicia repeat back what she wanted her to do?

3. Was it a good idea for Holly and Felicia to fly so soon after the incident? Why or why not?

4. What else could they have done to keep Holly and Felicia safe?

5. Why do you think the first sgt. wanted to know the reason Bethany didn't want her husband home early from deployment?

Chapter 32

1. Do you agree with Bethany that control is an illusion? Explain your answer.

2. Should Bethany report her husband and try to get help that way? What are the benefits? What are the risks?

3. Bethany is nagged by the thought that she's not honoring her wedding vows to love and respect her husband. Do you think she's guilty? Why or why not?

4. Bethany believes she has the option to call Family Advocacy or continue watching her kids fall apart. What other options can you think of?

Chapter 33

1. Was it wrong for Felicia to eavesdrop? Why or why not?

2. What do you think about their decision to let Felicia in on the truth about the men in their lives?

Chapter 34

1. What do you think Bethany's biggest fear is as she gets ready for her appointment?

2. What's the difference between feeling like you're "walking on eggshells" in order to keep from upsetting someone and just treating them right if the end goal for both is a happy and peaceful relationship?

3. What do you think about the pattern of girls marrying people similar to their dads?

4. Share your thoughts on the way Bethany explained to Felicia what it had been like to finally report Carlos. Do you think that's an accurate description?

5. Stacie didn't want Bethany to blame herself for any of it. What do you think of Bethany's conclusion for where the blame should fall?

Chapter 35

1. Do you agree with Bethany's decision to take Kenny from the treatment facility early? Why or why not?

2. What do you think Kenny felt when he found out his mom planned to leave him there?

Chapter 36

1. What do you think of Pastor Eric and Trudy's reaction to Bethany's news?

2. Can you identify Carlos' manipulation tactics after he delivers the news of his early return?

3. What emotions do you think Gloria experienced after talking with her dad?

4. Do you agree with Bethany's decision to tell Carlos that she was afraid for him to come home? What's the benefit of this? What could be the harm?

Chapter 37

1. How would you describe the way Holly may be feeling about Trudy and Pastor Eric's opinions?

2. Do you agree with the way Stacie described submission and the marriage relationship? Why or why not?

3. How do you feel about the way Stacie helped Holly understand Biblical interpretation?

Chapter 38

1. Explain what you think the cover of the journal may mean to Bethany.

2. Have you ever felt prompted to get, say, or do something for someone that ended up being exactly what they needed in that moment? Have you ever been on the receiving end of such a prompt?

Chapter 39

1. Do you agree with Stacie, that there's wisdom in being single? Why or why not?

2. Why do you think Carlos was so nice during their video chat?

3. Is Bethany right to do as Victor says, and keep her plans from Carlos? Why or why not?

Chapter 40

1. What do you think is the best way Stacie could help Bethany after they got the news that Carlos was already on his way back?

2. When Holly realized Danny was there, what were Holly's options and what do you think would have been the best? Why?

3. What were Felicia's options when she heard the conversation between Danny and her mom spiral out of control?

Chapter 41

1. Why do you think the most dangerous time in an abusive relationship is when the abused leaves, or tries to leave, their abuser?

2. What does it say about Rich's character that he's ready to drop everything to help, but at the same time, isn't forcing himself into the situation?

3. Why do you think Holly kept trusting men after being hurt so many times?

4. Why do you think Bethany became so angry after being confronted by Luciana?

5. What do you think Holly would want to say to Bethany if she were able to speak to her at the airport and why?

The *Daunted No More* story is not finished. Too many people believe that once someone leaves, it's over. Unfortunately, that is far from the truth, especially when children are involved. Join Bethany, Felicia, and Stacie in their next steps toward freedom in book two of the *Daunted No More* trilogy.

Resources:

DauntedNoMore.com has a resource page with an extensive list of resources available to victims and survivors of abuse in the form of phone numbers, websites, and even other books specifically related to:

- Teens (Sadly, teen dating violence is on the rise)
- Military Dependents/Veterans/Active Duty
- Americans Overseas
- Child Abuse
- Children Witnessing Abuse
- Sexual Assault
- Sex Trafficking
- Suicide Prevention
- Homelessness
- Legal Help

Watch the videos

S.R. Luviek talks about scenes from the *Daunted No More* trilogy and related events, giving you a deeper look so that you can avoid the trap, stop the generational cycle, raise awareness, learn warning signs, get help, or help someone you know. Videos will be posted on <u>DauntedNoMore.com</u>, YouTube, and FaceBook as they come out.

Follow S.R. Luviek on Facebook

- Be one of the first to hear about the release of new books

- Learn how you can get involved in the Daunted No More Project as it grows

- See new videos

- Help raise awareness

- Celebrate our victories together

ABOUT THE AUTHOR

S.R. Luviek lives on the West Coast and is the mother of two sons and two daughters. She served in the U.S. Army as an Air Traffic Controller before continuing her education in the fields of psychology, creative writing, and teaching. She's lived all over the United States as well as overseas. The Daunted No More Project starts with this first novel and continues toward its goal to educate young people in order to stop the generational cycle of abuse. S.R. Luviek believes domestic violence is preventable and aims to speak and teach youth and young adults to promote a raised awareness of prevention methods. Find out more about the Daunted No More Project at DauntedNoMore.com.

Made in the USA
Columbia, SC
22 October 2020